Real
Swansea
Two

Real
Swansea
Two

nigel jenkins

series editor: peter finch

SEREN

Seren is the book imprint of
Poetry Wales Press Ltd
Nolton Street, Bridgend, Wales

www.serenbooks.com
facebook.com/SerenBooks
Twitter: @SerenBooks

ISBN 978-1-85411-648-2

A CIP record for this title is available from
the British Library

The publisher works with the financial assistance
of the Welsh Books Council

Printed by CPI Group (UK) Ltd, Croydon, CR0 4YY

CONTENTS

SERIES EDITOR'S INTRODUCTION

Coming to Swansea takes almost as long as leaving. The way in along Fabian Way consumes eternity. Are we there yet? And as soon as we are, the glass pyramid of Plantasia, the gleam of Sainsbury's sitting where the old dock once was, the anti-aircraft gun on its plinth, the portico of Swansea Museum, we're gone. We're off on the long road out to Oystermouth, to Mumbles and Gower, the Swansea seaside beside us, and the hills rising up beyond. If Cardiff is shaped like a lozenge then Swansea resembles an arc, its arms bent around its golden and endless sands.

As Wales' second city the place has always had pretentions and the fact that they have never been quite realised has been Swansea's salvation. The Assembly Government did not settle here, nor did the National Stadium, nor the National Library, nor the great Welsh Opera House that now sits in Cardiff Bay. Instead the DVLA did, and the Maritime Museum and the Dylan Thomas Centre, the only home for poets in Wales that has really worked. Rather than strut into the *realpolitik* hash that is Wales's governmental future Swansea demurred. Instead of grappling with the problems of identity and representation, of inward investment and regional share, of talking to its hinterland while simultaneously being Europe's newest capital, as Cardiff does, Swansea simply went off on its own. The prows of Viking ships stare out to sea from the Guildhall tower, the rain falls constantly, and the population are pretty sure just who they are.

Down on the waterfront, beyond the Maritime Quarter, to the west of that sliver of ancient sand dune still there, pushing hard against the West Pier, the names of some of Swansea's Cape Horn rounding ships, copper traders, are lettered into the elegant sea wall. *The Jonas of Swansey, Blithe de Swanseye, Mohican, Zeta.* Robin Campbell was responsible. He of the great public artwork flood that began to wash across Swansea's redeveloping frontage in the 1980s, well ahead of similar interventions in other cities further afield. Campbell's artworks are everywhere down here. On boat shed doors, on pumping stations, on plaques on walls, as towers illuminating the continuing presence of land facing an ever encroaching sea. Here stand 'Zeta Mnemonical', 'Copper Flame', the 'Tower of Winds', 'Spolasco', the 'Lighthouse' and the 'Beacon'. High on the walls of the new apartments are engraved texts, visible when they were installed, pristine twenty or more years ago but weather-worn flat by today. The wind-borne sands of Swansea are not giving up on their attempts to face the city down.

Inland, among the chain stores and shopping malls, where that insidious mammon-driven branch of British culture that has taken the place of religion in our lives flourishes, Swansea loses its distinctiveness. All cities look like this. Glass, walkways, punters carrying packets, *Big Issue* sellers, the boundaries between the store and street dissolved, stacks of new clothing displayed below street lights, shoes, boxes, new goods glistening, money still leaving our wallets almost as fast as it used to before the economic fall arrived. To be a member of the city club, that hierarchy of British conurbations that compete against each other for economic effectiveness and demographic desirability, Swansea has to be like this. It twists and turns as it changes in a way unequalled by Cardiff and Newport or anywhere else in Wales. It has not ceased rebuilding its heart in the lifetime during which I've known it and shows no sign of changing its position for the decades to come.

Life here is slower than it is further east. Just a fraction. It takes that much longer to buy a newspaper, to ask directions, to order a pint. People walk more slowly than they do in, say, Newport, a fraction more leisurely but discernible nonetheless. Compared to how swift the fast life is in London, the city of Swansea is a bucolic backwater full of doze and haze. There is time here to look out to sea and to taste the air. It's a quality worth having.

I walk across the city in the company of Nigel Jenkins. I'm researching a book about the Severn Estuary. He's already completed *Real Swansea Two*, the book you now hold in your hands. He's planning *Real Gower*, his next venture in Seren's market-busting series of psychogeographic wonders. I want you to talk me through the city, I tell him, but avoid mentioning anything that is already in your books. That's going to be a hard thing to do. *Real Swansea*, the first volume has already captured the life force of this air-filled place, and *Real Swansea Two* will take that material up to a second level. But Nigel, a walking Welsh Encyclopaedia, poet of eminence, raconteur, tale spinner, and a prose writer with a line to die for, can do it.

We don't mention the Mumbles railway, the elevation of Swansea to the Premier League, the art wars with the council, the beach, the docklands, the myth behind the naming of Fabian Way, the graveyards, the swing bridge, the LMS railway, the copper industry, the restaurant district, Wind Street, the Vikings, the car parks, the Patti

Pavilion, the hospital, the ceaseless redevelopment, the art galleries, the literary greats who live here and those who once did, the books, the musicians, the eminent hordes. There's no discussion of Oystermouth, Neolithic walkways, methods of ancient fishing, boats or Swansea Jacks. No reference to curry houses, to parks, to the sand dunes nor the tallest building in Wales, the Meridian Tower, standing in splendid Welsh sky-scraping isolation facing Swansea's waves.

Instead we walk, sliding along the edges of empounded waterways, over the remains of docks, and the sites of great buildings. We pass the castle. Cross the Tawe next to where a great rail bridge once was. Pass the place where the world's first ferroconcrete structure once stood. View Childe Roland's wall-affixed concrete poem. Check more of Robin Campbell's art flurries and glorious intercessions. Pass the place where the fishing fleet lies tied up. View the controversial doors of the Boat Shed, the gnomic verses of Nigel's own creation that adorn the sides of the now up for redevelopment astral observatory, and the work by Scots genius Ian Hamilton Finlay lost among the blowing sand facing the distant sea.

We end atop that tall building. Sitting as high up as you can get in Wales without climbing a mountain. In a sea-facing seat in a pub that serves tea and cake. Below us is the beach that rolls on forever, fish traps with their distinctive vees clearly visible, the Severn Sea out there virtually shipless now. Swansea's days as a great port are over. The freighters rarely come. There's little coal leaving here, no metals, no manufactured goods. The Cork ferry sails no more. The sand dredgers go slow. The fishermen watch their quotas. There are yachts, pleasure craft, small boats. Swansea looks at the sea now, it's given up taking part.

We discuss the process of writing these books. Quarter the city, take in the outlying districts. Work out the connections. Make the place as big as you can. Walk the patch. Delve and ask questions. Read the histories. Meet the people. Dive deep into your own memories and where those are lost or non-existent latch onto others who are still in touch. Meet the famous and the local. Ask them to show you the parts with which you are less familiar. Uncover what you can of local mystery and find where the lines of energy are that make the place spin. Understand the city. Work out why it is and what it is and how it's here and what will happen next. Walk everywhere, never drive. Use your bike when appropriate. Take the bus and the train. Make notes, make more notes, write it down, then up. Fashion the many fragments you now have into a satisfying and much larger psychogeographic whole. A thing worth reading. That's how to make a Real book. Nigel is now a master.

Months after the walk I receive the *RS#2* manuscript, well ahead of schedule, splendidly done. This is it. Swansea made real for a second time. Jenkins has done an impressive job. Entertaining and informative, a voyage of discovery in depth, full of quirk and quality, opinion and controversy, history and topography, magic and academia. There's rain in here and, of course, sand. Swansea Jacks fill the pages. Worth waiting for. Yep. Pick it up, don't put it down.

Peter Finch

INTRODUCTION

Wales's first industrial town – where, indeed, modern Wales was born – finds itself today experimenting with how to survive in recession-hit, post-industrial times. Not that there is any Master Plan. Just as old Swansea was "doodled over the landscape"[1], so the city elaborates a new, twenty-first century identity largely through trial and error, happenstance and the chutzpah of a couple of winning goals at Wembley in May 2011 which propelled Swansea City into football's Premier League (and which to many a Jack solved all of Swansea's problems at a stroke – and forever).

For over 250 years, Swansea flourished on coal, iron, copper, tinplate and zinc. Then came the devastation of the Second World War, which left indelible scars, followed by the rapid decline of heavy industry. The greater Swansea area, which some have dubbed Swansea Bay City, may be bookended by two major steelworks – at Port Talbot and Trostre – but, since the 1960s, Swansea itself has been highly dependent on public-sector employment, with about 33,000 workers – over 30% of the population – currently employed in service industries (and all too exposed therefore to the untender whims of the coalition government in London).

Boom (for some) went bust in 2008, and major building projects such as the SA1 waterfront development around the Prince of Wales dock or the Royal Fern Park golf course and leisure complex at Llangyfelach lost momentum or stalled altogether, pending an improvement in the economic climate. The Swansea-Cork ferry service collapsed – yet again – in 2012, with a loss to the regional economy of £17m. But Swansea ticks over. If many urban pubs are struggling, as a result of the smoking ban and the economic downturn, the city's scores of restaurants are thriving, from SA1 to Mumbles.

Certain mothballed developments kicked back into life as a direct result of Swansea's elevation to the Premier League, in anticipation of an influx of football fans from all over the world wanting food, accommodation and entertainment. The team's promotion, it was claimed at the time, would be worth £30m to the Swansea Bay area and would see the club itself reaping £90m in terms of league payments, greater income and television money – whereas just eight years previously a penurious Swansea City, lacking even the funds to pay the electricity bill at the Vetch, nearly disappeared from the

Football League altogether. The *Sunday Times*, ahead of Swansea's inaugural Premier League match against Manchester City, said that if the team was a country, Swansea City would be South Sudan, the world's newest nation. Although the Swans lost 4-0 to Manchester City, in time they found their Premier League feet, coasting to an historic 3-2 win against Arsenal in January 2012 and two months later redeeming themselves against Manchester City with a 1-0 win, knocking the richest team in the world off the top of the league table. This continues to be celebrated as the most impressive result in the Swansea club's history, on a par with the All Whites' victory over New Zealand in 1935 and Gary Sobers' six sixes in 1968.

There has been world-wide fascination with a non-English side joining the United Kingdom Premier League. The 2011–12 lord mayor, Councillor Ioan Richard – the most industrious and cultured lord mayor to have shouldered the gold for many a year – was much in demand for interviews in both English and Welsh in the international media. It intrigued representatives of both Arab and Japanese television stations, for instance, that they could subtitle his remarks directly from Welsh to their own languages, without recourse to English, and channels such as World Sky Sports have also been keen to note what for many of their listeners is not only the novelty of Welsh bilingualism but even, in some cases, of the very existence of Wales.

Culture is a card the city has often been slow to play. Swansea has performed various main roles over the centuries: conquerors' citadel and administrative centre, trading port, agricultural market, the (short-lived) 'Brighton of Wales', a metallurgical crucible of world importance, the 'Intelligent Town' of scientific and technological discovery, a hub for services, education, leisure and – with an indispensable contribution from the Gower peninsula – tourism (in 2011, tourism was worth £317m to the city's economy). Sometimes these roles have overlapped; sometimes they've come round again, in altered form, as with the currently re-ascendant resort option. But Swansea doesn't need to be anyone's Brighton – or Cardiff, for that matter (the poisonous rivalry that can erupt between capital and second city, particularly on the sports field, is an infantilism, on both sides, beneath contempt). Swansea, at its most confident, has dared to be different. Just as Swansea was once, in the industrial era, Wales's 'Intelligent Town', so it is now, in post-industrial times – it seems to me – Wales's city of culture. The intelligent response to hard times, rather than diminution and retrenchment, is surely for Swansea to celebrate its extraordinary history and unparalleled location, its artistic and intellectual achievements, its sports and popular entertainments for all their worth. In hard times, you don't abandon your culture and heritage; you use it, in far more imaginative ways than have been attempted so far, to make those times better and to prepare for a better future. To *reverse* the infamous Nazi dictum: "When I hear the word gun, I reach for my culture."

It's tempting in straitened times for the disbursers of limited public resources to cut back on what they see as 'non-essentials'. Faced with the grim injunction to lop a punishing £60m off the council's annual budget of £340m – which is equivalent to the entire county highways budget – it's hardly surprising that many councillors felt anger and dismay at the stark choices they were faced with. As one of them put it, "What are we to axe – special-needs teachers or the Dylan Thomas Centre?"

It was, of course, the Dylan Thomas Centre – irrespective of the £3.6m that the Dylan Thomas 'industry' is said to be worth annually to Swansea's economy – which they deemed disposable. Fortunately, the University of Wales, keen to develop a public presence west of Cardiff, was on hand to catch the Dylan Thomas Centre before it fell, committing itself – or seeming to commit itself – to maintaining the centre as a formidable cultural powerhouse and as the focal point of the worldwide celebrations, in 2014, of the one-hundredth anniversary of the poet's birth. From its inception as Tŷ Llên, hub of the UK Year of Literature 1995, most councillors have been equivocal about the centre. Few attend its artistic events and many have been itching for years to close the place, several of them supporting plans in the 1990s to turn it into a Harry Ramsden's fish and chip shop. Swansea, at the official level, doesn't quite 'get' culture (there's barely a blue plaque to be seen) – while its artists get on with making it and its people get on with being it.

The city, undeniably, has severe economic and social problems. A report by the Centre for Cities in 2012 ranked Swansea bottom out of 64 British cities for its rate of employment (61.2%). I have friends from so-called Third World countries who have been shocked at the poverty they have seen in Swansea. The council reported in 2011 that in poorer parts of Swansea some children cannot speak properly when they start school. Swansea has the highest proportion of children living in poverty in Wales, with almost a quarter of the city's young living in workless households.[2]

And in spite of efforts to heal the historic divide between east and west, people living in east Swansea can expect to die thirteen years before those in west Swansea.

The Y-shaped city's multiple personality, with many a dark undercurrent, is among its perennial attractions. A century or so ago, the poet Edward Thomas (1878-1917) wrote from Swansea to his friend Jesse Berridge, "This is a sublime horrible town among the mountains at the edge of the sea. No town fascinates me so much..." (that "sublime horrible" judgement anticipating Dylan Thomas's more familiar – and kinder – "ugly, lovely town"). Few feel indifferent about the city, and many an 'exile' is susceptible to an aching hiraeth for the place. After a lifetime's gainful employment in London, a friend recently returned to Swansea, jobless and semi-homeless, choosing, as she said, "to be poor in paradise" over the affluence, exhausted air and relative *froideur* of metropolitan life.

The City and County of Swansea, stretching from Worms Head in the south-west to Penlle'r Castell on Mynydd y Gwair in the north-east, occupies approximately the confines of the medieval commote of Gŵyr (Gower). It's too big an area – geographically,[3] historically and culturally – to be encompassed in a single Real volume, hence this successor volume to *Real Swansea* (2008). The focus of both books is the city itself and its immediate suburbs. Accordingly, I have imposed somewhat arbitrary boundaries, creating roughly a square to contain my wanderings: the sea, naturally enough, to the south; the Neath Port Talbot boundary to the east, which runs down the middle of Crymlyn Bog; the M4 motorway to the north; and a line from Gowerton to Caswell in the west. Work has already started on *Real Gower*, which will cover most of what falls outside that rough square.

Notes

1. Wynford Vaughan Thomas.
2. In January 2012, Townhill had 55% of its children living in poverty, a level of deprivation higher than that of Tower Hamlets in London (52%). Other Swansea wards with high rates of child poverty include Penderry (48%), Castle (38%) and Bonymaen (35%).
3. 42,123 hectares.

EAST

FABIAN WAY

Although Fabian Way, running from the two bridges over the river Nedd to the southernmost road bridge over the Tawe, might seem – as the city's eastern gateway – to belong to Swansea, over half of its 7.6 km length falls within the limits of Neath Port Talbot. But, as the M4 lofts you 30 metres skyward over the Nedd, and Mumbles Head commands the near horizon, 'Home at last' is what the Swansea driver is likely to feel, braking for the 30 m.p.h. bend that, straightening seaward, will lower you, after 700 metres, onto Fabian Way itself and the last few minutes of your journey (if you manage to avoid traffic jams).

Constructed between 1946 and 1950, in noisily percussive concrete sections which have gradually been replaced by tarmac, this dual carriageway was known for years as the Jersey Marine, after the village and the beach – both of that name – between which it passes. Many still call this stretch of the A483 the Jersey Marine while wondering, no doubt, what the Channel Islands have got to do with it. The area was once part of the extensive Briton Ferry estate which passed by marriage from the Prices of Briton Ferry to the Mansels of Margam and, again by marriage, to the Villiers (pronounced 'Villers') and Vernon families, earls of Jersey, in the mid eighteenth century. They profited hugely from the industriali-sation of the Swansea and Neath valleys,[1] and numerous pubs and streets in the region called Villiers, Vernon and Jersey commemorate the association.

The name Fabian Way, spreading steadily eastward from St Thomas, has tended to supplant that of Jersey Marine, but its origin too is little known. An urban myth, which seems to have been hatched by the *Western Mail* in 2010, suggests that the road is named after the Roman general Fabius Maximus (c.280-203 BC), dubbed Cunctator or the Delayer, for his infamous delaying tactics. Although Fabian Way can be a notorious 'Delayer' of traffic, its name is derived not from Fabius Maximus but from a family of Gower farmers who moved to farm at St Thomas in the early seven-teenth century. The Fabians' whitewashed farmhouse,[2] demolished in about 1859, stood in the region of today's Inkerman Street and was a useful landmark for Swansea-bound mariners. The inlet below the farm became known as Fabian's Bay, and the road that passed between the farmhouse and the harbour also took the family's name.

Like most Swansea people, I've driven along Fabian Way scores of times. But it wasn't until May 2011 that I walked it. Given the relentless volume of traffic, it's not the most pleasurable of walks or bike rides (there's a cycle path on both sides of the road), but there's much to see that you'd never notice from a car.

Encroaching on my friend Lynne Rees's *Real Port Talbot* territory, I start at the eastern end of the old Briton Ferry bridge (1955), trying not to get too sidetracked by this intriguing realm of river crossing, railway, Brunel dock, marina, ship-breaking yard, pylons, abandoned industries and Gypsy encampment. Running parallel with the old bridge, 250 metres to the south, is the M4 flyover, completed in 1993, and, nudging up between them, the ever-ramshackle Warren Hill with its makeshift enclosures, sheds and lean-tos, caravans, piebald cobs and ponies. It was once an Iron Age hill-fort, training a watchful eye on river traffic below. On the opposite bank, similarly vigilant, was Hen Gastell, an early medieval western outpost of the kingdom of Glywysing, which in the tenth century became Morgannwg or Gwlad Morgan (Glamorgan), the land of Morgan. It's believed to have been a stronghold of Morgan ap Caradog ap Iestyn, lord of Afan (d. c.1208), in the twelfth century. Much of the top of this hill was removed by quarrying in the 1930s and 40s before it suffered the ultimate indignity of serving as a bridgehead for the flyover. Few realise, as they signal left for Swansea, that they are driving through a medieval castle.

And most are unaware, as they gather speed along Fabian Way, that they're hurtling through the middle of an 18-hole golf course, its two halves connected by an underpass – for pedestrians and cyclists – between the sixth tee on the east side and the fourteenth on the west. Laid down in 1894, this is the domain of Swansea Bay Golf Club, the oldest golf club in the Swansea area. And you'll deduce from the silhouettes-with-trolley-bags on the overlooking hilltop that there's yet another golf course up there: the public Earlswood course, once known by those in resplendence below as 'the artisans' course'. "Very good value for money," says my friend and colleague Neil Reeve, "although infested with golfers who don't know how to play and get in the way, often dangerously, of those who do."

The pukka golfers below seem to go about their mysteries unperturbed by the thousands of vehicles zooming imperiously through these serene fairways. It may be difficult to conceive of golfers – owners themselves, sometimes, of 'impressive' gas guzzlers – as agents of quietude, but that's how they seem this grey afternoon, as little noticed behind their screen of beech, alder, birch and gorse as the tens of thousands of ox-eye daisies that border the road, nodding their heads in the slipstream of every oblivious car. Even more secluded than the golfers are the yellow irises and tussocky bog grasses that throng the waterlogged roots of the (rare) carr woodland which stretches along the southern side of the road.

At the roundabout that filters traffic to and from both Jersey Marine village and Amazon's massive new distribution centre, I take a southerly diversion, heading for the beach half a kilometre away (a century ago, the sea came right up to what is today the road's edge; it'll be back soon). I don't expect to find many people there: the pull-in off the roundabout has room for only half a dozen cars. A large metal sign announcing Crymlyn Burrows Site of Special Scientific Interest lists various "DON'T"s, including the use of firearms: it's peppered with holes from airgun pellets. It's as well the tide is out. A muddy inlet, which can make a peninsula of the salt marsh and dunes, is shallow enough to cross on a higgledy-piggledy line of rusting wheel-hubs which someone has conveniently placed as stepping stones. The further I get from that

frenzied road, the sweeter on the ear are the skylarks, and by the time I reach the mouth of the Nedd and the unvisited beach all I can hear are the distant waves and the shushing of wind through the marram grass – apart from, just occasionally, the tormented, angry screaming of the machines of Sunday bikers. Otherwise, loud humanity is seen but not heard – from Baglan Bay power station, Port Talbot steelworks and docks on the eastern horizon to, looking west, Swansea, its docks and priapic seafront Tower. This four-kilometre length of protected coastline is one of the last stretches of Swansea Bay to be unmodified by industry.

Light industry and commerce, however, have been a feature of the northern side of Fabian Way for most of its history. The biggest player here from 1959 onwards was the Prestcold fridge company which was later acquired, for the manufacture of car components, by Ford, Visteon and subsequently Linamar. It closed in 2010 and what then became Swansea Gate Business Park has been looking for tenants ever since.

But business seems to be booming next door at Amazon who opened their vast 'Fulfilment Centre' – which is the size of ten football pitches – in 2008. It's Amazon's fourth distribution centre

in Britain and, with one in Leipzig, Germany, their biggest in Europe. Some 2,000 people work here, dispatching at peak times up to 300,000 parcels a day to internet customers all over the world. While the consumer goods whiz overhead on a kind of computerized railway, the warehouse workers – known as 'associates' in Amazon-speak – have to hoof it in special safety boots, many of them walking between 15 and 20 kilometres a shift, enthused (possibly) by Amazon's motto, "Work hard, have fun, make history".

Built on a prehistoric peat-bed between bog-fringed woodland and a deserted beach, Amazon's mega-shed might appear to be in the middle of nowhere. But ready access to the motorway network and the nodes of invisible trading routes means that, in common with well-connected LSSBs (large single-storey buildings) throughout the land, it's actually in the centre of everywhere.

The next big thing on Fabian Way is likely to be Swansea University's second campus on the recently cleared site of BP's tank farm – just east of Swansea docks, but largely within the bounds of Neath Port Talbot – which used to infuse the gateway to Swansea with a notoriously acrid stench. An influx of thousands of students here, together with the rise of Coed D'Arcy, the 4,000-home Poundbury-style 'urban village' at what was the Llandarcy oil refinery, will surely add to the volume of vehicles. Traffic can be so dense at peak times that one day in June 2011, for instance, it took an hour and a half to drive from the Jersey Marine roundabout to the Cape Horner pub, a distance of 5.5 km.

Swansea Council, stung by the impatience of traders and motorists, has been struggling with the traffic problem for years. The elegant if self-consciously 'iconic' Sidings Bridge (2007) over Fabian Way, just west of the entrance to the port, is part of a "park and ride" scheme which, with its express bus and cycle lanes, is intended to relieve pressure on Fabian Way.[3] The bridge's support mast bears more than a passing resemblance to a slantwise Skylon, the space-age totem at the heart of the 1951 Festival of Britain.

It's a losing battle, and in Swansea's 'traffic wars' it's usually the traffic that wins over pedestrians and residents. Scores of houses, businesses and pubs were swept away in the early 1960s when Fabian Street in St Thomas was widened to make Fabian Way. At the city end, the road today is six lanes wide and a formidable barrier between the established community of St Thomas and the moneyed dockside enclave of SA1.

A house on the edge of Fabian Way, which just managed to escape the devastating demolitions, became an internet sensation in 2011 – because it was thought to look like Hitler. The end-of-terrace house at 1 Port Tennant Road – which has a sloping roof

akin to the Führer's hairline and a front door reminiscent of his toothbrush moustache – caught the eye of local youth worker Charli Dickenson, who posted a picture on Twitter.

"We got stuck in traffic," she said at the time. "I looked over and suddenly thought to myself 'Oh my God, that house looks like Hitler', so I took a snap of it. Since then, it has gone really mad and the picture has appeared all over the world."

Another piece of accidental humour that tickled the wider world a few years back was a road sign on this stretch of Fabian Way that pointed the way to 'Tourist Destinations'. Its supposed Welsh version, 'Pennau Ymwelwyr', conveyed a less than reassuring message to visitors, translating ominously as 'The heads of tourists'.

The last building on Fabian Way, or the first as you head out of town, is the Cape Horner pub, a rare reminder hereabouts of Swansea's historic copper-ore trade with the Pacific coast of South America. It opened in 1963 on the thoroughfare whose widening had caused the demolition of half a dozen pubs, among them the Station Inn, the Cyprus, the Miers Arms, the Red House, the Midlands Vaults and – another pub with copper connections – the Chile Arms. Isolated on the corner of Miers Street, and closed at the

time of writing, this three-storey shoebox of a pub had been trying to survive as a restaurant, in competition with classier dockside eateries across the way. The Cape Horner's functions room on the middle floor was a popular meeting place for the Swansea left in the 1970s, hosting political poems-and-pints nights, protest gatherings and fund-raising sessions. One of the last events I remember there was a celebration in 1980 of Robert Mugabe's election as the first prime minister of a Zimbabwe liberated from white minority rule – a heady political moment that seems now a very, very long time ago.

Notes

1. By 1873, the Earl of Jersey owned some 2,877 hectares of land in Glamorgan, with an estimated annual rental of £36,928.
2. There's a sketch of the house in Swansea Museum, showing it half thatched, half tiled.
3. It was built on the site of a former railway sidings bridge, demolished in 2003.

CENTRAL

THE TOWN WALLS

Some of the towns established by Wales's Norman conquerors have extensive if not almost complete medieval town walling. But Swansea has no visible traces whatsoever – or so it seems. While sufficient fragments of the wall and its defensive ditch have been found below ground to enable the plotting of its course, the experts usually deny the possibility of finding anything above ground. It's all supposed to have been removed in the eighteenth century. But when I spoke to an authority on the subject, the city's former estates officer Bernard Morris (1933-2012), he intriguingly left the door slightly ajar. "Have a good look along the Strand between the bottom of Morris Lane and Quay Parade," he advised.

Excavations have shown that the town wall was not built in a uniform way, although it seems to have been, in general, nearly two metres wide, and constructed of local sandstone bonded with local clay, with water-worn boulders forming a thick exterior at lower levels. It was accompanied by a ditch along much of its length, about two metres deep and six metres wide.

Although it's not known when the town walls were built, they were certainly in existence by 1332. And there's no mistaking their purpose: to defend the colonizers and their purloined lands from the dispossessed natives. Welsh raids on Swansea – notably the devastation wrought by Llewelyn Fawr in 1215 and Rhys Grug in 1217 – prompted the castle's rebuilding in stone, and doubtless spurred on the lords of Gower to consider more effective means of keeping the natives at bay. The walls may have been the work, from 1306 onwards, of William de Breos III, and they'd have been constructed, like the castle, of that ubiquitous local material, Pennant sandstone.

They defined the shape of Swansea – even after their demolition – until the 1820s, when the laying down of Oxford Street began the town's westward expansion. Much of the early street plan is still in place: the Strand, High Street and Wind Street, Salubrious Passage, College Street and Welcome Lane, King Street and King's Lane.

Given the history-effacing, architectural banality of post-blitz Swansea, there's no better way of training the imagination on the dimensions of the medieval town than walking its walls – or, rather, the streets beneath which you believe their foundations might lurk. Equipped with a blown-up map of the city centre (walls highlighted in pink) and a wishful eye, my *compañera* Margot Morgan and I

begin our walk where Swansea began – the castle, whose eastern
elevation, overlooking the Strand, is said to constitute the sole indis-
putable length of town wall. We head down Castle Lane, under the
lee of the castle's arcaded southern wall, towards the Strand, looking
for a river-facing stretch of possible town wall, not down on the
Strand itself but set back about sixteen metres from the Strand and
running parallel with it – although it's not known to what extent the
river may have acted as the main defence of this side of Swansea.
At the bottom of Castle Lane, we turn right into the Strand – which
in medieval times, of course, was Swansea's riverfront. There's no
shortage of Pennant stonework along the Strand, but most of it –
the walls of warehouses or the sides of long passageways linking the
Strand with High Street and Wind Street – is oriented in the wrong
direction for the purposes of our quest.

At Quay Parade, we turn right to find major road works at the
bottom of Wind Street: deep trenches at precisely the spot where
the medieval South Gate was believed, until recently, to be situated.
We peer into them hopefully: nothing but black mud and gravel.
Having heard, though, that when the Salubrious Place development

was under construction a year or two ago the workers had discovered a stretch of medieval ditch near the Wind Street–Little Wind Street junction, we decide on a coffee in Frankie and Benny's, taking a corner seat as near as we can to where the ditch was investigated. This bit of ditch may have been associated not with the walls but with the suburbs that topped and tailed medieval Swansea outside its walls.

Frankie and Benny's is a typical New York Italian diner: black-and-white photos of crooners, film stars and Americana, and Ella Fitzgerald singing us in with 'Every time you say goodbye'. "The vowels of this woman are fantastic," says my Welsh-American jazz-singing companion. We ask the young waiter who brings us our (excellent) espressos to tell us about the Frankie and Benny chain. Oddly, there are no F&Bs in America, it seems, the land of the chain's founders. "But they're all over this country – and also in Europe," he says. "We're in Europe too," I venture. "Are you?" he says. He shows us a potted history of F&B: too much of a generalized Italian-American cliché to be true, in spite of the prominent wall display of F&B's supposed busts. Then he presents us, in view of our interest in F&B, with a glossy F&B calendar: all the wholesome American stereotypes are here, and all the 'national' holidays and saints' days except – you know it, even before removing the cellophane – St David's. A more telling omission is Thanksgiving Day. "They can't possibly be American without Thanksgiving Day," says Margot.

On, then, down an entirely reinvented Little Wind Street, past Chiquito and the Lava Lounge on our left, the NCP block on our right, before we turn right into York Street, checking some more promising black holes there: *dim byd*. We have probably, in any case, overreached Swansea's medieval bounds: the latest thinking is that the wall cut inland from the river, up Green Dragon Lane; it crossed Wind Street, where the South Gate would have been, and continued along the line of Salubrious Passage towards Princess Way. Princess Way follows, in part, the same route as the now lost Fisher Street which, as 'Vicus Piscatorum', is the earliest mentioned of all Swansea's streets.

We follow our map's wobbly pink line over Princess Way and, veering right, head up Rutland Street into the red-brick mopiness of St David's shopping centre. It occurs to me that one way for Swansea to address its chronic amnesia would be to mark out the route of its town walls with a course of some distinctive material –

Pennant sandstone, perhaps, with copper beading – set flush into streets and pavements and running across shop floors.

The builders of what for long was the C&A clothes store, and is now New Look, would certainly have known of the medieval defences: the foundations for C&A's colonnade, it transpired during construction work in 1974, were laid directly in the town moat.

The well-travelled statue of Sir Hussey Vivian – Castle Square (1886-1936), Victoria Park (1936-82) and finally the St David's centre – stands roughly where the Wassail Gate interrupted the defences. From there, we follow the wall along the western boundary of St Mary's churchyard, before it clips the corner of the churchyard, crosses the road and disappears through Primark. It travels diagonally for 90 metres through the block of shops sandwiched between Whitewalls and Princess Way, emerging through the door of Sports World, crossing Oxford Street and forging on through Marks and Spencer. I ask an attendant at an information desk near the store's greetings-card department how it feels to be standing on the walls of medieval Swansea. She gives me a professionally polite but pitying smile, as if trying to decide whether this nutter is drunk, deranged or trying on some evangelical foreplay.

Our wall leaves M&S through the goods entrance at the rear, cuts across the car park and heads straight through the block that occupies the corner of Princess Way and The Kingsway. We take a detour through the Hanbury and meet the wall heading from the doorway of the Pearl Assurance building and passing in front of the Dragon Hotel – where the old town's West Gate was situated. It then heads off down Orchard Street, ending up in the middle of the road at the south-eastern corner of the old Police Station. At this point, it turns at a ninety-degree angle down cobbled King Street (surely the draftiest alleyway in Swansea, thanks to the wind-funnelling effects of nearby tall buildings) to join High Street. Here stood the old North Gate, marking the medieval town's division between Bovton (above-town), what was north of that gate, and Donton (down-town), what was south of it. Iceland, on the corner of King Street and High Street, is where a clear section of the town ditch was recorded during building work in 1975.

According to most modern maps, King Street becomes King's Lane after crossing High Street, but many prefer to use the older name, Morris Lane, for this alleyway that slopes steeply down to where the Tawe once flowed. When in 1845 Henry De La Beche produced his shocking report on the squalor of Swansea's streets and housing, he described Morris Lane as "the dirtiest alley in the town"; all refuse was thrown into the lane and there it remained, unless rain washed it back into the houses. The lane has generally had a shady reputation. After a period as a 'massage' hot-spot in the 1980s, it declined into a state of ramshackle decay, serving no purpose beyond connecting High Street with the Strand.

It takes no great effort in the shadow of a considerable length of Pennant sandstone wall on the lane's southern side to imagine yourself under the lee of the old town wall itself. The bottom part of the wall, clearly distinguishable from the rest, could indeed be what's left of the town wall. And if it's not, surely the existing wall was built on the old wall's medieval foundations? Then there's the intriguing disjunction – a clean divide, with no attempt at interleaving the stonework – between two sections of the wall: it comes at precisely the point, about sixteen metres up from the Strand, that you'd expect the town wall to take a ninety-degree turn in a southerly direction.

Down on the Strand again, there's nothing of much promise until

we spot a compelling turret-like fragment, with a length of wall, to the side of and disappearing behind the red-brick (and incongruously suburban) Missionaries of Charity convent. The mission was inaugurated – by Mother Theresa of Calcutta, in person – in 1996, in a small terraced house on the steeply sloping Clifton Hill; it moved to this larger building in 2000. Run by a team of nuns from India, with their distinctive white and blue-banded habit, it provides a hostel for twelve homeless men.

Homeless

You're homeless, sure, if your dwelling's a box,
You're homeless if your blanket's *The Sun*,
But you can also be homeless if you live in a house
That's a mouldering, verminous run.
You're homeless if you're crammed in a crowded B&B,
You're homeless if you're rotting in 'A Home',
You're homeless if you're old and trapped downstairs,
You're homeless if you can never be alone.
You're homeless if there's no escape

From a husband who thumps you each night,
You're homeless if racists shove shit through your door,
You're homeless if you can't afford heating and light.
You're homeless if you live in fear of war
With nowhere safe to give birth,
You're homeless if there's never enough food on your table –
Yes, the homeless are many: most of the people on Earth.

Some of the men tell us what they have heard – that, yes, the structure behind the convent, which has clearly been extensively re-pointed in recent years, is indeed part of the old town wall. The 'in charge', as they say in India, is Sister Joseph from Kerala, who's been in Swansea since 2003. She invites me through and out the back to take a closer look. Wreathed in mouth-watering curry pungencies, I peer up and along, left and right, what must be one of the most formidable chunks of wall anywhere in Swansea. About 10 metres high and 25 metres long, it's an extensively patched and in-filled cocktail of building materials: Pennant sandstone, red sandstone, river stone, slag blocks, slate, granite, Victorian and modern brick. There are several blocked up old doorways and, let into the wall, two modern doorways opening on storerooms which, before the convent was built, says Sister Joseph, used to be archways where down-and-outs took shelter. Whether or not this structure, or parts of it, are original medieval walling, remains to be seen, but it would seem to be in exactly the right position, and that medieval-looking turret extruding from it is intriguing. (I'm later delighted to have my hunch confirmed by Ellie Graham of the Glamorgan-Gwent Archaeological Trust, who says that recent research has shown conclusively that the curving walls of the turret are indeed part of the medieval town wall. There's also the likelihood that that louring adjacent wall with its 'undercrofts' is at least in part a survivor of Swansea's medieval defences.)

We continue down the Strand and within minutes make another find. Opposite Parc Tawe, in the region of the footbridge over the Strand, is an extensive grassy bank and two lengths of Pennant sandstone wall running roughly parallel with each other and with Worcester Place. They look promising, but they seem too far up from the Strand. Then we notice, lower down the bank, and protruding from the red-brick side wall of the former Castle Cinema (now a Megazone 'laser tag' arena) a stubby chunk of rather likelier wall. Set back from the Strand by about sixteen metres, it would seem to fall directly in line with the course of the old town defences set by the wall of the castle itself, which is immediately the other side of the cinema. We have come full circle – with more questions than ever about Swansea's elusive town wall.

CASTLE SQUARE

Swansea is notorious, in the words of Joni Mitchell, for 'not knowing what it's got 'til it's gone'. The Mumbles train invariably heads the list of Swansea's squandered assets. To that growing list can be added Castle Square as a public space at the heart of the city – which ceased to be a space belonging to the public in 2008 when a gigantic television screen was dug in permanently in a corner of the square, churning out stultifying trivia non-stop, and rendering impossible the multifaceted conversation, at the personal and public levels, that is the delight of central piazzas the world over. Measuring 4.5 by 6.5 metres, and standing four metres off the ground – so that, alas, you can't assault it – the screen is one of twenty to have been inflicted on public spaces throughout the United Kingdom by the London 2012 Olympic Committee in tandem with the BBC.

You might be invited into Swansea's front room – for a protest meeting, say – but don't expect your host to acknowledge your presence by turning off the telly. Slobs R Us. Political demonstrations are no longer possible in Castle Square, a raised voice or a megaphone being no match for the vapidities emanating from the anaesthetising screen. Consumerism trumps ruminative silence or discussion every time. And don't expect the hyperactivity beaming from the telly – hardly more locally distinct than the cloned shops that surround it – to say much about the identity of Swansea. Council leader Chris Holley said at the time of the telly's switch-on (and the square's switch-off) that the big screen would "help generate a wonderful atmosphere in Castle Square" and "contribute to Swansea's reputation for sticking out from the crowd ...". Like loads of other city centres making amends for an impoverishing lack of television in people's lives.

You pave paradise and put up a parking lot. Or a television screen. Big Brother, it seems, we love you.

SALUBRIOUS PASSAGE

The intriguing name of this infamously urinous alleyway off hedonistic Wind Street is up there with Knob Lick (Missouri), Horní Street (Prague) and the village of Fucking in Austria as one of the 100 Rudest Place Names in the world, as listed in the book *Rude World*, published in 2006.[1]

Swansea people love it – not for the schoolboyish *double entendre*, but for the pleasure of rolling that glorious old adjective around the mouth, and for the flavour the alley exudes of a pre-Dickensian Swansea which time and the Luftwaffe long ago extinguished.

The grandiloquence of the street's name is hardly matched by its scale or appearance. Its essential element, a covered alleyway supported by six cast-iron pillars, is about the length between the two sets of stumps on a cricket pitch; the passage is floored with irregular flagstones puddled with piss which has been aimed vaguely at its graffitied walls by sozzled Wind Street revellers. An iron hoop, topped with a Victorian-style lantern, arches over its western end, neatly framing a view of Swansea's most contemporary building, the 29-storey Meridian Tower. You can see from Wind Street that the passageway has been driven between the second and third bays of a four-storey Georgian townhouse which

a plaque on its frontage suggests was commissioned by one 'Tho. Williams / Surgeon / 1803'.

Such passageways are relative rarities in today's Swansea, although there are other comparable Wind Street offshoots – Green Dragon Lane and St Mary Street in particular – which exert the same magnetic allure of urban lanes and back streets in cities world-wide.

> a waft of patchouli
> announcing in advance
> the old hippy

Its earlier name, Salubrious Place, would seem to lend support to the assumption that it was originally a late eighteenth- or early nineteenth-century 'court', a lane providing pedestrian access to a courtyard surrounded by (invariably overcrowded) buildings. The genteel interpretation of the situation is that the lane eventually developed into a pedestrian thoroughfare, during the 1780-1830 period when Swansea was attempting to re-invent itself as a 'Welsh Weymouth', and that this was the route walked by health-conscious Regency beaus and their gels, off to partake of the salubrious zephyrs of Swansea sands.

The seedy romance of the place certainly appealed to the poet Adrian Mitchell (1932-2008) when he was Dylan Thomas Fellow during the 1995 Dylan Thomas festival. He enjoyed showing visiting writers "the delights / of Salubrious Passage, my favourite ghostwalk, / under which I heard the Italian Love Gods play."[2]

But I detect in the passage's naming a distinct tang of Swansea irony, if not sarcasm – for Salubrious Place was all too insalubriously close to the stinking town ditch, into which huge quantities of household refuse were thrown. And 'salubrious' is not a word that could be applied, without a twisted smile, to conditions in the cramped 'courts' of old Swansea, which by the late nineteenth century had become insufferable slums. More recently, prostitutes – known as Wind Street Walkers – used to hover at the passage's mouth, where these days a beggar is often slumped.

> Salubrious Passage:
> froth-lips wants pence please
> for the last bus home

As you emerge into the light beneath that iron hoop, there are stones about you, if not ghosts, with tales to tell. Immediately to your left, there's an exposed patch of curvaceous walling, done in slim Pennant-sandstone blocks, which seems much older than the structure it now finds itself supporting. A few metres beyond, you'll find yourself walking on the remains of a fossilised beach, formed by the action of waves on sand in the Carboniferous era, between 290 and 354 million years ago:[3] the passage of thousands of feet over this sandstone flag, since it was quarried locally a hundred or more years ago, have darkened the crests of the ripple marks, making them easily visible – at the same time, no doubt, as diminishing them imperceptibly.

The Victorian tone of the open part of the street is augmented by the antiquated lanterns that adorn Metropole Chambers (1927) and those fringeing the No Sign Bar's polythene-covered smoking patio. The name Metropole Chambers recalls the nearby Metropole Hotel, or the George as it was in the nineteenth century, when it was a prestigious berth for ships' captains. The part of the hotel fronting

Wind Street survived the blitz, but its living accommodation took a mighty hit. Its upper regions remained derelict through the 1950s, the cupboards in its dusty corridors agape with gently decaying stacks of linen and bedding. It finally collapsed in the 1960s.

As numerous 'To Let' signs indicate, there hasn't been much happening in Salubrious Passage since the recession began to bite in 2008. Among the boarded up businesses is what used to be Dylan's Bookstore – still with its exuberant sculptural flourish of cherub, steel ribbons and stone books – which Jeff Towns ran here for 25 years before decamping reluctantly in 2004 to larger premises in King Edward Road, Brynmill. He regretted not being able to take the address with him, which he regarded as probably the greatest for a bookshop anywhere in the world. A collector of anecdotes about the street, Jeff recalls "the wonderful story about Salubrious Passage where Dylan Thomas used to visit a friend who had a shop there.[4] The pair heated up coins on a Bunsen burner, dropped them onto the pavement below and waited for people to try to pick them up."

Jeff's shop was originally no more than a lock-up, which may once have been the stables for a long-gone pub opposite called The Shades. He rented it for a tenner a week from "a wonderful, eccentric and ancient solicitor, Evan Hines, who had offices opposite. When Evan died, his executors offered me the freehold of my shop, which I bought. It was very small and I needed more space. Next door was an old gents' urinal – a kind of Clochemerle-style *pissoir*. Evan Hinds could overlook it from his office and complained incessantly to the council about goings on inside its marble stalls – he claimed it was Swansea's premiere 'cottage'. The council's response was to brick up the entrance and leave it to pile up with garbage."

Jeff bought the urinal and redeveloped the shop, incorporating the pissoir and raising the roof to include a kind of minstrel gallery for extra bookshelves. Soon, though, the business outgrew that space and Jeff decided to add a complete second floor. "The architect Brendan Minney [1941-2012] of Penmaen designed a sweet 'A' building with a small faux turret on top of which I placed a cherub, made by Rob Conybeare." (This little fatso with quill is a close relation of cherubs found lurking elsewhere around town.) "I had just been in Barcelona and had admired the work of Antoni Tàpies, so we added the steel ribbons that flowed down to three giant marble books that I sourced from a monumental mason. They were like solid and flightless kites mounted on the pine-end of the

building. They needed words, so what better for Dylan's Bookstore than to incise the opening words from his greatest lyric, 'Fern Hill': 'As I was young and easy'."[5]

Jeff tells me that in the early twentieth century the shop had been a barber's emporium run by another eccentric character, 'The Great Vitoski', an émigré, possibly from Poland, who claimed to have cut hair on Broadway and boasted of famous show-biz and mobster clients. "Legend has it that he had numerous signs offering his services in various languages, which he alternated in the window depending on what ships were berthed in the docks. He also kept a foul pot of stew boiling on a small stove. One day, early in my time in the passage, I was standing outside in the sun when a passing old-timer stopped, took a pace back, and surveyed the building wistfully. He began to reminisce about Vitoski, but then he came close and with a nudge and a wink whispered gleefully that it was the first place in Swansea you could get – nudge, nudge – 'them French letter things!' I like the idea that my shop was always a place of 'letters' – of one kind or another."

If business in Salubrious Passage is struggling, the same cannot be said of the word 'Salubrious', which is proliferating. The final manifestation of the Dylan Thomas Bookstore in Brynmill (which closed in 2012) was housed, by way of tribute, in Salubrious House, and the word has attached itself to new buildings in the vicinity of the passage, such as the Salubrious Court residential block at the end of the street, and the leisure and entertainment complex Salubrious Place, which declares itself in letters a metre high at the Wind Street-Quay Parade junction's gateway to the city. Little scope there, though, for spicy *doubles entendres*.

PRINCESS WAY

Princess Way, which could have been an attractive tree-lined boulevard akin to Barcelona's Ramblas, is a typical Swansea fudge, pedestrianised in its northern half, partially pedestrianised in its southern, and with a half-baked sense of direction.

Opened in 1952 by a princess shortly before she became a queen, the then concrete-surfaced Princess Way, bordered for much of its length by post-blitz concrete-and-glass storefronts, lay roughly along the line of bombed out, and much narrower, Goat Street and, in part, Fisher Street.

What was originally the moat of the castle gradually filled up with silt and rubbish, so that for much of the eighteenth century the east side of Goat Street was used by the burgesses for grazing animals, digging saw-pits and raising dung heaps. On the west side was a row of houses, in one of which the English poet Walter Savage Landor (1775-1864) lived for a while.

If I were to tell you that on the corner of College Street and what was Goat Street more than a hundred people were burnt alive as they sheltered in the basement of the Wesley Chapel (1840s) during the third of the Three Nights Blitz (21 February 1941), I'd be perpetuating a well-worn urban myth. The Italianate chapel, commemorated by a head-height plaque in College Street, was certainly a casualty of the bombing, but everyone in the basement was led to safety before its destruction.

For much of the first decade of the present century, the northern, pedestrianised end of Princess Way was in redevelopment limbo. After years of uncertainty, its new configuration began to take shape: the roundabout and pedestrian underpass at its junction with The Kingsway were demolished in 2006; the Pearl Assurance building was adapted for residential use (part of a welcome repopulation of the city centre); and David Evans, the last of Swansea's

grand department stores, was demolished in 2007, to make way for a £30m shopping complex – of underwhelming design – which eats into a substantial tract of the street.

When the gleaming brass and wooden doors of David Evans closed in 2005, with the loss of 245 jobs, it was, as the local media inevitably declared, the end of an era. David Evans, which was built on the site of the Theatre Royal (1807-98) and traded there for 140 years, was posh. Its post-blitz building (1954) had fourteen box-set windows, each dressed individually to project an image of elegance, high fashion and taste. The floor manager in the 1950s would personally greet the more exalted customers – Lady Jenkins, Lady Evans-Bevan, Lady Gregg – in their furs and perms, airs and high-heeled graces. The ground floor, as late as 2005, exuded class and brassy glamour, with its heavily made-up beauty consultants touting Lancôme, Guerlain, Helena Rubinstein, Revlon and other select brands.

After David Evans closed, but before it was demolished, the Swansea-based Glamorgan-Gwent Archaeological Trust opened five trenches within the store and spent about a year investigating medieval (and later) remains beneath the floor of what had been the women's clothing department. They unearthed the old castle ditch,

which was about two metres deep and which had filled up, since it was last used for defensive purposes, with domestic refuse and horse dung. Their most exciting find was two abraded shards of Roman pottery, the first evidence of a Roman presence in Swansea itself, as opposed to the surrounding area.

All that has been saved of the 1954 building, thanks to the tireless campaigning of local historian Paulette Pelosi, are seventeen ornamental medallions, depicting fashions through the ages, which decorated the top storey of the store on both the Princess Way and Castle Square façades. Paulette, whose motto is "Life is looking up!", encourages everyone to raise their eyes above shop-window level and relish the generally ignored quantity and variety of Swansea's architectural embellishments.[6] "I've always found that the very act of pointing a serious-looking camera at a Swansea landmark arouses attention," she told me, "Everyone begins to look up!" Hardly anyone noticed the medallions until Paulette began pointing her camera at them and appealing in the local press for them to be saved. Her campaign succeeded, and the medallions – the work of the largely forgotten sculptor John Matthews – are now to be seen in the garden of Swansea Museum. The first, which was at The Kingsway end of the building, depicts Eve unadorned. The series works through the ages – from the tenth century to Victorian times – before concluding with a modern almost-Eve in nothing but a bikini.

One of the street's few blitz survivors is the Cross Keys pub, a corner of which, with the castle, is Swansea's oldest building: note the fourteenth-century lancet windows by the main entrance. It was built in 1332 by Bishop Henry de Gower as the Hospital of the Blessed St David, effectively an almshouse catering for "blind, decrepit or infirm priests and other poor men" of the bishop's vast diocese of St David's. As the historian Glanmor Williams has observed, "in the midst of this Norman town, which had tried to keep the Welsh out, the cult of the latter's best-known saint was nevertheless honoured." By the end of the sixteenth century, it had become an inn, with the sign of the crossed keys of St Peter commemorating its religious origin – and an inn it has remained (it also housed, in the nineteenth century, a slaughterhouse). The Cross Keys used to be a low-ceilinged, intimate pub, crowded if there were more than twenty drinkers in its friendly little bar. But now, having suffered a series of disproportionate extensions, it's like some Disneyfied baronial hall, loud with excitable plasma screens and corporate in its lack of character.

St Mary's church opposite did not survive the blitz. It was rebuilt, in the 1950s, much in the style of its 1890s predecessor, and is possibly the sixth church to stand on this site. Although Swansea is a city, St Mary's is not its Anglican cathedral: the cathedral of the diocese of Swansea and Brecon is 72 km away, in Brecon. Ceri Richards' 'Deposition' (1958), one of three of the painter's large-scale works to be seen in Swansea,[7] hangs here. And there's striking contemporary stained glass from locally trained artists such as Rodney Bender, Kuni Kajiwara and Catrin Jones.

Among notable gravestones on the north side of the churchyard are a slab embedded in the paving commemorating William Jernegan, architect of much of Georgian Swansea, and, a few metres away, an upstanding scroll of pink marble whose wordy inscription commemorates Major Lewis Roteley (1785-1861), hero of Trafalgar (and slum landlord).[8] The inscription describes how a severely injured Rotely, after Nelson had received his fatal wound, "kept the [*Victory*'s] deck and succeeded to the command of the remnant of the detachment of Marines left alive in the ship on that day." At his home, May Hill House, Roteley would entertain dinner guests by producing relics of the battle, the biggest trophy being

Nelson's blood-stained stockings.

Swansea sometimes gets things half right. A £2.4m regeneration of the southern end of Princess Way, completed in 2006, saw two lanes of traffic removed and an enhanced pavement area – with decorative stonework, five street-art beacons, and sixteen polished granite benches – designed to answer the attractively landscaped environs of the National Waterfront Museum on the other side of Oystermouth Road. But it remains a space dominated by traffic. No walkers cross the road where coloured markings tell them to, because there's no reason for them to cross at that point: the place most pedestrians choose to cross is twenty-five metres further up the street, where they have to play Russian roulette with the traffic. And I've never seen anyone sitting on those magnificent benches, or any dosser sleeping on them (their design forbids it). They all face outwards, as if in homage to the traffic, and don't talk to either of the pubs – the Cross Keys and the New York – that top and tail the southern end of Princess Way.

The New York, which opened in 1963 with a Long Island Bar and a Manhattan Lounge, underwent something of a royalist cringe in 1987 and renamed itself the Duke of York, when a son of the woman who opened this street acceded to that title. But they've dumped the Duke and it's the New York again. As Ellington's, it was for many years the hub of Swansea's jazz scene, with live music in its upstairs room four nights a week.

OXFORD STREET

It was the development of Oxford Street in the 1820s that began the town's westward expansion. Why is Swansea's main shopping street so long and straight? Because it was laid down on the line of one of Swansea's three ropewalks.[9] These were sheds about 400 metres long and 9 wide, which supplied the port's voracious demand for rope.

The Market has always been the street's focal point, although everything east of its junction with Union Street, along with the market itself, was destroyed in the blitz, and rebuilt in a hurry, concrete shoe-box style, after the war. If the damage was less severe west of Union Street, there were casualties nevertheless. Some shops destroyed in that recessed part of the street at the southern end of Picton Arcade were replaced by three or four Nissen hut shops which survived well into the fifties. One, I remember – a grocer's called Genders – had an overhead network of taut wires; shiny brass pots whizzed along them like miniature cable cars, ferrying cash to and from the counting house – an hypnotic spectacle for a five-year-old.

Two magnificent palaces of entertainment survived the bombs, the Carlton Cinema (1914) and, next door, the best loved of all Swansea theatres, the Empire (1900). Renowned for its music hall and variety shows, it did much to spark the careers of both Harry Secombe (1921-2001), eastside Swansea's most famous son, and the comedian and comic actor Frankie Howerd (1917-1992). As a conscript during the Second World War, Frankie Howerd spent several years in barracks in Penclawdd. He'd relieve the monotony of army life by attending the Empire's weekly variety shows, where he'd sit with pen and notebook purloining gags for his own future routines. The Empire could not survive competition from the cinema and television. My parents took me to the Empire in 1956, for my first ever (enthralling) experience of theatre – *Babes in the Wood*, starring Stan Stennett, with Morecambe and Wise support-

ing as 'the baddies'. We went back the following year for the Empire's final panto, *Jack and the Beanstalk*. By the end of the decade the Empire had been demolished; the unutterably banal 99p Stores building occupies the site. The sole remaining trace is in Nelson Street where, between Franco's Café and what used to be Enzo's hair stylists, there's an unusually tall entrance to a covered service alley: this is the old Empire's 'back door', its scenery dock. (Nelson Street was perhaps best known to Swansea youth for its long-lasting joke shop, Blacks, stuffed with such irresistible parental irritants as whoopee cushions, plastic dog turds and stink bombs.)

The Carlton, or at least its bow-windowed, dazzlingly white Carraraware frontage, is still with us – as Waterstone's bookstore. Built for the Swansea Electric Cinema Company in a daring fusion of classical and art-deco styles, the Carlton was one of Britain's earliest showpiece cinemas. It's the master work of the architect Charles Tamlin Ruthen (1871-1926) whose other distinctive Swansea buildings – in his trademark Edwardian baroque style – include Pantygwydr English Baptist Church (1906-07) in Brynmill, the Mond Buildings (1911) in Union Street and the Exchange Buildings (1913-14) in Adelaide Street. The Carlton, as the *Post* declared when it opened, was "the last word in cinemas", with a café and palm-court orchestra on its first floor, a dramatic

staircase (still there) twining up through the entire building, and a roof over the staircase that could be slid back in warm weather so that customers, before or after the film, could take their refreshments in the open air.

Of the many films I saw there, *Ben Hur*, shown in August 1959, was, for a ten-year-old, the most thrilling. Bumper audiences were anticipated at the Carlton for *The Inspector*, a big-budget movie in which Three Cliffs Bay in Gower featured as a beach in Palestine, with fake palm trees and castle. The film opened on 8 October 1962, but perhaps because Three Cliffs figured only in its final ten minutes, *The Inspector* seemed to leave Swansea filmgoers underwhelmed, and it finished after less than a week.

After the cinema closed in the late 1970s, there was a popular campaign – posters, meetings, Carlton T-shirts, letters to the press – to save it from demolition, led by four local architects calling themselves ACES (Action for the Care of the Environment in

Swansea). The council rallied to the cause, and there was a public enquiry, which I attended as one of the campaigners. This was, literally, a class act. The developers' case was argued by a no-nonsense Bradford man, with a reputation for turning old buildings into rubble. Pitted against this down-to-business Yorkshireman were the plummy tones of a barrister with a silk Paisley handkerchief overflowing his breast pocket, who deployed witheringly Wildean rhetoric to argue the case for the building's retention. It was riveting theatre – and none of us minded that on this occasion the toff's argument won and the Carlton was saved. The building reopened as Waterstone's in 1995.

Bookshop

I'm browsing in 'Barddoniaeth'
when up stomp two unlikely lads,
hooch-swiggin and eyes a-poppin
at the lovers on the cover
of my *Acts of Union* ...

"It's never ...?"

"Tis, mun, the fuckin works."

"On the front fuckin cover of a fuckin book!"

"Give it ere ... fucking poetry."

"*Fuckin* poetry ... or fucking *poetry*?"

"Fucking *poetry*."

"Fuck it."

   The restless reinvention experienced by Oxford Street shops in the later twentieth century was stoutly resisted, until its closure in the 1980s, by one old business, Griffiths the ironmongers, on the corner with Plymouth Street, opposite the Eli Jenkins pub[10] on the other corner.[11] This agricultural emporium was about the last memento of Oxford Street's long association with Gower farmers, whose carts and traps would line the street, until well into the twentieth century, when they came to town with produce for the Market and to do some shopping of their own, if not some carousing in the pubs. Some of these were inns with proper stables in their yards, but many farmers availed themselves of more informal arrangements, resting their horses in people's gardens. Because none of the older houses had a back entrance, the farmer would have to lead his horse through the front door, along the passage and out into the garden via the scullery. On the farmer's shopping list would almost certainly be some items from Griffiths' or one of the other ironmongeries that used to be numerous in the town centre. In the farming community in which I was raised, Griffiths the ironmongers was a by-word for all conceivable agricultural needs. To enter Griffiths' dimly lit and densely cluttered cave was to step back half a century or more, and to savour ways of farming life that had largely passed into history. You name it, Griffiths would be sure to have it: castrating tongs, chicken wire, scythes, billhooks, pitchforks, halters, headstalls, seeds and seed-fiddles, ropes, buckets, nails and screws, cross-cut saws, anvils, pig-slaughtering benches; among the treasures hanging overhead were a couple of zinc baths, of the kind used by miners in front of their kitchen fires, for which there'd been little demand for decades. There are no shops of such character left in the whole of Swansea, and hardly any shops in Oxford Street under local owner-ship: almost all conform to the cloned banality of the kind of corporate businesses and 'retail outlets' to be found all over Britain. Griffiths' now belongs to a chain of mobile-phone merchants.

> "Big Issue!"
> on every corner, mad dogs
> and Englishmen on ropes

Once upon a time (i.e. c.1995, the year Swansea hosted the UK Year of Literature and Writing), Swansea could have had a genuinely twenty-first-century – and truly central – central library had the city fathers summoned the nerve to go ahead with Will Alsop's innovative design for a national literature centre – which was to have been built on the car park in front of the Grand Theatre, site of the old Oxford Street National Schools (1848; demolished 1989). This multicoloured, glass palace-of-the-word on stilts, outright winner of an international competition organised by the council, proved too much ultimately for the arbiters of munici-pal taste. Reaching for the ever-ready excuse of 'shortage of cash', they hastily consigned it to the realm of the Swansea-that-might-have-been. Alsop recycled his design for Peckham library and scooped one of the most prestigious international prizes of his career. This own-goal for Swansea caused much mirth in the sophisticated capital – until Cardiff did more or less the same thing with Zaha Hadid's design for an opera house; the two cities between them made Wales an architectural laughing stock for years to come.

The junction with Wyndham Street, in Oxford Street's largely residential Sandfields section, is roughly where the old ropewalk would have ended. Here Oxford Street seems to celebrate its liberation from the rigours of rectitude by taking a leisurely tilt southwards for its remaining 400 metres.

UNION STREET

With its pawnbrokers, moneylenders, bookies, charity shops, burger bars, clone retail outlets, empty premises, abandoned upper rooms and cheapskate architectural potching, Union Street illustrates as well as any the decline in identity and purpose suffered by city centre shopping streets throughout the land.

> the lip-glossed one,
> her *Cosmo* bought, sneaks
> a sneaky sniff of it

Because my father, who was an agricultural valuer as well as a farmer, had an office on the first floor of 15 Union Street – in premises owned for years by the downstairs business, Bradford & Bingley (now rebranded as Santander) – this was the first Swansea street I came to know well. I wonder what my conservative old man would have made of the 'business' done hereabouts by his granddaughter – my eldest daughter Angharad – as a busker outside Swansea Market's Union Street entrance. During her student years she'd often pitch up here to serenade the shoppers with her folk music, violin case open at her feet to receive the takings: £30 or £40 an hour was not unusual, and around £70 an hour at Christmas time – a tidy little earner.

For most of my life, it's been a one-way street, funnelling traffic in a northerly direction, alongside the Market, across Oxford Street and into The Kingsway. It seemed almost against the natural order

of things when a few years ago the council, having pedestrianised three quarters of the street, reversed its one-way flow in the remaining quarter, sucking vehicles in from The Kingsway before despatching them eastwards down Park Street.

Although the Market was reduced to a shell during the 1941 blitz, Union Street suffered relatively little damage, apart from a massive crater in the region of the Exeter Hotel, a site since occupied by H. Samuel the jeweller. Much of the business done by old Union Street was conditioned by its proximity to the market and by the needs of farmers as well as shoppers. In 1876, this short street, little more than 150 metres long, boasted eight public houses, which by the 1950s had been reduced to two, the Dillwyn Arms (today's Virgin Media) and the No. 10 (now a Holland and Barrett health-food store). Well into the 1970s, there was still a branch of that once essential agricultural emporium Griffiths the ironmongers[12] in lower Union Street. Having called there for, say, a galvanised bucket, a Gower farmer might wander up to Smith the boots for a new pair of hobnails or some Wellingtons, festoons of which used to hang on strings outside the shop. Then he might call to see my father at T.E. Jenkins & Son about the sale of a field, before tucking in to pie and chips at the Union café next door (now

Oxfam) or the Dorothy café across the road. If fish was his fancy, he might take a seat at Peter Jones's in lower Union Street, remembering before heading home to buy some linctus at Jack Gilbert the chemist.

Other businesses I recall from not so long ago include Thomas Thomas the wholesale warehouse (now Abbey National; the owner's artist daughter, Brenda, once made a dinosaur for Ringo Starr), Halford's bikes (now Clive Ranger), B. Barer the jeweller, Sol Solomon the tailor above the Dorothy café and alongside Twinney watch repairs (Swansea no longer has a tailor's); then, at the top of the street, Lovell's café (excellent for knickerbocker glories), the self-consciously classy Burlington restaurant, and Calder's, the gentlemen's outfitters. There were two butchers: Woodley's on the east side of the street and Woodward's opposite, next door to my father's office. Thursday was half-closing day, staunchly observed by most retailers. My brother Martyn, who took over from my father, used to observe some curious business going on next door most Thursday afternoons: legs of lamb, strings of sausages and joints of beef flying out of the rear upstairs window of Woodward's and landing on a flat roof below, to be spirited away by nightfall.

Many of these shops had considerable character, none more so than Duck, Son & Pinker,[13] the piano, sheet music and record shop, at number 11. Entering between two display windows, you'd be assailed by the smell of beeswax polish and the sound of piano-tuning. The long central walkway was flanked on either side by pianos of all shapes, size and price. At the far end, separated by glass panels and swing doors, was the record department, where I bought my first ever 78, 'The Ballad of Davy Crockett'. Soon the new, 'unbreakable' 45s came in, and, as frequently as the pocket money would allow, I'd find myself striding along the brown linoleum of Duck, Son & Pinker to pick up the latest hits by Cliff, the Shadows, Helen Shapiro, Chubby Checker, the Everlys.

Like many Union Street frontages, that of number 11, now occupied by Cheltenham & Gloucester, has been hideously 'updated' and simplified, the upper floor having been obliterated by an overreaching slab of repeating concrete panels.[14] Elsewhere, bay windows have been lopped off – as if a face could be improved by the removal of its nose – and original features slighted in the service of 'corporate identity'.

A proud survivor of the general humdrumming is the ornate, mock-Tudor frontage of 'Ye Olde Wine Shoppe No 10', with its

multiple leaded lights, its chorus of gables, its playful lantern above
a jetty with corbels carved in the form of griffins, hawks and what
looks like an aggressively thirsty duck. It was among the most
distinctive pubs in Swansea, but nothing survives of its beguiling
interior. The building, dating from about 1790, was the Glamorgan
Arms before it became the No. 10. Like the Dillwyn Arms in lower
Union Street, and umpteen pubs of yesteryear, the No. 10 was laid
out to a traditional three-bar plan: public bar, snug and, at the end
of a side corridor, lounge bar – floored, in this case, with red quarry
tiles, and lofty of ceiling, its headroom continuing beyond a
balconied first floor. On a plinth in this space towered the presiding
genius of the No. 10, a stuffed Bavarian bear named Archie, who'd
been left behind by a circus in the 1800s. Archie survived the Astey
chain's drastic remodelling in 1967, but not the closure of the pub
in 1990. Some believe that the mangy bear propped in a corner of
the Queen's in Gloucester Place is Archie, but that tormented wreck
(known as Boris) is not the bear I remember from those mornings
when I'd sidle into the back bar of the No. 10 – the pub whiffing still
of cleaner's disinfectant – to spend half an hour with an underage
pint of dark and a book of poems, Archie frowning down on me
from among the skylights.

If one edifice in Union Street can be described as grand, if not grandiose, it's Charles Tamlin Ruthen's Mond Buildings (1911) built of Portland stone in his characteristic Edwardian baroque style as headquarters for the National League of Young Liberals. It was paid for by the industrialist and politician Sir Alfred Mond (1868-1930), co-founder in 1900 of the Mond Nickel Company in Clydach (which became the largest nickel works in the world). Here, Ruthen was getting confidently into his stride for his master-piece, the Carlton Cinema (1914) round the corner in Oxford Street, indulging himself in giant Ionic columns, curlicues, bows and recumbent cherubs, and crowning his rich confection with an open, domed cupola guarded by rampant dragons. Its upper floors are home today to a couple of dance studios.

> lights on red –
> from above, as cars idle,
> the tippety tap of dancers

During the 1970s the Mond was one of Swansea's main student haunts. The guitarist Brian Breeze performed regularly at the Students' Union bar there, and was renowned for his (then) *pièce de résistance*. If, during a long set, he felt the need to relieve himself, he'd launch into an electric rendition of *The Dam Busters* theme tune and head for the toilet, his guitar lead being just long enough to allow him to reach the urinal. He'd be followed to the stalls by a large group of male fans, who'd gather round to admire this formidable feat of multi-tasking – and then, zipped back up, and playing all the while, he'd return to the stage.

On the marble staircase of the Mond Buildings I once fell in something like love with a complete stranger. Our passing gazes locked, for a moment, in mutual attraction – but we said nothing and moved on. It's only, perhaps, the poem I wrote that keeps the experience alive, at least for one of us.

The Long History of a Brief Glance

And what did we do? but walk on by,
huddle back like mutes
among the blind faces, the flags of noise –
no word between us but the dark
statement of nameless eyes: *complete stranger,*
I know you well –
Then nothing of you
save a flash of heel, a breath of patchouli …

I've met them, such eyes,
in some sometimes of the weariest cities: they'll
reach to you in mirrors and in the passing of trains;
down vacant throughways crowded with feet
they'll come, dark eyes, to meet you
with silence, with nothing less
than their love:

and as you dance in them you dare
to lose them,
to sleep the night, like any other,
in a separate town.

In nineteen hundred and seventy six
I passed her on a stairway,
she ascending, me going down:
we, you and I, made a night of our eyes,

and in that night I touched you, we
touched beyond the moment
our innermost realms –

till the light broke us back
to move forever
away through the crowds.

Thirty years later
I close my eyes to see you, to
lose you again.
And space that emptied of you
refills with failed sunlight, begrimed marble –

the smell of patchouli warm from your skin.

A souvenir of a romance that seems not to have flourished hangs high overhead in the anti-bird mesh which envelops the building: a girl's silver bracelet, as irretrievable as lost love.

Above both of the Mond's ground-floor entrances, sandwiching premises recently abandoned by Barclays Bank, you can read the stirring injunction, 'Make yourself necessary'. Not a thought that seems to have occurred to Union Street for a while.

THE KARDOMAH CAFÉ

"Prynhawn da," the Italian owner greets me in nicely consonantal formal Welsh, "sut ydych chi?"[15] Tuscany-born Pietro Luporini, who's been attending weekly Welsh classes at Three Crosses for some years, always likes to give the language an airing with customers who he knows speak something of *yr hen iaith*.[16] And over the decades he has come to know thousands of customers, if not always by name, then certainly well enough to exchange friendly, joshing banter as his loyal regulars come and go, unseduced by the soulless uniformity of nearby trendy chain establishments.

The last remaining Kardomah Café in Britain is surely the most famous of them all. The Kardomah Coffee Company, a tea and coffee importing business, was founded in Liverpool in 1845. In the early 1900s, it started opening cafés, and by the 1930s there were about thirty Kardomahs, including those in Swansea (1905),

Cardiff and Newport; there was even a Kardomah in Paris.

This proudly Swansea institution – in Portland Street, just north of the Oxford Street entrance to Swansea Market – has been in the care of the Luporini family since 1970. They've been at pains to keep it much as it was when it opened in 1957, replacing the original Kardomah – Dylan Thomas's "Home Sweet Homah" at 13 Castle Street – which was "razed to the snow" (as he wrote in *Return Journey*) during the 1941 blitz. Italian design was all the rage in the 1950s, when central Swansea rose like a featherless, hobbled phoenix from the ashes of war. Part of Morris Buildings (1956) – named after the Swansea mayor, MP and zealous redeveloper Percy Morris (1893-1967) who, in 1957, called for the demolition of Swansea Castle[17] – it initially incorporated the butcher's premises next door, until it was sectioned off, giving the café its present chunky L-shape.

Pietro joins me at a window table for a chat about the Kardomah, while his son Marcus, managing director of the business, takes our order: a cappuccino for me and an espresso for Pietro.

"No Italian," says Pietro, "drinks cappuccino in the afternoon."

As elsewhere in Wales, Italians have made a huge contribution to the café, restaurant and wider culture of the locality. The first wave, mainly from Bardi in the north and Picinisco in the south, settled in the early 1900s; a second wave arrived in the 1950s, establishing businesses which have long been household names in Swansea: Sidoli's, Macari's, Valerio's, Arcari's, Demarco's, Velardo's, Avo's, Pompa's, Belli's, Cresci's, Cascarini's (of Joe's ice cream fame), Greco's, D'Ambrosio's, Pelosi's. Seven Swansea café proprietors lost their lives in the shameful *Arandora Star* episode, when hundreds of Italians who had been classed as 'enemy aliens' by the British authorities were shipped off to Canada on a vessel which was torpedoed by a German submarine; 50 of the 446 who died were from Wales.[18]

Acknowledging that the original Kardomah – a converted Congregational chapel where Dylan Thomas's parents were married in 1903 – was a rather different establishment from its replacement, Pietro nevertheless enjoys his café's association with the renowned Kardomah Boys. When I made a documentary of that title with BBC Wales in 1997, he was happy for us to film, on a busy weekday morning, a reconstruction of Dylan Thomas and his pals – among them Fred Janes, Daniel Jones, Vernon Watkins, Tom Warner, Charlie Fisher, "poets, painters, and musicians in their beginnings" – "drinking coffee-dashes and arguing the toss [about] music and poetry and painting and politics. Einstein and Epstein, Stravinsky and Greta Garbo, death and religion, Picasso and girls..." The young actors, in character, took a table among the other customers, but the Kardomah Boys of old would have stationed themselves in the former chapel's gallery, looking down on the respectably bourgeois and, they'd trust, shockable clientele below.

Little was salvaged from the rubble of the old café, apart from its magnificent counter, which is still to be seen at the Welcome to Town restaurant in Llanrhidian, and a few souvenirs that bedeck today's Kardomah. Hanging by the door, there's a menu panel from the old establishment, advertising such delights as '3 Egg Omelettes' and 'Pan Fried Calves Liver & Bacon'. There are nearly a hundred items on the modern menu, but Petro still gets the odd customer asking for the calves' liver.

"Although it's not the old Kardomah," he says, "it's the Kardomah at heart, and I think at least two of the original Kardomah Boys, Daniel Jones and Fred Janes, came to the opening in 1957."

With 25 members of staff and so many regular customers, "It's really like a family," he says. The longest serving member of staff is

Nella Foinski, originally from Bardi, who joined the team in 1973. In the late 1990s, staff morale plummeted and Pietro lost two good chefs when the business was blighted by the prospect of demolition, as part of the – ultimately unrealised – multimillion-pounds Castle Quays scheme. This grotesquely grandiloquent project, championed by the council with a philistine zeal which would have gladdened the heart of Percy 'Wrecking-ball' Morris, would have involved the demolition of everything between Castle Street and Union Street, over 250 metres away, and the building of a stockaded shopping block closed to the public at night. Funnelling huge volumes of traffic into the heart of the city – at a time when other cities, such as Birmingham, were abandoning ill-conceived traffic-centred shopping hubs – it would have incorporated ramps to ferry delivery vehicles up to a lorry park on its roof. The people of Swansea, invariably wiser than most of their representatives, took strongly against the scheme. Protest meetings, led by the actor Helen Griffin, were held in the Kardomah, and over 20,000 people signed a petition against the plans. (Pietro was glad to reciprocate by investing money in Helen's prize-winning film about racism, *Little White Lies* (2006).)

"It was a really bad, stressful time," Pietro remembers. "But I was determined not to be beaten by the developers. The public reaction was brilliant. People said they wouldn't let the Kardomah close, they would stand in the way of the bulldozers."

Surviving, therefore, another potential 'blitz', the Kardomah went on to further burnish its fame as a setting for the 2009 *Dr Who* Christmas special (David Tennant's final appearance as the Time Lord). Just after Easter that year, the café was festooned, for the cameras, with Christmas decorations, and extras were filmed bundled up against the non-existent cold.

The Kardomah appears safe for the time being from developers' whims, and, with Pietro and his wife having seven grandchildren, there would seem to be no shortage of a younger generation poised to continue the family's Kardomah tradition. There may not be much Italian spoken by the Luporinis these days, but Welsh has to some extent taken its place. Of the three grandchildren who attend Welsh-medium schools one shares exactly the same name as his grandfather. "So eventually and at long last," he says, "there'll be a Pietro Luporini *yn hollol rhugl yn Gymraeg*."[19]

THE GRAND THEATRE

An encounter with the odd cherub in the city centre is not something you should necessarily attribute to tired emotionalism: it could be real. For cherubs, as bold as brass, are to be seen here and there, having been liberated – assisted by the artist Robin Campbell – from the dress circle of the Grand Theatre in Singleton Street. We've met one already in Salubrious Passage and there's another atop the housing association flats in Christina Street. But the biggest concentration of cherubic mayhem is, unsurprisingly, in Singleton Street itself, diagonally opposite the Grand, where six of them swarm over the tower-like structure that houses the stage door of what used to be the Milkwood Jam rock venue.[20] With hammer and chisel in hand, these are busy worker cherubs (or *putti*,[21] to be correct), whereas their thespian siblings in the dress circle seem to be engaged in little more than fondling the foliage while ogling the ripe, bare breasts of the Amazonian matrons alongside.

What John Newman has called the "rollicking high relief plaster-work" of the Grand's two balcony fronts is an essential component of the theatre's Victorian ambience – although the original 1897 building has been enveloped since the 1980s by major extensions on three sides, in a daring mixture of styles. The distinguished Neath-born director Michael Bogdanov (1938) described it to me as "the best conversion of an old Victorian theatre in Britain. The way the stage functions is terrific. You can drive a lorry onto the stage and unload your set. Every facility, the wig room, the dressing rooms, radiate off the stage in a horseshoe, which is exactly as it should be, so you can feed the stage properly."

Swansea, notoriously careless of its heritage, is lucky to have the Grand. The theatre has lurched, for most of its history, from crisis to crisis, and could so easily have gone the way of the much loved (but not enough loved) Empire in nearby Oxford Street. In 1963, the council – hooked, as ever, on highways – wanted to demolish the Grand in order to widen the road, but by 1969, when the town became a city, there'd been a change of heart: you cannot call yourself a city, they seemed to have decided, unless you have a municipal theatre.

In the airy foyer, I meet up one summer morning with the Grand's co-manager designate Paul Hopkins and Peter Richards, director of the Grand-based Fluellen,[22] the theatre company which has spearheaded a significant revival of mainstream theatre in Swansea since the company's formation in 2000.

We begin our Grand tour in the car park opposite. Here you can see how the major 1980s augmentations have been wrapped around the 1897 building, whose twin triangular roofing pediments, giving way to truncated towers, protrude from the glass 'ribcage' walkway which has been added at dress circle level. Both old and new styles frame the original, quirky lettering that spells out 'Grand Theatre', playfully at odds with the classical understatement of the most recent architecture.

What these developments tend to obscure is that the Grand was built on the corner of Singleton Street and Princess Street.[23] Sadly, Princess Street and James Street, which ran parallel with it to the west of the Grand, were among half a dozen notably close-knit terraces to be demolished in the 1970s and early '80s, to make way for the Quadrant development (1980), the new bus station's manoeuvring apron and a car park – a regrettable clean sweep which nevertheless presented the theatre with an opportunity. The top end of Princess Street, roughly opposite the Vivaldi Italian restaurant,[24] has been 'filled in' by the Grand's foyer, the theatre's eastward expansion taking in much of the United Welsh bus garage-cum-station, which stood between Princess Street and Plymouth Street.[25]

A sense of the theatrical seemed to infuse the atmosphere in this part of town. There was, for instance, Leonard from Pennard, greeting 'friends' with a blast from his transistor, accompanied by his own stentorian 'singing', and directing cars and buses with a sawn-off traffic cone. In the Gower Inn, opposite the eastern doors of the bus depot, you might have run into Boyo Smith, a newspaper seller on Plymouth Street, who wore silver spurs, cowboy boots and a stetson as he swaggered in and out of the Gower 'saloon'. And in Princess Street itself, a few doors down from the theatre, there was Dulcie and Graham Davies's Volunteer Arms, or the Vols, the hub of this warm and welcoming community, and more or less an annexe of the Grand. The Vols clientele had theatrical tastes of their own and would enjoy cavorting in fancy dress, particularly on Saturday nights: cowboys and cowgirls, pirates, Davy Crockett, Ena Sharples.

The scene to the west of the theatre in those days was also very different. Dillwyn Street, which today feeds seamlessly into the multi-lane West Way, came to an abrupt halt in the region of the Singleton pub, where there was a T-junction. Facing you here was one of Swansea's first Indian restaurants, the Bombay Grill, which advertised itself in huge white letters painted across its slate roof. The demolition of James Street, on one side of the Bombay Grill, and much of William Street on the other – along with the Bombay itself – made West Way possible and enabled the Grand to expand westwards, with new dressing rooms, bars, a restaurant and a garden. I can't cycle down West Way, through the ghost of Swansea's early 'Injun', without slavering for a chicken Madras.

The Grand, like the rest of Sandfields, is built on sand. When the council bought the theatre in 1976, they were forced to take drastic measures to stabilise the building, by drilling holes beneath the foundations and filling them with concrete. Two buildings on this site preceded the Grand. The first was Rolls and Hoare's Brewery (later, the Old Brewery), one of about 15 Swansea breweries in the 1860s; its clock can still be seen on the tower of the Norman church of St Teilo, Bishopston, where it was installed in 1886. The second was the Drill Hall, which was sometimes known as the Prince of Wales Theatre. The site was acquired by the actor managers and theatre impresarios H.H. Morell and Frederick Mouillot. They built the Grand, one of five Swansea theatres by the end of the nineteenth century,[26] specifically as a playhouse, not a variety hall.

The Grand, throughout its entire history, has always struggled to make money from plays. As every management has found, Swansea audiences love opera, operetta, musicals, panto, light entertainment and excitements such as *Hair*. They do not have much taste for drama, particularly serious drama – unless it comes with some television star topping the bill.

In the late 1960s, with an unbounded appetite for drama (and, no doubt, the odd, unspoken crush on an actress or two), I'd pitch up every week to see whatever the Grand might offer in its weekly rep: Chekhov, *Boeing, Boeing*, Ibsen, Shaw, *Dial M for Murder*, *Roots*, *A Taste of Honey*, Pinter, Neil Simon, *Arsenic and Old Lace*, *Doctor in Love* – all grist to the mill of a callow youth who hoped to become a writer. But the audiences for these plays, even for the frothiest frivolities, were pitifully small, amounting sometimes to no more than twenty or thirty souls, lost among the red plush of that echoing auditorium.

Such have been the pressures from cinema, television and the 'celeb' culture of recent times, that the Grand's *raison d'être* as a playhouse has sometimes been lost. Like many theatres facing similar pressures, it turned itself into a 'flicks' for much of the 1930s and '40s, becoming the Swansea Cinema; and in 1969, when it was losing £200 a week, its then owners, the Willis family of Cardiff, applied for permission to turn it into a bingo hall. At this point, the council stepped in to run it as a civic theatre, eventually buying it outright for £100,000. Maintaining a balance between popular entertainments and more thoughtful fare has remained a challenge. There's little in the main-stage programme that might qualify as serious drama.

"I hear people being disparaging about the tribute bands, comedians and psychics," says Peter. "But it's because such acts are on the programme, and are popular, that we can put Shakespeare on in the arts wing."

It's in the arts wing's studio theatre (1999), approached by a metal staircase spiralling up through two floors, that the majority of Fluellen's productions are staged.

"I started Fluellen," explains Peter, "because I felt, having lived in London for about thirty years, it was shocking that you couldn't find professionally produced Shakespeare more than two or three times a year here. There was a need to plug that gap. The audiences have been very solid and sometimes, indeed, spectacular. There is still an audience to see classical theatre. It's just that you can't do it for a week in the main house any longer. I agree with Bogdanov: the more theatre there is, the more people will come."

The main auditorium remains much as it was in 1897. The notorious dress-circle pillars, which affect the sight-lines of about 200 people, could have been removed during the renovations, but it was decided, for authenticity's sake, to keep them. To the right of the stage there's the plaque laid by Adelina Patti (1843-1919), who was the most famous singer in the world when she did the honours at the theatre's gala opening.

A mystery that long exercised Paul was the mismatch between the theatre's current capacity of 1,126 people with the 2,500 of former times – until it became clear that in the Grand's early days there would be standing room in the pit in front of the stage. Not every performance, these days, registers a capacity crowd, but the theatre, nevertheless, "takes a hell of a kicking, with some 300,000 passing through every year, and 250,000 of them passing through the auditorium."

Even with a capacity audience, the four boxes, in two tiers either side of the stage, are rarely used. Neither Peter nor I have ever sat in a theatre's boxes, so we try one of them out. There are five seats in each, with an increasingly poor view of the action the nearer you are to the stage. A box, clearly, is to be seen in, rather than to see from. Each has a little 'tiring room' or ante-chamber to the rear, for refreshments and, doubtless, the occasional canoodle.

On our way down the main stairway to the stalls, we pause to salute the portrait of John Chilvers (1920-2008), without whose unswerving commitment as the Grand's artistic director and manager through some deeply dispiriting times there would be no Grand Theatre today. I remember him as a considerate, neatly bearded man who, before every performance, would station himself in the old foyer, in dinner-jacket and black bow tie, smiling a greeting to patrons as they filed in, many of whom he'd know by name. During the day, if not rehearsing a show on the stage, he'd be found at his administrative tasks in the manager's office, with his black Labrador, Tom, snoozing at his feet.

The Norwich-born director was hired initially, in 1957, for only one season, but he ended up running the theatre for 25 years, until his retirement in 1982, having directed over 530 shows. Farce was his forte, but he was versatile in all genres – as Peter well remembers.

"When I met him (for the only time) at a reception in London, I asked him how he had accomplished so much in such a short time.

GRAND THEATRE
SWANSEA.
STAGE MEASUREMENTS

Pros Arch 29 FT 6 WIDE X 24 FT HIGH MAX.
8·998 MTS. X 7·320 MTS.

Pros Wall to Back Wall 45 FT 10-16·265 MTS.
Back Wall to Setting Line 43 FT 2 -13·116 MTS.
Width of Stage 95 FT - 28·975 MTS.
Fly Floor to Fly Floor 72 FT 4 - 22·662 MTS.
Bar Length 43 FT - 13·115 MTS.

Stage to Fly Floor 29 FT 6 - 8·998 MTS.
Stage to Fly Rail 33 FT - 10·065 MTS.
Stage to Intermediate Gallery 49 FT 6-15·098 MTS.
Stage to Rail 53 FT - 16·165 MTS.
Stage to Grid 71 FT 2 - 21·706 MTS.

He replied that after several years directing rep he had fallen into a sort of directorial shorthand or 'painting by numbers' where art, to a certain extent, went out of the window and some essential pragmatism replaced it. For instance, he plotted every production so that his leading man always made his first entrance upstage left and his leading lady always made her entrance upstage right, and everything seemed to follow on from that. This, I suppose, is what made John Chilvers so special – the ability to make little gems of theatre out of what was basically a conveyor belt."

From the stalls, we hop up onto the stage where the set is being built for the second production of this summer's rep season – which opens tonight. There's a panel on the stage's back wall setting out its measurements. Peter points out that although the depth of the stage to the back wall is now exceptional, and the new fly seems to tower above us forever, the aperture of the proscenium arch remains relatively narrow – calling for flexibility in the design of touring shows.

We pass by the stage door, watched over by a young woman ensconced in her glass booth with a novel. Seems like an ideal job for a keen reader, although she has to be at her post by 7.00, when the cleaning staff come in. Before the renovation, there were only four dressing rooms, but now there are fifteen. Actors tend to plump for No. 1, traditionally the best appointed and the nearest to the stage. What they often don't realise about the Grand is that there are two unnumbered dressing rooms even nearer the stage, Oxwich and Caswell, each with a Gareth Thomas painting of those bays, "so that actors from away can have some sense of where they are," says Paul.

In the basement, beside the entrance to the orchestra pit, there's a door labelled 'Trap Room', which is directly beneath the stage, creaking overhead with set-building activity. There are two trap doors here, not used, says Paul, since a Little and Large show in the 1990s.

We conclude our tour with a coffee in the Footlights bar and restaurant, which is humming with early lunchtime activity.

"I have been around a few theatres in my time," says Peter, "but this is one of the nicest in every respect. You have a genuine sense of community here."

Tastes, as ever, change. I ask Paul what direction the main-stage programme might take in future, after a long run of psychics, vampires and other excitements. Musicals, he thinks. "They've always been popular, but they may become more so."

"Perhaps," suggests Peter, "a musical about a psychic vampire?"

ST HELEN'S ROAD

Of all Swansea's commercial streets, the one with the most character is St Helen's Road. In its one-kilometre length, from Mumbles Road to its junction with The Kingsway and Dillwyn Street, St Helen's Road packs in an anarchic jumble of architectural styles, places of worship, shops, food bazaars, a brothel, a Masonic Hall, businesses – and restaurants, especially Asian restaurants. The air hereabouts is wreathed in mouth-watering aromas from the thirty or more eateries that jostle for custom on (mostly) the southern side of the street.

Until the mid-nineteenth century, St Helen's Road was the main western route out of Swansea. It was a country road passing through fields, the few gentry houses that dotted its length enjoying uninterrupted views, over Swansea Burrows, of the Severn Sea, as it wasn't until 1850 that building began on the Sandfields terraces. At its junction with Brynymor Road there were two tollgates. One was for Mumbles-bound traffic which, until Mumbles Road was constructed in the early 1820s, was obliged to take a notably indirect route to its destination: past the Slip (on the seafront), then through Singleton Park to Sketty Green, then past the old oak which gave its name to Derwen Fawr, and finally through Blackpill to Mumbles. The other was for Gower-bound traffic, as Walters Road did not come into play until the late 1850s: the horses and their vehicles would swing right into Brynymor Road, gathering strength for the punishing uphill scramble to the Uplands.

At its Mumbles Road end, where my walk starts, St Helen's Road experiments with a boulevard feel, exuding an air of spaciousness as it skirts Victoria Park and the generous greensward that enisles the Guildhall (1934). "Unadulterated fascism," was the poet Harri Webb's (1920-94) verdict on the design of the Guildhall as I drove him past it years ago. (In a 2011 episode of *Dr Who*, 'Let's Kill Hitler', the Guildhall stood in for Hitler's Reichstag headquarters.) Another poet of that generation, John Tripp (1927-86), was also perhaps articulating a critical view of the civic architecture when, on a later occasion, he had me stop the car so that he might take a piss *en plein air* on the lawn in front of the Guildhall. It's likelier, though, that the homebrew was pushing for a means of expression.

I doubt that either poet would have taken much delight in a newer chunk of supposed civic gravitas on the opposite side of the road, namely the Alex Gordon Partnership's Crown Court (1988), built on the site of Swansea's tramcar depot (the last trams ran in 1937) and the site, before that, of the St Helen's Iron Foundry. The court's dourly weathered white Portland stone exterior is all too suggestive of grim and grey proceedings within. It is supposed to have been influenced by the postmodern playfulness of the Maritime Quarter. According to that normally discerning critic John Newman, it's "an essay in mannerist wit."

> 'love you, bye': he
> pockets his phone, then books another
> illegal parker

Abandoned churches in search of new roles is a main St Helen's Road theme. The first we come to is an old Nonconformist chapel which has been turned into the Imam Khoei Islamic Centre and Arabic School – one of several St Helen's Road institutions serving the spiritual needs of the area's growing Islamic population, many of whom are involved in the Asian, and specifically, Bangladeshi restaurant trade. Most of Swansea's – indeed, Wales's – supposed Indian restaurants are in fact run by Bangladeshis, the majority of whom come from the north-eastern city of Sylhet, which is one of the richest cities in Bangladesh, thanks largely to investment by expatriates living in the United Kingdom.

A popular curry house on the other side of the road is Miah's, where you can dine among the beams and rafters of the commodious roof-space of what was once St Paul's Congregational Church (1881) (and briefly, in the 1980s, the Studio Cinema, with blue movies in the crypt). This was the church of one of Swansea's most loved twentieth-century figures, the beret-topped Rev Leon Atkin (1881-1976), Labour councillor, friend of the poor and homeless, bane of Swansea's establishment, anti-fascist – and proper of the bar at the nearby Brynymor and Westbourne pubs. Leon Atkin, who preached a social gospel, made the crypt a refuge for the homeless, particularly during the blitz and the bitter winter of 1947. He was renowned for the valiant stand he took against Sir Oswald Mosley and the British Union of Fascists when they held a rally at the Plaza Cinema on The Kingsway in 1934.[27] The atmosphere in the cinema, which had been infiltrated by anti-fascists (including Dylan Thomas) in spite of the scrutiny of Blackshirt 'Biff Boys', grew increasingly volatile as the demagogue worked his supporters into a fascistic frenzy. Anyone in the employ of a Jew, Mosley railed, should resign their job. Leon Atkin, who'd managed to sneak in with his dog-collar hidden by a scarf, said that his boss was a Jew. 'Then you should find a new employer immediately,' said Mosley. At which point, the Reverend, rising from his seat and removing his disguise, countered with a question, 'Could you give me some idea who my new boss should be?' The crowd's laughter broke the fascist spell, and the Welsh anti-fascists' 'Hen Wlad fy Nhadau' battled with the Blackshirts' 'God Save the King' as fists began to fly and the police moved in to break up the meeting.

Opposite Miah's is that venerable Swansea ice-cream parlour Joe's which also has branches in Mumbles and Parc Tawe, and sells to retail outlets much further afield. "Everything else is just ice cream!" its adverts boast, confident of a product that on hot days and holidays will see queues spilling out of the parlour and disappearing

down the street. On a summer weekend, the branch will sell 190 gallons of the stuff, the equivalent of 11,400 cones. The Joe's story began in 1898 when one Luigi Cascarini came to Swansea, from the Abruzzi Mountains in Italy, to establish a café business. Joe's was founded in 1922 by Luigi's son, Joe, whose distinctive recipe – a closely guarded secret to this day – quickly established itself as Swansea's ice cream of ice creams. Joe died in 1966, but the business he founded has been continued by five subsequent generations. It must be the world's sole producer of a Welsh-cake flavoured ice cream.

A curry house older than Miah's, just up the street from Joe's, is the Anarkali. Established in 1978 by Ashiqure Rahman, it claims to be south-west Wales's first tandoori, and has won several British Curry Awards. Locals tend to pronounce it 'AnaKAAARlee', and I've heard literary types call it the Anna Karenina, but the correct pronunciation is 'AnARkali', with the emphasis on the second syllable; it means pomegranate blossom. Anarkali was a legendary slave

girl from Lahore, in what is now Pakistan, who was supposedly buried alive between two walls on the orders of the Mughal emperor Akbar, for having an illicit relationship with prince Nuruddin Salim, who later became the emperor Jahangir. The tragic story of Anarkali, whether apocryphal or highly embellished, has inspired innumerable works of art, literature and cinema – and launched a thousand 'Indian' restaurants the length and breadth of Britain.

The distinctive spirelet which tops Miah's calls across the junction with Brynymor Road to its probable inspiration, a similar but older spirelet on top of what was originally Swansea Hospital (1869). Swansea's – and Wales's – first voluntary infirmary was built on the seafront in 1817 alongside the late eighteenth-century Bathing House, which had been defeated by its remoteness from town and by a ridge of pebbles that impeded access to the beach. In 1835, a new infirmary was added to the 1817 one, but by 1850 it was unable to cope with the demands of a rapidly expanding population, and advice was sought from Florence Nightingale about the design for a new Swansea hospital. She declared that the 50-bed Swansea Hospital, designed by the London architect Alexander Graham, would be "the finest and most perfect small hospital in the kingdom". But, with the population continuing to mushroom and with some 600 furnaces in the Lower Swansea Valley causing horrendous injuries to industrial workers, that 'small' was all too soon the problem. By the early twentieth century, in-patient resources at what had become, in 1890, Swansea General and Eye Hospital, were severely strained. The pressure was relieved only when Singleton Hospital opened in the late 1960s. Most of the old hospital buildings were demolished in the late 1980s, to be replaced by sheltered housing for the elderly. What remains of the old hospital is the handsome administration block, topped with that clock-bearing spirelet – a landmark in winter, but largely hidden by surrounding trees in summer.

Opposite the old hospital, on the corner of Beach St and St Helen's Road, is the former Lloyds Bank branch where the poet Vernon Watkins (1906-67) worked as a clerk for 41 years. It's now a branch of William Hill, the bookmakers, but a relief carving of the Lloyds rearing horse emblem is still a prominent feature above the red-brick building's entrance. Vernon had no desire to emulate his father, who was manager of Lloyds Bank in Wind Street (at numbers 25-26, now the Revolution bar). A relatively undemanding, humdrum job such as clerking suited him fine. At the end of every working day, he'd forget all about the bank, climb aboard the 14 bus (still running today) and head home to the cliffs at Pennard – and his real work, poetry. On one famous occasion his imagination seems to have anticipated its release a little prematurely: it had been left to Watkins to shut up shop but, his mind already on higher things, the poet hurried home having forgotten to lock the door of the bank.

Shortly after this point, where boulevard has by now narrowed to street, St Helen's Road begins to get into its extrovert stride. While the sedate north side of the street comprises in the main rather grand late nineteenth-century residences, many of them offices, the terraced south side is a busy clutter of small shops, restaurants, take-aways, and Asian food markets spilling their exotic wares out onto the pavement. Shoppers bustle, some in saris or hijabs, while men, often bearded beneath kufi prayer caps, or dressed in kahn tops or galabias, mill about chatting, smoking, fixing a deal, or passing to and from the mosque.

no one, here,
stoops to the peach that lies
in the gutter

There was a time in the 1960s when you'd be hard pressed to find in Swansea any food more adventurous than a banana. A green pepper or a can of lychees was occasionally spotted, but it wasn't until Chinese and Indian restaurants became relatively common, from the mid 1970s, that oriental vegetables, herbs and spices began to be readily available. These days, think of any ingredient you fancy, and you can be sure that the cornucopian bazaars of St Helen's Road will stock it – from halal goat meat to Bombay duck, from okra and pak choi to yams, plantains and gourds of all sorts, from garam masala and jeera to couscous, papads, and hoi sin sauce – and most of these foods far cheaper than in the multinational supermarkets.

And if you don't feel like cooking, you can take your pick from dozens of eateries: the Rose Indienne, Mango's, the Yummy Yummy Chinese takeway, Pizza Venice, Didier and Stephanie's French restaurant, Topo Gigio, Pizza Hut, the Paddyfield, the Surma,

Southern Fried Chicken Indian Takeaway, Garuda, Vojon, Tantalizer African Bar and Restaurant (where you could get in the mood for a visit to Bunnies 'massage parlour' above), Evergreen Cantonese, BBQ King, Food to Go. Some seem to last only a matter of months before changing name and identity, but others, such as the Viceroy of India, have been part of the streetscape for years.

When the former Apostolic Church was being demolished to build a Tesco Express, evidence of an earlier presence on this site, the Agricultural Hall of 1870, came to light, in the form of an arched entranceway proclaiming in relief the building's name and date (in Roman numerals), and surmounted by a stylised sheaf of wheat.[28] This relief is preserved on a low, oblique plinth at the rear of what is now called Ty [sic] Heledd and can be seen from Oxford Street. Among the literary and musical entertainments presented at the Agricultural Hall (later known as the Old Assembly Rooms) was an early performance, in 1876, by the Swansea Jubilee Singers who modelled themselves on the famous Fisk Jubilee Singers, a black American choir whose 'weird slave songs' were rapturously received when they toured south Wales from the 1870s onwards. Such performances could be said to represent the tentative beginnings of a Swansea jazz and blues scene.

> cyclist yawning,
> leaving in his wake
> a trail of yawns

The biggest former church on the south side is Argyle, built for the Presbyterians in 1873 – in a grand classical style, with portico, pilasters and soaring columns – during Swansea's chapel-building boom of 1870-90, when no fewer than 25 chapels were constructed. It was designed, by Alfred Bucknell of Sketty, to accommodate 900 worshippers, at a time when Swansea's population stood at 51,000. Chronic dry rot and a dwindling congregation forced Argyle's closure in the late 1980s, and it suffered a devastating fire in 2004, before its resourceful redevelopment as apartments.

The chapels were in shameless competition with each other in matters of size and style. A conspicuous material indicator of spiritual prosperity was Bath stone, that golden brown Jurassic limestone characteristic of buildings in Bath and the Cotswolds. As the nearest source of Bath stone was the West Country of England, it was not until the railway reached Swansea in 1850 that this prestigious building material could be imported.

Bath stone is the making of Argyle's façade as it is that of the flamboyant and far grander St Andrew's Presbyterian church diagonally opposite. Built in a 'light and airy' Gothic style in the early 1860s by wealthy Scottish drapers, and reminiscent of certain churches in Glasgow, St Andrew's twin towers dominate the skyline in this part of town. No less inviting of attention are some stony details which, had nineteenth-century worshippers paused to consider them, might have unsettled believers already discomfited by the revolutionary findings of Charles Darwin and Alfred Russel Wallace, which were being denounced from many a pulpit. Richard Porch, in his fascinating exploration of the stones of Swansea,[29] points to the banded appearance of the heavily weathered limestone gateposts of St Andrew's, with strata alternately heavy with fragmented fossil shells – then free of them. "The banded appearance of the gatepost was probably caused by successive prehistoric storm events (cyclones or hurricanes) that caused the laying of each band [on the sea bed] via a rapid deposit," he writes. "Each band may represent half a day's sedimentation. Think of it – you can still see the effect of a prehistoric storm [from the Upper Jurassic period] on St Helen's Road." Even more disturbing of creationist assumptions is the Pennant sandstone paving leading up to the church, which is covered in ripple marks made by the ebb and flow of water on a prehistoric riverbed some 280 to 310 million years ago.

No historian of Swansea has a keener eye for stony wonders and oddities than Richard Porch. Richard has noticed, a few metres east of St Andrew's, an anomalous disruption in the Pennant sandstone walling in front of the newly opened Masala Bazaar. He describes it as "a curious assembly of stones that looks as though the wall has been built around them" and identifies it as a combination of Carboniferous limestone and Sutton stone, which would have come from a hillside near Ogmore-on-Sea. He speculates that this blocky squiggle could be the remains of an old water butt or fountain, possibly from early Victorian times.

I rarely pass the Masala Bazaar building, on the corner of George Street, without thinking of one of Wales's most popular poets, Harri Webb. Born in Catherine Street on the north-western edge of the Sandfields in 1920, Harri spent most of his adult life (after naval service during the Second World War) in other parts of Wales, chiefly as a librarian at Dowlais, Merthyr Tydfil and then at Mountain Ash. He was active, above all in the 1960s and 70s, as both poet and political rebel-rouser – of a nationalist, republican and socialist stamp – who was determined that Wales was "marching backwards into independence, everybody desperately pretending that we are going somewhere else." Harri exulted in putting the boot in where necessary, scandalising the genteel, and upsetting political opponents; he relished flying in the face of that "ghastly good taste" which, he said, was "one of the pervading weaknesses of the Anglo-Welsh generally."

I first met Harri in the mid 1970s, round about the time he gave up alcohol. Some months into his new, healthy regime, a friend remarked how well he was looking. "Yes," said Harri, "and by the time I die I shall be perfectly fit." This wasn't quite how things worked out.

Old age came cruelly early to Harri Webb. By the time his fourth volume of poetry was published in 1983, he had more or less closed down as a writer, having embarked on a series of illnesses, including a stroke in 1985, which rendered him housebound in his ground-floor, mountain-top flat in Cwmbach, Aberdare. In the summer of 1994, he suffered a strange and highly contagious virus that necessitated a long stay in a quarantine unit. He lost his beard and even his Zimmer-assisted mobility. Obliged to abandon any idea of a return to the semi-independent life he'd led in Cwmbach, the old sailor sought a last haven, in November of that year, in a rest home in the building which now houses the Masala Bazaar[30] – about 300 metres from his birthplace. Soon after he moved in, I took him

a bag of Welsh cakes, and we managed to have a conversation of sorts. It seemed, perhaps, that he was slowly recouping some strength. But on New Year's Eve he died, just as many other local writers were carousing among crowds on the seafront, celebrating the launch of the Swansea-centred UK Year of Literature and Writing 1995.

Two distinguished buildings remain to be noted before St Helen's Road becomes The Kingsway, at opposite sides of its junction with Page Street. Firstly, the two-storey, red-brick Quaker Meeting House or Pagefield House (1858; it was built in a field acquired from a Mr Page). The fourth building to be occupied by the Society of Friends since their arrival in Swansea in 1655, this handsome Tudor-Revival structure, with its pale stone quoins and ornate bargeboards, reminds us of the significant role played by Quakers in the development of Swansea. They were particularly prominent in the copper industry and in shipping. The Quaker entrepreneur George Haynes (1745-1830) made a significant contribution to Swansea banking and pottery, and was founder of Wales's first newspaper, *The Cambrian* (1804-1930).

Another Quaker, the businessman and Harbour Trust chairman Roger Beck – who gave his name to various Swansea features, including Swansea University's hall for mature students, Tŷ Beck House, in the Uplands – was instrumental in raising the funds to build the other notable building here, the red-brick and Portland stone YMCA, the work of one of Swansea's most imaginative architects, Glendinning Moxham (c.1860-c.1935). There are plaques in the foyer commemorating both the laying of the building's foundations stones in 1912, on the site of the former Longlands Hotel, and the YMCA's opening in 1913.

Although open these days to old and young men and women, of all faiths and none, when the YMCA was founded in London in 1844 its aim was to put Christian principles into practice and house young men living in squalid and unsafe conditions. If a working man moved into an unfamiliar town such as Swansea, he could seek out the YMCA and be sure of a cheap bed for the night. Much has changed since then, but the organisation's core commitment to supporting the disadvantaged and vulnerable remains constant. Its wartime roles have included acting as a makeshift emergency hospital for servicemen wounded in the First World War, and in the Second World War it was a billet for American soldiers. During the blitz, it could easily have gone the way of the rest of the bombed-out centre, had it not been for the servicemen who manned the building during bombing raids throwing fifteen firebombs off its flat roof.

In the YMCA's Page Street elevation, there's a door to the Llewelyn Hall, which was added in 1920 and named after Sir John Talbot Dillwyn Llewelyn (1836-1927) of the renowned Penllergare dynasty, sometime Conservative MP, mayor of Swansea and president of the Welsh Rugby Union, who had been a member of the YMCA's original building committee. Numerous plays, pantos and school entertainments have been staged at the Llewelyn Hall. Dylan Thomas acted here, from 1929 to 1931, with both the Swansea Grammar School Dramatic Society and the YMCA Players, who specialised in thrillers and farces. My own junior school, Craig-y-Nos (or Lloyd's), then of Eaton Crescent, was among several to avail itself of the hall's facilities. I remember dressing up as a soldier, aged seven or eight, for some Christmas extravaganza at the Llewelyn Hall, my first ever stage experience, and as an adolescent I used to attend performances there by the Swansea Youth Theatre, which at that time was a showcase for emerging talents such as Eleanor Thomas and Gareth Armstrong.

A drawback of the Llewelyn Hall was its situation directly beneath the YMCA's gymnasium, whose galumphing activities could impose some distracting percussion on, say, the balcony scene of *Romeo and Juliet*, or the intensities of Tennessee Williams's *Suddenly Last Summer*. Although the arts rather than sport would eventually claim me, I used to enjoy our school's weekly gym classes at the YMCA, where our coach was the dedicated gymnast Walter Walsh. Mr Walsh could exhort even chubby kids like me to unanticipated heights, such as the tops of the gymnasium's ropes. The year I managed to climb a rope and touch the ceiling must have been 1957, because I can never think of the YMCA's gym without two hits of that skiffle era coming to mind, Nancy Whiskey's 'Freight Train' and Johnny Duncan's 'Last Train to San Fernando': "If you miss this one / You'll never get another one / Biddy-biddy-bam-bam to San Fernando". My special pal and I used to 'Biddy-biddy-bam-bam', *sotto voce*, as we scurried around the gym on busy routines like skipping or climbing the wall bars. Then in lulls, as we lay panting on our backs before sits-ups and leg-lifts, snatches of the more plaintive 'Freight Train' – "Please don't tell what train I'm on / So they won't know where I've gone" – might pass between us, percussed irregularly by the metallic rallentando of the abandoned ropes still swinging from their beam hooks. Strange to be able to recall such moments – but not the name of my special pal.

This end of St Helen's Road has a reputation for begging, vagrancy, vandalism, boozing and drug-taking, with businesses complaining about heroin addicts shooting up in broad daylight. The boozers and junkies seem particularly drawn to the environs of the yellow-brick Sun Alliance building. Traders there have complained to the press about bottles, syringes and excrement being left behind overnight. Why anyone would want to cosy up to what is one of the most hideous buildings in Swansea beats me – unless, like those poets at the other end of St Helen's Road, these *damnés de la rue* are also making a critical point about the architecture.

BROTHELS

I'm sitting in the No Sign bar in Wind Street with a former student of mine – let's call her Scarlet, her chosen professional name – who used to work in a Swansea brothel. Not that brothels advertise themselves as such: massage parlour, gentlemen's club, health club are the preferred euphemisms. Scarlet has kindly agreed to walk and talk me through a semi-clandestine side of Swansea of which the majority see and hear little. Only occasionally will a news story bring it steamily to light, as when, in 2009, male prostitute Paul Grabham murdered his prostitute wife Kirsty Grabham in their flat in Rosehill Terrace, Mount Pleasant, and dumped her body in a suitcase beside the M4 near Bridgend.

"Prisons are built with stones of law," wrote William Blake, "brothels with bricks of religion."[31] Religion is no longer the force in Welsh life that it used to be, but brothels and sex workers are still with us, even if their procedures and habitats are constantly adapting to shifts in the law and changing social mores. 'Nymphs of the pave', 'sirens of the Strand' or 'bats' as they were sometimes known in old Swansea (because they came out only at night) have been part of the local scene for as long as there's been a port at the mouth of the Tawe.

These days, it's more of a 'massage parlour', luxury apartment or escort kind of trade rather than a street-walking business, and in recent years Mansel Street – about 300 metres away from the Central Police Station – has been the hub of such activity. In the port's heyday, the numerous pubs, 'dancing houses' and 'women's lodging houses' in and around the Strand were the focal point. By 1865, over 330 known prostitutes were working in Swansea, many of them no doubt operating out of an extensive slum – in what is now the Alexandra Road area – which was frequently denounced as "a hotbed of theft, brutality and immorality". By 1912, that figure had fallen to about 100, but they still managed to turn Castle Street and Wind Street into "dens of iniquity, riot and theft". The wealthy, as ever, have made their own, discreet arrangements – chiefly, these days, involving escorts – but for impecunious desperados, on both sides of the deal, the encounter may sometimes take place in notably squalorous, if not dangerous, circumstances. Until the recent refurbishment of High Street began, men would go looking for sex in the warren of railway tunnels behind High Street station, the resort of homeless street drinkers and hardy women who'd sell their bodies for as little as a fiver a time. One was nicknamed Gaslight Lil, the inference being that she'd been on the game since before the advent of electric lights.

Scarlet, who spent about a year working in the brothel – not as a prostitute but as maid and receptionist – was offered her job when, employed by a cleaning agency, she turned up to clean some premises above an Indian take-away in Dillwyn Street, at the western end of that night-life jam-pot The Kingsway.

"There was this girl there, really sexy, who'd come down from Manchester, and she was setting up a brothel. She didn't want the usual bed-and-box-of-tissues establishment. She wanted to set up a gentlemen's retreat, to bring a real bit of Manchester class to Swansea. In the bed at that time – four-poster, wrought iron, silk sheets – was her boyfriend. 'Want a line of coke?' he says. Well, why not, innit?"

Scarlet's job included changing the bed (each client had fresh sheets and towel), doing the laundry, topping up the candles, replenishing the lubes and condoms, cleaning the sex toys, writing the copy for the portfolio and designing the website, cooking for the girls, washing their clothes and making up names for them, and chatting to clients both on the phone and as they waited to get horizontal with a girl.

Her basic wage was £50 a day, but with tips from the girls she'd sometimes improve that by £100. And the days were long: 9 a.m. until midnight or 1 a.m. The girls, including Scarlet, would start the morning with a glass of free champagne each, and keep topped up throughout the day with regular infusions of Buck's Fizz. "We were pissed most of the time."

Clients were charged £120 for a half-hour session, of which the girls would receive £70 and the boss, 'tantalizing Tori', £50. "She was different from other places, which tended to be cheaper: the girls weren't just pieces of meat. £70 per client is very good. The price was all-inclusive – not separate prices for different services, like kissing or hand shandy, that you get in other places. I was dressed the part and would get the men worked up while they waited, showing them the portfolio, acting sexy, winding them up so they'd come quickly and you could get them out of the place faster. Portfolio, shower, dance – that's how the show began. It would get some of them so excited they'd come almost before they got started. There'd be quite a turnover of clients. It was backed up because it was a brand new brothel, and we'd often have to hide the clients from each other."

Swansea's older establishments resented the competition from this new business. They'd attempt to sabotage it by leaving bad reviews on the website, repeatedly phoning in to block the lines and prevent incoming calls, sending bouncers round to threaten to smash the place up, and infiltrating spies to steal Tori's winning ideas.

There were three or four girls on Tori's books, including a pole dancer, an 18-year-old known as Angel, and an economics postgraduate from Swansea University they called Lucia. "Tori was seriously anal about cleaning and would not employ women addicted to drugs," Scarlet tells me. "Heroin and crack are problems with girls in other places. Most had been abused and raped. Some enjoyed working there. It was theatre. It was the women together. Laughing at the men as soon as they had their backs turned, but pretending to be really nice. We used to just rip it out of the men – who thought we really loved them.

"We worked as a team, and it was hard work, for all of us. When the girls were having a period, they'd be told to stuff a sponge up 'em, so that they could carry on working. Most of the blokes were normal, everyday guys, with only maybe one in ten being a bit pervy. There would be on-line warnings put out generally about the dodgy ones. Safety did come first. The clients would often be young, good-looking guys, probably really shy. 'Ah, love 'em,' we'd often find ourselves saying. It's all scary for them when they come in. Sometimes the men would just want to talk, about how difficult their lives were. Not bad guys, just ordinary guys who loved sex and weren't getting enough of it at home.'

Occasionally, the police would pay a visit, and they'd have to hide a girl or two, as the law sets a limit on the number of girls who can work in a brothel. Scarlet would also be instructed to remove all the condoms from the boudoir drawer, to foster the illusion that theirs was a spa-type establishment. The laws around prostitution in Wales and England are far from straightforward. It's generally assumed that prostitution – exchanging sex for money – is illegal, but that is not the case. However, soliciting and running a brothel are illegal. But what, in the eyes of the law, is a brothel? In Scarlet's time, an establishment worked by just one person, with or without a maid or receptionist, was not classed as a brothel. The law changed following the serial murders of five Ipswich prostitutes in 2006, to permit two prostitutes and, possibly, a maid/receptionist to work legally in a brothel.

Swansea's city-centre brothels, of which there are fewer than half a dozen, seem to be tolerated: by their neighbours, which are mainly business rather than residential properties; by the police, presumably because they tend to be in largely non-residential parts of town; and by the *Evening Post* which cheerfully cashes in on the sex trade in its 'Personal' notices, tucked between the car adverts and the sport – where you can find everything from a 'Stunning

Transexual' and 'Happy Niki's Reviving Massage' to a 'Buy one get one half price' deal at Chantells and 'No-strings fun in Sketty'.

We begin our crawl of the euphemisms by heading up Wind Street towards High Street station. Just before we reach the stylishly refurbished Grand Hotel, there's a dusty door on our right, to the 'classy' (and apostrophe-free) Park Lane Gentlemans Club, where, says its website, "Our girls are beautiful and will always do their best to please you. Our fees are a reflection of this." A 'regular adult massage' will cost you between £40 and £60, but you might prefer to splash out on a one-hour massage at £100 to £200, or a 'Double (twice) massage' at a similar rate. (Is the higher rate, I wonder, for the ugly and the old?). Kissing will cost you an extra £10. So too will toys and a uniform.

We turn west into Alexandra Road and pass between the Police Station and Magistrates' Court on the threshold of what, until about 2010, was Swansea's sex-trade mecca, Mansel Street. There used to be three 'establishments' here, until the recent closure of Passion Gentlemen's Club; the building (1934) is now the latest home of the Elysium Artspace, an enterprising gallery for young and adventurous artists which began as Exposure Gallery in College Street in 2003. The artists have only just moved in,[32] and are staging their inaugural exhibition on this huge building's three floors, which they have left largely as they found them when the sex-workers moved out: holes in ceilings, garish wallpapers ripped away in jagged sheets to expose either bare walls or older layers of paper, chintzy paintwork and mouldy old finishes, fragments of cheap, dusty carpet, and expanses of concrete or bare wood flooring.

"There were used condoms of various colours littered all over the place,' says Jon Powell, one of the Elysium's directors. 'They were dropped behind radiators, in odd corners and beneath floorboards. We found an empty tube of lubricant jelly, a red garter under a floorboard, a red skimpy tube top stuffed behind a radiator, and a pair of tights with a hole ripped in the rear stuffed behind a radiator in a room which, disturbingly, was decorated with yellow, child-like wallpaper. We also found a love letter of sorts."

Some of the builders who have lately visited the gallery to provide quotes for renovation work remembered being clients of Passion. Apparently, on the top floor there were pool tables, a bar and a jacuzzi, with mirrors on the walls and ceiling, where you would be wined and dined before withdrawing to one of the smaller rooms.

One of the builders told Jon: "I used to come here a lot, I did, until they started getting in girls who were cheap and looked a bit rough, so I started using next door."

Jon also found a couple of time sheets, with girls' names, room allocations, and amounts paid. At that time, there seemed to be five main girls working there – Nicole, Lucy, Elisha, Reni and Sophie – and they entertained eight or ten clients a day in rooms called Pink, VIP, Gold and Studio, at roughly £40 or £50 a time, with the establishment retaining about half the proceeds.

Immediately next door, and just two doors away from the Undeb Bedyddwyr Cymru (the Baptists Union of Wales), is the ever-open but rarely used front door of Studio 95. Most clients are backdoor men, 'parking at rear' (*double entendre* intended, if you like, but it'll cost you) being a desirable feature of these establishments. Scarlet goes in to check out the prices. "It's really cheap," she reports, "£40 for a full personal service, and the girl gets £20 of that. It's clean, though, and they've got a cash machine. But there's nothing much happening there."

Bunnies, further up the street, seems even cheaper: £30 until 5 p.m., of which the house takes half, and £40 thereafter, with £5 for extras. It's open seven days a week, from 11 a.m. until late. Parking, of course, at rear. The girl Scarlet spoke to was about 18 or 19, and she'd been working there for three weeks. "I asked her what it was like and she said, 'Love, it's like a girls' night out.' It seems a really nice place. Made me want to go and work there. Hope they change the sheets. Bet they don't."[33]

A slur-y beggar reeking of booze taps us for cash 'for a burger' (the euphemisms abound) as we turn down towards The Kingsway to check out Scarlet's old workplace in Dillwyn Street. But it's been abandoned, as has the take-away below it. The blackout material is peeling from the brothel window, giving us a glimpse of the sun-faded satin swags of the boudoir.

"I wonder what happened to Tori," says Scarlet. "I hope she survived. She drove us hard, but I liked her. It was fun working there and I learned a lot. There were loads of laughs, even though you felt like a slave sometimes. But I wouldn't say the girls were victims. It was like a business which seemed all normal and glamorous, but there was this sadness about it. The whole place felt like that. But when you're making that kind of money – what other jobs get anywhere near it?"

Blissfully Blissful

blissfully blissful and two
lovely kids no
language please
in front of the ladies

he's lunching under lilac
his lady wife
away for the week

couldn't live now
without her
nor imagine life
if she
were unfaithful not
that she would be
Woman is mannes loye and ál his blis

she's away for the week
one more pint
then it's down to the beach
to take in the totty
after that maybe
a ride into town
the new massage parlour
a fiver your back
a tenner the front
and twenty for 'relief'
the big F itself is
not for sale
and anyway who
wants to risk disease?
how then on earth
could he break the bad news?

unfaithful? no
he couldn't tell her of course
– emotions and things – she
wouldn't understand
but blissfully blissful and wanting

for nothing
not in all the world

save relief now and then
from a hired hand

WALTERS ROAD

Walter Road or Walters Road? The latter, probably, for sound historical reasons, although the former tends to prevail these days, supported by the street's sole name-plate, on a house at the junction with Burman Street. The confusion used to be reflected in name-plates at either end of the street, one with an 's' and one without.

The version with an 's' makes the better sense when you realise that it was one James Walters (1813-1888), scion of a wealthy family of grocers and chandlers, who built this tree-lined boulevard in the late 1850s as a private road through his Ffynone estate. What became the main route from central Swansea to Gower was, until then, farmland known as the White Stile fields, through which the Penclawdd cockle-women would wend their way – having washed their feet at Olchfa[34] and then donned their boots, to look their best for town – on the final leg of their 13km walk to Swansea Market.

Walters had recently bought the land, which stretched from Page Street to Eaton Crescent, from the marine artist and pioneer photographer the Rev Calvert Richard Jones (1802-77; Jones's 1841 daguerrotype of Margam Abbey has become famous as the earliest of Welsh photographs). Having fallen into debt, Jones had needed to realise some assets by selling off part of the extensive Heathfield estate, which he had inherited in 1847 and on which he too was busy building streets.

Walters's vision for the development of the area, which included streets on both sides of his central boulevard, is characterised by elegance and spaciousness, aspiring to the Victorian ideal of a rural ambience in an urban environment: broad roads (both Walters Road and Ffynone Road are over 20 metres wide), a grand crescent (St James's), a park (St James's), occasional sweeping gardens (the delightful properties at Belgrave Gardens), terraces of two, three or more storeys, with bay windows, gables and ornate bargeboards, pedimented doorways, elaborate cast-iron railings, and an abundance of classical detail – in short, a model of Victorian urban

design celebrated by contemporaries as one of the finest thoroughfares of Wales. And there is also variety. Each of Walters Road's
consecutive terraces, sandwiched between adjoining side streets,
sounds a distinct variation on the classical theme, suggesting that
Walters granted leases to private developers to do their own thing
on separate plots – but in accordance with his overall vision.

An architectural anomaly is the four-storey, flat-roofed Belgrave
Court block of flats at the top of Walters Road, an early twentieth-
century edifice built by the Watkins dynasty of property
speculators. Probably its most distinguished occupant was
Glasgow-born Arthur Whitten Brown (1886-1948)[35] who, with
John Alcock, made the first ever non-stop transatlantic flight on 14
June 1919. There's a plaque to his memory above a door. A century
later, we tend to take our transatlantic 'hops' for granted, but Alcock
and Brown's flight – from St John's, Newfoundland to a bog in
Connemara, a distance of 3,026 kilometres – was a 16-hour, death-
defying epic. With Alcock as pilot and Brown as navigator, and with
nothing but dead reckoning to guide them, they survived an engine
fire, a non-functioning radio, continuous cloud, snow and ice. At
one stage, Brown had to walk on the wings of their open-top, two-
seater bi-plane to knock ice off. Aged 32 at the time of his
world-changing feat, he had another three decades of somewhat

anti-climactic leftover life to kill – which he spent as the manager of a light-bulb factory in Swansea. Mounted on the wall of his office in Wind Street was one of the propellers of the modified Vickers Vimy bomber in which he and Alcock crossed the Atlantic. The propeller, eventually donated by Brown to the RAF College Cranwell has not been seen since its disappearance from the college's museum. Brown, who was devastated after his only son was killed in action on D-Day, died at Belgrave Court; an accidental overdose of Veronal was said to have been the cause.

Transport of a more traditional kind used to be represented by a stone horse trough on the pavement immediately in front of Belgrave Court. It vanished in about the 1970s; but still in place nearby is a foot-high stump of weathered milestone on which the only fully discernible word is 'Swansea'. Where carts, drays, wagonettes and hansoms once paused, to slake equine thirsts after the long, uphill haul from town, the Gower buses briskly come and go.

It would have been clear to James Walters by about 1852, when the first sod was cut for the new South Dock (today's Marina), that the guts were about to be torn out of Swansea's modish heartland of the Burrows, where most of the town's well-to-do had settled in elegant Georgian terraces. They'd need somewhere else to live – and he would build it for them, in even grander style. Walters Road was intended from the outset as a residential boulevard, and so it remained until the Second World War. The Three Nights Blitz of 1941 prompted a dramatic 'change of use': many families vacated commodious dwellings that were all too close to the lethal night-time action; then, bombed-out shops and businesses – keeping safer, daylight hours – rushed in to fill the vacuum. It was an exodus, in chiefly a westerly direction, from which Walters Road and many neighbouring streets have never fully recovered.

Notable bombed-out businesses to move to Walters Road included the Ben Evans department store ('The Harrods of Wales'), J.T. Davies the chemist, Long's the jeweller, Crouch's the jeweller, Ruby Graham the classy ladies' couturier (in the bow-windowed premises currently occupied by the Royal Welch Fusiliers Club), the gentlemen's outfitter Sidney Heath – and innumerable solicitors, estate agents, financiers and insurance companies. After the reconstruction, which wasn't completed until the later 1960s, some of these concerns returned to their former plots. But many stayed put, to be joined in due course by hotels, restaurants, cafés, hair salons, vets, dentists and offices of all sorts.

street-sassy blonde
treats herself – no one looking –
to a leonine yawn

The later twentieth century saw increasing numbers making their home in Walters Road, mostly in 'new build' settlements such as the houses around St James's church or the red-brick Brunel Court apartments – rather than in the upper floors of the old terraces, many of which remain empty and uncared for. This modest residential influx has helped nurture local bars and restaurants.

Opposite St James's church, at the top end of Walters Road, is the latest of all late night-spots. It's long been a popular haunt among those who prefer candle-lit conversation to the yelling of monosyllabic inanities over robotic blitzpop. All ages, and not only the under 25s, are welcome here. When closing time, not so long ago, meant closing time, you'd approach a curtained and seemingly lifeless Mozart's, and tap appealingly on the bay window. A chink of light would show, followed by the tired face of the then patron, Carl, a burly Austrian with a white beard. If he decided you were friend rather than snitching foe, he'd wearily open the French window, and hours of congenial 'after hours' would be yours in the cosy front-room bar. "Time, ladies and gentlemen, please" is never a call I have heard at Mozart's.

In a couple of larger rooms at the rear, especially at weekends, the volume's turned up for extravaganzas such as Mozart's 'Funked Up!', 'WALES'S ONLY 100% VINYL NIGHT', as the posters proclaim, of funk, soul, disco, Latin and reggae. And on two Thursdays a month, the dusky back bar becomes The Crunch, an atmospheric open-mic night for local poets, doggerelists and ranters to strut their wildly varied stuff. With the Dylan Thomas Centre, it has played a vital role in creating, for the first time in Swansea, a poetry 'scene'. Cardiff, thanks to key literary players such as Peter Finch and Chris Torrance, has had a vibrant poetry scene since the mid 1960s, bringing together on a regular basis, at different venues and under various banners, the city's literati – to read and slam, to generate magazines and happenings, to form splinter scenes, to exchange the best of their talents with the wider poetry world. Swansea's makers, for all their international renown in certain cases, have been more atomised, rarely gathering in public for more than one-off readings, and rarely generating a head of communal, creative steam – until 2008, when the young

American poet Graham Isaac, who had just completed a creative writing MA at Swansea University, joined forces with Adam Sillman of Mozart's to set up The Crunch. He knew what he was doing. The challenge was to leaven the space-cadets and self-indulgent chancers with sufficient serious practitioners and published guest poets to keep the audience's interest and to persuade them to come back for more. Which they do – standing room only on most Crunch Thursdays.

If you were to dine at a different Swansea 'eatery' every night of the year, you'd still not exhaust your options by the year's end. This was far from the situation when Bizzie Lizzie's opened its basement doors at 55 Walters Road nearly thirty years ago. Although Swansea could boast Indian, Chinese and chain establishments such as Berni Inns, there were few independently run restaurants, and almost none with an imaginative menu. Bizzie Lizzie's – with Colin Presdee's Drangway in Wind Street – would break that mould.

It began in the early 1980s as Toby's (the old sign featuring a terrier of that name gathers dust out the back), and it was run for a while by the late Duncan Atkinson, a cheery charmer who relished good food and real ale, and had a devil-may-care attitude to licensing laws. Poets and artists loved the place. I remember many a carousal with the likes of Dewi 'Mav' Bowen, Mogg Williams and Terry Hetherington, and visiting writers such as Adrian Mitchell and John Tripp. One spring day in 1983, I took the Czech poet Miroslav Holub (1923-98) there for a light lunch, after a visit to the Miners' Library at Maes-yr-Haf in the Uplands and prior to a reading that night at Swansea Arts Workshop in Gloucester Place (now the Mission Gallery). The lunch turned out to be anything but light: a vast portion each of rabbit casserole which, said Miroslav, was "Like trying to eat an angel." All too accustomed to the then repressive ways of the Czechoslovakian regime, Miroslav had a sharp eye for the sometimes surreal heavy-handedness of official-dom. "Look what I found in the Miners' Library, my favourite souvenir of the whole trip," he said, reaching into his wallet pocket and pulling out a wad of toilet tissue, every sheet stamped, to the poet's delight, with the words 'Government property'. Miroslav was similarly taken by the locked goals on the university playing fields, and had me take a photograph of him standing beside a goal-mouth barrier on which was inscribed 'No unauthorised games'. He thought it would make an excellent New Year's card.

Unlike wily Carl at Mozart's, Duncan did nothing to disguise his reckless after-hours welcome to all. I was there the night the inevitable happened. Three or four policemen burst in, ordered the bar closed, told us all to stay put, and then took down everyone's name and address. No prosecutions followed, but that was the end of Mr Atkinson's carefree tenure.

A Conservative club – the Salisbury, at 128 Walters Road – might seem an incongruous venue for a rock-n-roll wake, but that's where, one blustery afternoon in October 2005, the family and friends of the guitarist (and sometime plumber) Clive 'Snob' Roberts have gathered to wish him farewell and to reminisce about his contribu-tion to many top local bands, among them the Blues Bunch, Deke Leonard's Iceberg and the Flying Aces. The approach to the Salisbury Club's first-floor functions room is regal and British, with large black-and-white portraits of Prince Charles, the Queen and the Duke of Edinburgh accompanying you up the ornate, carved stair-case. Not a word of Welsh, naturally, anywhere in the building. But enter the L-shaped functions room at the top of the stairs, and you'll find an entirely different world celebrated in the photographs on the walls: bluesmen – black and white, ancient and modern – many of whom have played here at (what is at least one night a week) the

Tawe Delta Blues Club.[36] The club, which started at the Heathfield Club, Mount Pleasant in 2000, is run by former Everly Brothers and Dire Straits drummer Terry Williams and his wife Louise. Urban rather than country blues is their preferred strain, electric and ear-fizzingly loud – which a feminist friend of mine, assailed by it weekly in her Mount Pleasant home, refers to as 'cock rock'.

With a white floral guitar on a deserted stage, there's no music this afternoon, just affectionate chat about Snob in particular, and music and life in general. Time lethally passes. The place is full of ageing musos – Clive John,[37] Brian Breeze, Mike Bollom, Martin Ace, Roger Henderson, Georgina Ace, the loud and lusty Dai Rees – who tend to greet each other, as the heart-attacks, strokes and cancers mount, with warm reassurances about how well they're looking. A notorious Swansea thug, sipping half a bitter, is looking too old these days to do too much physical harm – although he could no doubt summon 'the boys' to fix a deal or quell a challenge.

Until 2009, the Salisbury Club was a gentlemen's club (in the literal rather than 'massage-parlour' sense). Chaps only; chapesses admitted only at certain times and in certain rooms. When Mrs Thatcher pitched up at the Salisbury in the mid 1990s, she was turned away with the regretful sigh 'no women'.[38] She'd have been even less welcome – largely on socio-political grounds – in the Tenby next door, a famously 'colourful' boozer and more naturally the habitat of blues aficionados. Here the poet Peter Read encountered the formidable Dai Cwmbwrla, immortalising Dai's "pink vest over white shorts", and the advert for "Strongbow, the best cider in the world" tattooed on his chest, while his back boasted "Swansea City are ace". After Peter read his poem 'Dai Cwmbwrla' on Radio Wales, he heard that Dai was "looking for him". He thought it wise, at that point, to re-title his poem 'Dai Vest' and to steer clear of the Tenby for a while.

The pub's owners have tried to change its image from time to time, importing Chesterfield sofas during one make-over, and changing its name – in recognition of its proximity to the Con Club – to the Churchill. But the Tenby, in spirit, it remained, and the old name was soon restored. When the pub closed in 2010, its many fans feared that its closure, like that of too many distinctive Swansea boozers, might be permanent, but it reopened towards the end of the year, after a major refurbishment and with a new landlord deter-mined to keep at bay the business-wrecking drug-heads, some of them clumsy with knives, who have come to haunt this part of town.

he leaves the pub,
having paid the jukebox,
in the middle of his song

MANSEL STREET, DE LA BECHE STREET, GROVE PLACE, ALEXANDRA ROAD

Walters Road continues towards High Street and the railway station as four much shorter lengths of thoroughfare: Mansel Street, De la Beche Street, Grove Place and Alexandra Road. Who were these people?

Mansel Street, built by the Rev Calvert Richard Jones as he developed his Heathfield estate in the mid 1800s, was named after the great photographer's half-brother (he liked to name his streets after family associations: Verandah Street was named after his boyhood home, Veranda, a mansion at Singleton; Calvert Terrace was named after his father, Christina Street after his daughter, and Portia Terrace in Mount Pleasant after his second wife). Although, as a man of leisured means, the Rev Jones may not have devoted too many hours to the curing of souls, he would no doubt have blenched at Mansel Street's reputation in our own time (until about 2010) as the hub of Swansea's sex-trade, and, with the lower Walters Road area, a mooching ground for boozy beggars and druggies.

As Mansel Street becomes De la Beche Street, the small shops and businesses give way to much bulkier architecture: the abandoned and wisteria-sprouting Albert Hall, whose three ventilation cowls are prominent features of the city's roofscape. It opened in 1864 as the Music Hall, having been designed in a relatively plain (and therefore inexpensive) style by William 'Coppernose' Richards, author also of the Mansion House[39] (1863) in Ffynone, among other Swansea buildings; when the Music Hall was extended in 1881 it was renamed the Albert Hall, after Queen Victoria's late consort. For half a century, the Albert Hall was at the heart of Swansea's cultural life, featuring performances by such stars of the day at Madame Patti, John McCormack, Penfro Rowlands and Charles Dickens.

In 1896, the ruthless colonialist Henry Morton Stanley (1841-1904), who was born John Rowlands in Denbigh and spent his adult life denying his Welshness, addressed a large gathering at the

Albert Hall and told them bluntly that he had been "wondering as to whither this craze for Welsh will lead to" [sic]; he had seen a goodly portion of the British Empire and warned that "wherever the aborigines were found clinging to their traditions, they were sunk in obscurity and unimportance". I can imagine this message going down well with many of my great-grandparents' generation who were sedulously de-cymricising themselves. My paternal great-grandfather had come in from threadbare rural Carmarthenshire to the glowing hearth of Swansea business life, establishing himself in an urban plas in Ffynone called Goedwig. Meet the family c. 1900: Meurig, Dilys, Eluned, Eira. Meet the family again, thirty odd years later: Ian, Roger, Noel, Rowland.

Yr Iaith[40]

> She who has forgotten
> remembers as if yesterday
> the scythe they left rusting
> in the arms of an apple,
> the final bang of the door
> on those sheep-bitten hills.

In Abertawe, in Swansea
there were killing to be made,
and they politely made theirs.

She spent a lifetime loving
the taste of white bread, a lifetime
forgetting the loser's brown.
And on their middle floors
the brass gleamed, the crystal sang,
while away in the attic
dust fingered
the violins and the harp,
and far below stairs a discreet
and callused tongue complained.

Years she remembers
of cuff-link and shoeshine,
but nothing, she says, nothing
of those dung-filled yards.

It's autumn now, an evening
that ends in colour t.v.
and the washing of dishes.
I ask her, as I dry,
Beth yw 'spoon' yn Gymraeg?
Llwy, she says, *llwy, dw i'n credu,*
and she bites into an apple
that tastes like home.

And meet the family today: Angharad Siân and Branwen Delyth, fluent speakers of Welsh. It has taken the best part of a century to cure the family's cultural cringe.

The oldest of Swansea's surviving nineteenth-century theatres, the Albert Hall suffered, like the others, from the growth of cinema at the expense of music hall, so it 'joined the opposition' in the 1950s, being the first in Swansea to host midnight matinees. These were hugely popular among the late pub-going crowd, who'd form great queues snaking from the cinema's entrance in Cradock Street round into De la Beche Street. On one famous occasion, as the film-goers poured onto the street after the show, they were serenaded by one of their number, a certain Harry Secombe, whose compelling tenor voice brought the traffic to a standstill.

The Albert Hall closed as a cinema in 1977 and spent the next thirty years as a bingo club, with 10,000 punters a week piling through its doors during the good times – which were also the smoky times, as more than half of the clientele were smokers. The imminence of the 2007 ban on smoking in enclosed places, together with dwindling custom, resulted in the closure of Mecca Bingo's Albert Hall operation hours before the smoking ban came in. There'd been room at Mecca's larger club in Carmarthen Road to build a heated outdoor shelter for smokers, but limited space at the Albert Hall forbade that option. The future for this Grade II listed building has never looked more uncertain, although a campaign was launched in 2011 to refurbish the building as a 3,000-seat venue for big-name acts which Swansea, currently, can't accommodate.

A bright future for the building immediately next door, the former Dynevor School, which closed in 2002, was assured in 2006 when one of its past pupils, Dr Rowan Williams, the Archbishop of Canterbury, returned to open Swansea Metropolitan University's Dynevor Centre for Art, Design and Media. The Centre consists of two radically different buildings "yoked by violence together" (as Dr Johnson complained of Donne's imagery): the sombre Pennant sandstone edifice of the old school (1894) and the vapid quotation from Swinburne which has been tacked on to it.

Although the school – built where once the stream that gushed down Mount Pleasant gathered as Washing Well Lake – was partly destroyed in the blitz of 1941, there remain no obvious traces of damage. But if you cross the road and examine a limestone pillar outside the offices of Rees Richards & Partners, you'll see that a sizeable chunk of it has been sheered off by flying shrapnel. The curiously ornate premises which Rees Richards now occupies escaped virtually unscathed, but the firm's former headquarters, the historic The Laurels a few metres away – where the new Central Police Station stands – was obliterated, its safe still white hot among the ruins hours after the attack.

The names of two of these consecutive thoroughfares, De la Beche Street and Grove Place, commemorate eminent Swansea scientists.

London-born Sir Henry Thomas De la Beche (1796-1855), FRS, who has streets named after him also in Sketty,[52] Morriston and Llanelli, is best known as the founding director of what is now the British Geological Survey, and for the first-ever geological

survey, from his base in Swansea, of the south Wales coalfield (1838-1852); he also conducted pioneering research into the causes and prevention of explosions in coalmines. His father, a slave-owner with a sugar plantation in Jamaica, was born plain Thomas Beach, but, fancying he was descended from Norman barons, he changed his name to the Frenchified De la Beche (surely it should have been De la Plage?). Those Jamaican slaves kept young Henry afloat on an income of £3,000 a year, enabling him to live the life of a gentle-man geologist. But by the time he moved the Geological Survey to Swansea in 1837, emancipation was well under way (the last Jamaican slave was freed in 1839), and he was obliged to rely on geology as the means of support, thereby establishing geology as a profession it was possible to pursue outside the universities.

In 1845, De la Beche produced a devastating report for the Health of Towns Commission on the dangerously insalubrious state of Swansea: the Lower Swansea Valley area was plagued by noxious fumes; malformed streets and alleys were badly paved; ramshackle houses were overcrowded; urine streamed from homes without privies, and dung – animal and human – piled up in the streets; most people were reliant for their water on polluted wells and streams; typhus and consumption were rife. His report stung the authorities into implementing improvements, as did his comparable observations about Brecon and Merthyr. De la Beche may eventually have had local streets named after him, but when he died – in London, some years after leaving Swansea – *The Cambrian* accorded the bearer of such unwelcome news only the briefest of obituaries.

The scientist commemorated by Grove Place, Sir William Robert Grove, FRS (1811-96), was a Swansea native and Swansea Grammar School alumnus, his family home being that handsome Grove Place villa blitzed by the Germans, The Laurels. There have been signs in recent years that this "veiled figure, known only to historians of science and a small number of engineers and physicists" – to quote Ronald Rees's absorbing study of eminent Swansea scientists, *Heroic Science* (2005) – may be verging on the wider recognition his achievements deserve. He got a decent entry in *The Welsh Academy Encyclopaedia of Wales* (three times the length of De la Beche's), and in 2003 Grove and the exciting prospects for the revolutionary fuel cell he invented – at Swansea in 1839 – were featured in the *New Yorker* magazine. It was the law, rather than slavery, that sustained this self-taught physicist, whose chief fascination was electricity. Having developed the two-fluid electric battery, and used such a battery to provide electric light for his lectures at the Royal Institution in London, he then constructed a gas battery which produced electric current from hydrogen and oxygen reacting on platinum electrodes. Although this fuel cell, as it was subsequently renamed, was far more efficient than the steam engine, the implications of Grove's discovery were largely ignored at the time: steam power was in the ascendant, and there seemed to be no shortage of the fossil fuels on which it depended. Grove's fuel cell, says Rees, was "a classic example of the right invention made at the wrong time." It wasn't until the 1960s, when NASA applied fuel-cell technology to the space programme, that both industry and governments began to take Grove's invention seriously as, potentially, a non-polluting source of power for most forms of transport. If, as many believe, we are on the threshold of the hydrogen age, then Grove "is assured of a place in the Pantheon alongside Edison and Bell."

The 160-metres-long Grove Place has room for little more than the new Central Police Station, opened in 2001 on the site of the old central fire station (1959-97), and the Magistrates' Court. The aloofly utilitarian cop shop is humanised to some extent by the six-

metres-high stainless-steel 'Fingerprint Monolith' (2010) erected on the pavement outside its car park. Informative and playful, it's the wacky work of the ingenious public sculptor and 'automatist' Andy Hazell (1959), who lives in Knighton, Powys. The 50mm thick slab of steel is cut through with lines of text which describe the sinuous contours of a gigantic fingerprint. The top two thirds deal with the history of the police, from the establishment of local militias and night-watchmen, through '1890 whistles replacing rattles in raising the alarm', '1880 The 'Pickelhaube' helmet is introduced', '1927 police telephone boxes are built at busy intersections', '1946 999 is introduced', '1961 the fingerprinting department is established', to developments such as 1964's amalgamation of the four south Wales forces (Cardiff, Merthyr, Swansea, Glamorganshire). The lower third consists of a range of common abbreviations, such as TWOC (taking vehicle without owner's consent), BOB (breach of bail), D + I (drunk and incapable) and BOP (breach of peace).

It was at the Magistrates' Court across the road that I was once robbed by a policeman. Having refused to pay a fine of £40 for the 'criminal damage' I (among others) caused to a fence during a peace demo in 1986 at the so-called US Oceanographic Research Centre at Brawdy in Pembrokeshire – which was a key element in America's preparations for nuclear war – I was taken down to the cells beneath the court and relieved by a policeman of all the cash in my pocket, about £1.50. I was given time to cough up the rest – and released. When, a short while later, I again refused to pay the fine, the magistrates sentenced me to a week in Swansea jail.[43] Not bothering with the single penny with which this time I'd baited my pocket, a policeman took me straight to a transit cell where, for an hour or so, I listened to the youngsters in neighbouring cells ribbing the policemen passing to and fro, getting bawled out in turn, and moaning for cigarettes and lights for cigarettes – the abiding obsession of prison life. There was nothing to read but the graffiti, including 'Kill the poor' scratched in a join between the bricks. I wondered how often the youthful habitués of these cells – poor beyond doubt – had been here before: they seemed well-known to the police and to each other. And I wonder now, decades later, how much of their chaotic lives those scions of poverty may have wasted in jail.

Two beacons of hope for modern youth, both managed by Grwp Gwalia, are to be found on opposite sides of Alexandra Road: the Foyer, the imaginatively adapted former Working Men's Club (1885) which provides housing and training for disadvantaged 16- to 25-year-olds; and the Llys Glas arts and culture complex which Grwp Gwalia has developed at the old Central Police Station.

The Foyer is one of Wales's most innovative social housing projects. Built by Grwp Gwalia in 1997, and conserving just the front and the eastern side of the distinctly French-looking Working Men's Club – which was otherwise virtually derelict – it was the first of seven projects across Wales designed to address the problem of youth homelessness. The Second Empire tone of the original red-brick and Bath-stone exterior belies the airy modernism of the rebuilt interior, in which 28 small bedrooms and various communal rooms are disposed around a central area called the street, where parties and various craft and life-skills sessions are held. The concept comes from France: foyers were introduced there after the Second World War to provide mobility for young people moving from town to town. There may be a 'three strikes and you're out' rule, but the project's architect, Phil Roberts, and the people who run the Foyer are determined that the place should not have the institutionalising feel of a hostel. Mediterranean colours, timber framing responsibly sourced, light flooding in, solar panels on the roof contributing to ecological sustainability, and an unmistakeably inspirational ambience: architectural determinism at its most benevolent.

The old Central Police Station (1913) is one of many distinguished buildings designed by Swansea's imaginative borough architect Ernest Morgan (1881-1954). Occupying a commanding angle site between Alexandra Road and Orchard Street,[44] the Police Station survived the blitz – but only just: for graphic evidence of bombs and flying shrapnel see the pitted red brick walling of its Orchard Street elevation. The Police Station occupies the site of the Alexandra Skating Rink, roller-skating being a popular pastime in late Victorian and Edwardian times. And it was a short distance south of this site at Capel Gomer – where today the Orchard Street multi-storey car park stands – that in 1814 Joseph Harris (Gomer; 1773-1825) launched the first weekly newspaper[45] in Welsh, *Seren Gomer*, as a "General Weekly Informant for the whole of the Principality of Wales"; although it survived for no more than two years as a weekly, it ran in one form or another until 1983. Gomer is commemorated by the heroically banal Capel Gomer (1962) at the top of Cradock Street, which replaced the more dignified late nineteenth-century Mount Zion chapel demolished by the Luftwaffe in 1941.

The Llys Glas complex at the old Central Police Station includes artists' studios, function rooms, student accommodation, the Cyrenians' Celfi Gallery, the offices of the Citizens' Advice Bureau, and an arts café bar called Tapestri. With the Welsh School of Architectural Glass next door, the Glynn Vivian Gallery opposite and – adjoining the Glynn Viv – Dylan Thomas House, historic home of the BBC in Swansea and now (mostly) Swansea Met's music department, Alexandra Road has become much more of a cultural quarter than boozy Wind Street once pretended to be.

The area once had a very different profile, being compared in the nineteenth century to London's infamous Seven Dials slum. The provision of what is now a tree-lined boulevard containing some of Swansea's most distinctive public buildings was intended to sweep away a notorious breeding ground of crime and squalor. It was "covered with small, unsightly, unhealthy houses, inhabited by the criminal and abandoned classes," wrote Samuel Clearstone Gamwell[46] (d. 1896) in 1880, shortly after the road was laid down. Known initially as Yeo Street, after Frank Ash Yeo (1832-88), the industrialist (and former Swansea mayor, future Gower MP) who had most actively pursued the slum's clearance, its name was changed to Alexandra Road after the Danish princess who opened it one afternoon in October 1881, shortly after her husband, Prince Edward, the Prince of Wales (and future King Edward VII), opened the dock that bears his name.

The last 80-metre stretch of Alexandra Road, between Orchard Street and High Street, once had considerable character; now it has none – unless vacuity and concrete brutalism are accounted characterful.

On the south side of the street stands the 13-storey Alexandra House (1975), a stupefying slab of offices, where once there stood the four-storey Great Western Hotel, with shops and restaurants on the ground floor, arcing elegantly round into High Street. One of the eateries here was the Orient Indian restaurant, possibly the first of Swansea's curry houses, which was particularly popular with local musicians at the end of a night's gigging. It wasn't unusual to find half a dozen bands there on a Saturday night, with their VWs and converted ambulances parked outside, covered in fans' lipstick messages. The Orient wasn't licensed, but if you were in with the staff they'd gladly top your Coke up with rum. Guitarist Brian Breeze told me of one memorable night when a band manager known as Cracky (the late Graham Dean Jones) smuggled into the Orient a sports pistol which was one of his band's on-stage gimmicks.[47]

"Cracky worked himself up into a pretend fury with the proprietor, Abu, shouting and getting angrier and angrier until, in an eye-popping rage, he suddenly produced the gun and aimed it at Abu, who was crying 'No, Mr Cracky, no!' He fired the gun, there was an almighty bang, and Abu, clutching his chest, fell to the floor, crying 'You've killed me, Mr Cracky!' But of course nothing at all had come from the gun apart from one hell of a noise. The place was full of horrified customers."

In the middle of the road, near its junction with High Street – at which there was invariably a white-cuffed policeman directing the traffic – was an island with ornate metal railings surrounding the entrance to underground toilets. As the worm burrows, these toilets were only a few yards away from another underground establishment, a notorious drinking den run by the former Welsh heavyweight boxing champion Jimmy Wilde (1911-90; not to be confused with a more famous Jimmy Wilde (1892-69), 'The Tylorstown Terror' who became the world's first flyweight boxing champion in 1916). Swansea's Jimmy Wilde took his title in 1935 when he beat Charlie Bundy, and the following year he came close to lifting the British championship, flooring Tommy Farr three times at Swansea's Vetch Field; the fight ended in a draw, but he was beaten in the rematch and Farr took the championship. During the Second World War, he ran a gym near High Street station (the American Rocky Marciano's boxing career began there), and in 1946 he fought – and lost – the last of his 49 fights. Not for Jimmy Wilde, though, the sad afterlife of many a has-been boxer, punch-drunk and raddled with booze, sparring with reflections in shop windows. In the late 1950s, he opened the Alexandra Guest House: between G.&J. Ferris newsagents and Station Jewellers (the last shop on the north side of the street), there was an alleyway and above it, sticking out over the pavement, a sign inviting you to 'Take Courage at the Alexandra Social Club', which soon became known to everyone, especially the out-of-hours clientele, as Jimmy's. Half-a-crown admission for non-members. All-night drinking. Rooms for hire, if you got lucky.

Mine host – remembered as a hard but fair man who looked after his friends – was always immaculately dressed, in white shirt and dickie bow. The club itself was somewhat less than immaculate.

"The place was never cleaned – it was filthy, disgusting, you daren't even lean against a wall," remembers poet and translator Malcolm Parr, who nevertheless relished its anarchic ambience. He has a fund of stories about Jimmy's: dancers falling off the bar, smashing glasses on the surrounding tables; sex-hungry sailors; prostitutes, famous actors and singing stars; wide-boys fencing stolen goods. "The police loved the place, because if there was anyone on the run they knew they'd find him at Jimmy's."

Jimmy Wilde in later life rose to the challenge of one last fight: the struggle to get listed-building status for his premises. What was known originally as Siddall's Buildings had played a significant role in the development of the town's socialist and labour activism, and he was determined that his place should not suffer the same fate as the handsome hotel block across the road. It was a fight he was doomed to lose. Earmarked for demolition, the building was gutted by fire and, in 1986, demolished – as were all the other colourful properties on that side of the road. The site is now a car park.

THE MACABRE CAFÉ

Drugs came to Swansea, as sex came to Philip Larkin, in the 1960s. Psychedelic posters, Timothy Leary tracts left threateningly on parental coffee tables, freaky lightshows at Dream and Bystanders gigs: such were the ominous 'signs' that your teenager was well on the way to drug-addled ruination. Although, in fact, relatively few 'actually inhaled' much in any purposeful sense, most being more or less content with the rebellious trappings, the stuff was certainly there for the dealing – chiefly hash, speed and LSD. And where better to fix yourself a deal than the notorious Macabre Café in Mansel Street, with its black-washed interior, minimal lighting, skeletons and coffin-top tables? To be seen entering the risqué Macabre – next door to what is now the K2 Indian restaurant, and later, for a while, the Sound Hole music shop – was to burnish your street cred among friends – and to condemn yourself to perdition as far as Mam and Dad were concerned.

My friend Lainie Defee (b. Jennifer Searle) used to go there often. "It was the favourite Mod haunt," she told me in an email from Oklahoma, where she settled in the 1970s. "We – of course – called it the Morgue. The cheapest thing on the menu was baked beans on toast. I ate a lot of those. My dad used to drop me off there, and I recall vague warnings of it being on the police radar for drugs."

In its relatively short existence (c.1966-69), the Macabre – at least in its early manifestation – was hardly the den of iniquity that parents and the bus queues opposite imagined it to be. There'd often be two dozen scooters parked outside, festooned with rabbits' tails, tiger tails (free with Esso petrol), and banks of mirrors, the lower ones angled for the ogling of girls' legs. "Older people no doubt looked askance at us," says Peter Williams, who used to cook at the Macabre. "They didn't understand this new thing. Cars were all black then, and life, like the telly, was black and white. Then along came the Beatles and suddenly you had coloured cars."

The Macabre was opened by the late Martin Life and his wife Eve to cater for the Mods of west Wales, while diagonally across the way in Christina Street – where today's Siop Tŷ Tawe sells Welsh books and CDs – was the Christina Café, the Rockers' h.q. – "full of blondes in beehives," Peter remembers. "Now and then, we'd have the odd rumble with the Rockers, but nothing too serious, because we all knew each other. People used to say, 'Mods and Rockers, Brighton and all that, I was there', which is bollocks, as they'd never have made it there on those machines."

Peter, whose (slightly younger) brother is the former Dire Straits drummer Terry Williams, has spent most of his life as roadie and sound engineer with numerous world-famous acts, among them Swansea's own Badfinger, Joan Armatrading, Sad Café and (whisper it) the Bay City Rollers. But he got his first job, after school hours, at the Macabre.

"I hadn't even cooked cornflakes before I cooked there. The menu was sausage, egg and chips or egg, chips and sausage or chips, egg and sausage, and Coca Cola and Sprite. There were no check trousers or anything like that. You'd just be sitting there drinking a Coke, and then someone would come in wanting egg and chips. Martin used to pay us like this: there was a big coffee tin full of pennies, beside the Dansette record player, and he'd shove his hand into it at the end of the night, pull out a handful of pennies and that's how much you got. There were no pre-packaged chips in those days, and we were paid by the volume of spuds we peeled. We'd be out the back peeling the spuds, and chucking every other spud over the wall of the Bamboo Boutique next door: one for Martin, one for the garden."

Not being a licensed establishment, the Macabre was open all hours. Bands used to pitch up around midnight for their post-gig egg and chips and Coke. "We had Chris Farlowe in there one night," says Peter. "He'd been flown over by helicopter, after singing his number one hit 'Out of Time' on *Top of the Pops*, to perform at the Ritz, Skewen, then the Regal, Ammanford the next night.

"Drink in those days wasn't a big thing. Drugs were just coming in, although nothing more than a bit of blow. But you didn't bring it into the café, Martin wouldn't allow it. You'd go round the back lane."

The Macabre began to live up to its dodgy reputation, says Peter, "when the heavies took it over – people like Micky Baker and Killer Morgan, both now dead. They were off their heads in there, it was frightening. One night, Killer Morgan was lying on a coffin, peaking on acid, and they got a saw, the blunt side down, and were trying to cut his leg off. The police wouldn't touch those boys. Far too dangerous. It was all finished by about 1969."

The 'drug scene' of nearly half a century ago, for all the strident alarmism of an older generation, seems almost quaint today, in view of the hundreds of lives blighted, in most western cities, by much more powerful and addictive drugs such as crack and heroin, aided and abetted, as ever, by booze and by a relentlessly criminalising and counter-productive 'war on drugs'. The police say that Swansea's drugs dependency is as severe as that in some inner London boroughs. A 2011 report[48] found that Swansea is consistently the highest in the United Kingdom for positive testing for heroin and cocaine in people arrested for 'trigger offences': the British average for positive drug tests is around 23%, while in Swansea it is over 35%.

With a 180% increase in heroin users in Swansea between 2006 and 2009, there's no shortage of theories (and prejudices) about what has become one of the city's most devastating social problems. There are children in poorer parts of Swansea who enter nursery classes so impoverished through their parents' drug addiction that they start school unable to speak even their own name. What it means in human rather than statistical terms is communicated most poignantly in a documentary film, *Swansea Love Story*, launched in December, 2009 on *Vice* magazine's VBS.TV website as part of their Rule Britannia series of love letters to a decaying Britain. Made by Andy Capper and Leo Leigh (son of film-maker Mike Leigh), *Swansea Love Story* came as a shock to many. It features two homeless addicts, Cornelius and Amy – among other damaged souls – whose guiding fixation, apart from each other, is cheap cider and heroin. The far from unintelligent Cornelius Collins tells us how, as a child, he followed in the footsteps of his father, an addict and a dealer, and 18-year-old Amy describes how her mother got her hooked on drugs and put her to work, aged 14, in a 'massage parlour'; they both became alcoholics, she says, after she gave birth to Cornelius's stillborn baby. Some have found this scrupulously non-judgemental work of 'immersion' journalism too unbearably painful to watch beyond the first of its six ten-minute parts, but it's not without touches of humour and it even manages the odd flicker of hope – showing, for instance, the determination of one of the addicts to kick his habit and to stay "clean and serene".

An undercover operation by Swansea police in 2010, in which an officer posed as a homeless busker, resulted in twenty-five local heroin dealers being jailed, among them Cornelius Collins, who was sentenced to twenty months inside.

The film-makers, who spent weeks among their subjects, worked in league with Swansea Drugs Project which has become an indispensable lifeline for people with drug and alcohol problems. Founded in 1983 by a group of local residents (among them Martin Life), it's one of the oldest and most innovative substance misuse agencies in Wales, having pioneered the first needle exchange programme in the country. It opened a substantial new centre – with a flamboyant glass portico, and painted a fizzing electric blue – on Mansel Street in 2010, a few doors west of where the Macabre once rattled its alarming bones.

THE OLD CENTRAL LIBRARY

Wales, at long last, has an English-medium national theatre, which seems, this time, to be more than some thespian's short-lived pipedream. It's a balmy evening in early April 2010, after the coldest winter in thirty years, and I'm milling around in the courtyard between the old Central Police Station and the old Central Library, sipping a glass of wine which came 'free' with a very expensive packet of crisps, contemplating a mountain of discarded books, and waiting for the second of National Theatre Wales's twelve inaugural productions, *Shelf Life*, to spark into action. The show's an unlikely collaboration between John E. McGrath's NTW, Welsh National Opera and Swansea's own tirelessly experimental

Volcano theatre company – all stitched together by directors Paul Davies and Catherine Bennett, and dramaturg D.J. Britton – which, we are soon to find, works admirably.

Volcano, who often like to stage their extravaganzas in numinous buildings, have not been alone in falling for the charms of the old library, with its captivating domed reading room reminiscent, in miniature, of the British Museum's. It was a prime location for the BBC's 1985 mini-series *That Uncertain Feeling*, starring Dennis Lawson and Sheila Gish, and based on Kingsley Amis's 1955 novel about the amorous (mis)adventures of a feckless and lecherous librarian in Aberdarcy (a thinly disguised Swansea). The novel had earlier been adapted for the 1962 feature film *Only Two Can Play* (1962),[49] starring Peter Sellers and Kenneth Griffith, but curiously the Glynn Vivian Art Gallery was used instead of the Central Library. Presumably, the film-makers felt the Glynn Vivian looked more like a library than the real one.

Since the old library was emptied of its books in 2007 and its functions transferred to the new central library in the seafront Civic Centre, it has been in the care of the Welsh School of Architectural Glass, who are not quite sure what to do with it.[50] But filmmakers, including the makers of *Dr Who*[51] and *Sherlock*, have been queuing up to use the circular reading room,[52] and it's a lull in filmic proceedings that gives Volcano and co a three-week run of this faded beauty of a building.

For 120 years, it served as a storehouse of knowledge. Fact and fiction, gossip and wisdom – it was all collected here. Volcano are interested not only in the narratives and information gathered in the books, but in the stories accumulated by the building itself. What does it mean to close a library? What have libraries been in the past and what might they become? What future for the book in this relentlessly digitising age?

Swansea's first public library opened in Goat Street (roughly commensurate with what is today upper Princess Way) in 1871. It was far too small from the outset, and was replaced by the Central Library and School of Art in 1887, built in Italian-classical style on land which previously housed "dens of debauchery and obscenity", to quote a local magistrate. It was clearly meant to exert a significant improving influence on the moral and intellectual life of the town, although not all members of Swansea's upper echelons were in favour. The Morriston colliery owner John Glasbrook, who had successfully delayed the founding of a free library, had claimed in 1870 that "people have too much knowledge already; it was much easier to manage them twenty years ago; the more education people get the more difficult they are to manage."

A contrary view was expressed by the former (and future) prime minister William Gladstone who, invited to open the Central Library on 6 June 1887, declared that "Without the blessings of reading, the burden of life would be intolerable." A small bust of the Liberal leader used to be kept in the reading room; it's been replaced tonight by a theatrically large portrait of Gladstone, which, after being paraded through the courtyard on a ceremonial litter, is ensconced in the reading room, to preside over the proceedings with a bemused eye.

With audience numbers limited to only thirty per performance,

Shelf Life's two performances a night are sell-outs. While we wait for that litter, the actors and the WNO's community choir to sweep into the courtyard, a lone performer beneath a tasselled pagoda wipes old hardbacks with a wet cloth, dilating whimsically on the glory of books. As daylight turns to dusk, I notice how the sky, contaminated by dust from the eruption of Iceland's Eyjafjallajökull volcano,[53] has turned an extraordinary green. As the book-wiper's eulogy peaks, she plunges the volume into her washing-up bowl, and into the court-yard irrupts the cast, with the choir in full voice, modestly attired to look like librarians, but sporting here and there Dionysian masks.

This tension between measured decorum and sensory abandon – sex in the stacks, nudity among the desks – is an insistent, allur-ing undertow throughout the evening. As the choir sing about libraries, an aerial dancer suspended on a rope from the rim of the reference library's roof twirls as she swings in ever wider arcs, jotting notes on scraps of paper and, with growing effort, pinning them on increasingly far flung parts of the drum's stone wall. Between songs, there are snatches of drama, as when a Nordic blonde pursues a young man with a rolled up newspaper, beating out of him an admission of sexual 'infidelity'.

We are then invited into the stacks, at ground-floor level beneath the library. Bathed in red light, these narrow, brick corridors of book-bereft, wooden shelving remind the woman in front of me of the Roman catacombs. Fragments of stacking instructions are pinned here and there:

WELSH POOL
Authors with bardic or literary titles filed under family surname
"Ceiriog" = Hughes, J. Ceiriog
"Crwys" = Williams, M. Crwys
"Gwenallt" = Jones, D. 'Gwenallt'
"Emrys ap Iwan" = Jones, Robert Ambrose

And there are intriguing snippets of graffiti to be stumbled on, some perhaps original, some almost certainly 'Volcanic': "Bong on"; "Librarians make novel lovers"; "GOM = God's Only Mistake" (which is what Gladstone's detractors called the 'Grand Old Man'); "Kardomah Gang's hideout was razed to the snow – DT"; "Today is not what it should be".

Here again, in a cosy alcove, is the book-washing one, still waxing lyrical about literature, while whisking up in a measuring jug milk, eggs (with shell) and cinnamon, before decanting the brew into a mug and drinking it. She's going out shortly, she says, and would we like to accompany her while she puts on her make-up? She leads us into a nearby section where there are five life-size posters of the *Shelf Life* actors, naked. This would seem to refer to the story – which I have yet to find reliably authenticated – that following the Three Nights Blitz of 1941 the stacks were used as a mortuary for some of those killed in the bombardment. (Later, it's said that although the books smelled of burned flesh for years afterwards, people continued to borrow them. Is this more Volcanic ash? What to take literally and what not, from these mythic remembrancers?). Chatting as she applies her make-up, the player asks what we think of her lipstick – Paviland Ochre. Only Phil George of the BBC and I seem to get this gigglesome aside.[54]

We are then directed up some steps, at the top of which the Nordic blonde is skipping vigorously, reeling off all her dreams and ambitions – before halting abruptly, to declare that she's fulfilled not one of them. Then, in return for, say, a hug or a swivel of a customer's hips, she gives each of us what seems to be a genuine, individually numbered reader's ticket, before ushering us into the magnificent reading room, where a central round table is piled high with cheeses, grapes, olives and loaves of bread, and candlelight gleams on silverware and glasses.

The idea here, explains the company, is that "We have imagined one last meeting of the custodians of the library – ghosts or angels, or mortals like us, opinions, arguments, vanities and hopes: the old library hears them all and it trusts that you, our readers, will enjoy the experience ..."

With most of the books and reading desks removed, the relative silence here is of a different kind from the intensely busy quiet of the reading room's heyday, when all manner of researchers – self-improving dockers, political activists, professors from the university – would be found here side by side, immersed in reading and note-taking. Built at a time of enlightenment, the rigidities of the class system were nevertheless inscribed in the building, with an entrance at the rear for the lower orders, while 'polite society' entered at the front. A paternalist care for the people's moral well-being was reflected in various acts of censorship. In 1899, for instance, it was decided that the racing tips in daily newspapers should be blacked out. Rules and regulations in the early days included: no animals, no smoking, no spitting, no eating, no talking, no tracing pictures, no striking matches, no children under 14 except with the librarian's permission; and anyone found selling or pawning a library book would be liable to prosecution for larceny.

Our numbered tickets entitle us to a free book each, which we retrieve by climbing the stairs to the balcony. No. 21 gets me Bill Bryson's *Short History of Almost Everything*. An acquaintance with a restless love life gets *The Kama Sutra*.

Then the 'final meeting' begins, as we descend from the balcony to take our seats facing the round table, around which the six players – who, by now, have become our friends – loosely gather to eat, drink, reminisce, philosophise, shout, murmur and kiss. From time to time, one or other of them peels away: to clamber up the wrought-iron supports of the balcony, for instance, or to stand on a column of books to recite a Tony Curtis poem about Singleton Hospital. They film each other with a hand-held camera, the images being shown on makeshift screens. During a somewhat worthy peroration delivered to us by an actor with his back to the others, the Nordic blonde and a cheeky young beardie gradually strip naked, freezing in a seated, reading position whenever the orator turns towards them. Although the actors are evidently under orders to frustrate both narrative and extended, coherent dialogue – by refusing to respond or react to each others' statements – the 'meeting' nevertheless delivers many funny, provocative, wistful vignettes. The most moving is a hesitant and bashful recollection of a first love, communicated in evasive, fragmented, incomplete words and phrases: I've rarely heard such fumbling inarticulacy express, with stunning definition, such a depth of feeling.

It's dark enough, by now, for eidetic images of Swansea street scenes to be projected onto the glass of the dome itself, and it's time, alas, for the party to end.

A week or two later, I return to the scene. No round table. Everything back to what looks like normal. But it isn't, quite. Gladstone's still there, and the colourful star in the middle of the floor, which the table had partly occluded, is not the library's original design: it's a legacy from *Dr Who*. And the books that once again fill the library's shelves are not books at all, but a sleight of theatrical hand … awaiting, any day now, the return of the Time Lord.

THE WELSH SCHOOL OF ARCHITECTURAL GLASS

Hanging on the back of an office door in the Welsh School of Architectural Glass[55] in Alexandra Road, there's a shrine of sorts, its central feature being a brown Dai cap which last saw action in 1972, the year in which its owner died. It belonged to the distinguished stained-glass artist Howard Martin, founder in 1935 of an institution which he hoped would make Swansea as famous for glass in the twentieth century as it once had been for china and porcelain.

He was to be granted his wish. Any discussion of contemporary glass spirals back inevitably to Swansea. Other places figure on the map – Edinburgh, London's Royal College of Art[56], Pilchuck in America, John Petts' classes of the 1950s in Carmarthen – but nowhere offers such a complete specialisation in the art of designing and the craft of assembling stained-glass windows, and few courses can claim such longevity. In 2010, it celebrated its 75th anniversary, still in the Art School building where it began, and in the process of taking over the old Central Library which occupied the lower portion of the building. Like the Art School, it has had various names and governing bodies over the years, but it is today part of Swansea Metropolitan University.

Swansea-trained glass artists of international renown are to be found all over the planet, among them Kuni Kajiwara and Sachiko Yamomoto in Japan, Elaine Bell and Deborah Coombes in the United States, Yanos Boujioucos in Greece, John Abramczyk in New Zealand, Mark Angus in Germany, Martin Donlin and Graham Jones in England, and Sarah Hall and David Pearl in Canada (and Swansea). In Swansea itself, there are over twenty professional stained-glass artists, several of whom have significant international reputations: Amber Hiscott, Alex Beleschenko, Catrin Jones, Chris Bird-Jones, Vanessa Cutler and Rodney Bender (a recent head of the school). Such is the influence of Swansea-trained virtuosos, both at home and abroad, that they have sometimes been referred to as the Swansea Stained-Glass Mafia. "Through its remarkable glass program," wrote Sarah Hall in 2001, "the gray, rainy city of Swansea has been the genesis of thousands of square feet of colour and beauty in libraries, museums, churches, commercial settings and public buildings around the world."[57]

The story starts with painter and educationist William Grant

Murray (1877-1950), the charismatic Scot who is credited with having made the most significant single scholastic contribution to Welsh visual arts of the twentieth century. Grant Murray's forthright and visionary attitude declared itself at the outset. His interview in 1909 for the dual post of head of the new municipal School of Art and Crafts and director of art for Swansea remains the stuff of legend. T.J. Rees, Swansea's director of education, reported that Grant Murray said that "his first impression was that [the leaky art school] was one of the most dismal buildings he had ever been in. The lighting arrangements were also bad and unless the Council was prepared to spend money, he hoped they would not appoint him to the position"; in his opinion, the Art School, founded in 1853 (although not established in Alexandra Road until 1887), was as good as dead, and he had no wish to be associated with its funeral. To Swansea's and Wales's good fortune, he got the job.[58]

Trained in Paris and influenced by the Impressionists, Grant Murray inculcated an openness to international styles which has been a hallmark of the Swansea stained-glass experience ever since. He was also concerned to nurture indigenous talent, using the scholarship system to give the industrial working class an opportunity to study art. "There will be no Welsh school of Painting," he argued, "until Wales can train its students and Wales can support them when trained." He was determined that Swansea, rather than Cardiff, should "take a definite lead in founding a National Art".

Analysing the reasons for the strength of Swansea's artistic life from the 1930s onwards, the poet and scholar J. Gwyn Griffiths wrote in the *Western Mail* on 29 June 1964: "If Swansea is far more alive culturally than Cardiff, the basic reason is that it is far more Welsh. It has recognised a cosmopolitan element which has sometimes proved invigorating, but it has not been swamped by it; and its rich hinterland is still vitally Welsh in culture and language."

Outstanding talents nurtured under Grant Murray's inspired regime include Ceri Richards, Fred Janes, Mervyn Levy, Will Evans, Archie Griffiths, Evan Walters and Kenneth Hancock; and among a later generation, Vera Bassett, Mike Freeman, Will Roberts, George Little, Valerie Ganz, Ivor Davies and Glenys Cour (one of Wales's greatest colourists, Glenys has tutored generations of Swansea glass-art students).

The school's momentum was seriously impeded by the Second World War, after which Wales's centre of artistic gravity began an eastward, anglicizing drift towards Cardiff. Nevertheless, the foundation had been laid in 1935 for what is probably Grant Murray's most enduring legacy. In that year, he invited a brilliant former student, Howard Martin, to teach an evening class in stained glass. Grant Murray had long felt it was an 'insult' that no stained glass was being made in Wales.

Born in 1907 to a working-class family in Morriston, Howard Martin had served an apprenticeship as a lead-light worker and was self-taught in stained glass. In 1934, with his cousin Hubert Thomas (1913-95), he established in Morriston – in a corrugated iron shed at 62 Martin Street, built for him by his father – Wales's first known stained-glass studio, the firm of Martin and Thomas, which was revived in 1948 as Celtic Studios. It soon became world famous. The stained-glass course also, in the post-war period, went from strength to strength under Howard Martin's direction.

Celtic Studios employed talented graduates of the stained-glass course. Their staple in the busy '50s and '60s was ecclesiastical glass, but Howard Martin welcomed secular commissions for pubs, houses, cinemas. Then, as today, an innovative stained-glass artist was often constrained by the unadventurous expectations of commissioners. Many clients have rigid views about content and style, born of prevailing suspicions about 'modern art' and the widespread expectations of this particular art that it should be some vague imitation of Victorian imitations of medieval glass. Given the freedom to develop a brief, Howard Martin was a genuine innovator. Opposite High Street station there's a closed and semi-derelict pub which was known as the Station and later the Pullman. The bar used to have three magnificent Howard Martin windows, with confidently modernist treatments of transport motifs – but they have disappeared. It's possible that some canny prospector squirreled them away, but likelier, given Swansea's insouciant disregard for its heritage, that they were tossed into a skip. His superb cinema-related panels for the Art Deco Windsor Cinema in Neath were treated with more respect and saved for future use when permission was given in about 2006 to demolish the building.

Howard Martin's enthusiasm for Continental practice, rather than post Arts and Crafts English lyricism, continued under Howard Martin's successor at the school, Tim Lewis, the son of a collier from Pontarddulais, who, having retired from the school in 1996, continues to practise at his Glantawe Studios in Morriston. He revolutionised not only the course in Swansea but the direction of glass art in the United Kingdom, not least through his enthusiasm for the increasingly abstract German contribution to the discipline. He'd invite the leading glass masters of Germany – Georg Meistermann, Johannes Schreiter, Joachen Poensgen, Ludwig Schaffrath – to work with his students in Swansea, and send Swansea students to serve apprenticeships in Germany.

One such was my friend Amber Hiscott, who developed a close working relationship with the formidable Schaffrath. During one of his Swansea visits, she and her partner, the stained-glass artist David Pearl, invited me to eat with them and Ludwig in Magpie Cottage, the wind-blown and mice-infested chalet they rented in a field on the cliff at Rothers Sker, Mumbles (now long since demolished by those persistent westerlies). A big man in every sense, with a reputation as the most monumental of all the German glass masters, renowned for his work in cavernous churches and huge public buildings, the great Ludwig seemed unfazed to find himself huddled, with us, over an ancient fan heater in a tiny asbestos shack that quivered with every gust banging in from the Severn Sea. The conversation was interrupted now and then by the need to activate the mousetrap, an upturned biscuit tin propped ajar by a stick support, which, attached to a string, would be whipped away as soon as a mouse darkened the trap's cheese-baited door. My friends would then, gentle souls, take the mouse for a drive and release it far enough away from Magpie Cottage to discourage its return.

Amber and David were among a generation of students to benefit from a major project which Howard Martin passed on to Tim Lewis in 1970: the stained-glass cloister of Maxwell Fry's Bridgend Crematorium. The German influence, changing from a figurative focus to one of abstraction, is palpable in this project, which took ten years to complete. The best of Swansea-produced glass art has usually been ground-breaking in terms of both design and technique, but even the most experimental of Swansea-trained artists tends to value the solid grounding they received in what modish postmodernists have sometimes derided as a backwater. "The fact that we were in a supposed backwater was incredibly useful," Amber told me. "All the other colleges were aping the worst aspects of modern art and dispensing with the basic skills – to make some 'modern statement' that was really rather trite."

The major advances pioneered by Tim Lewis and his students were not embraced by Celtic Studios which, after Howard Martin's death, began a slow decline. In the early '60s, when Celtic Studios were exporting great quantities of stained glass all over the world, as well as producing for the domestic market, they had a staff of thirteen. But when I visited their 5 Prospect Place premises in 1987, the team had dwindled to just five. The terraced Georgian building was a cluttered and dusty place, and, with all the acid etching and lead work which the craft entails, a far from healthy working environment. The studios had turned their hands to more restoration and 'period work' than perhaps a hungrily contemporary studio would be happy with. They were doing what Hubert Thomas, the surviving principal, called "modern work", although he told me – after I'd sheathed my Bic – that he had "no time at all for this bloody old German tramline stuff". The times had changed, but Celtic Studios were not changing with them. Shortly after Hubert Thomas died in 1995, Celtic Studios closed.[59]

Most of the school's alumni these days work as individuals, rather than in a studio set-up. High-profile projects outside the area include works by Rodney Bender and Amber Hiscott at the Millennium Centre in Cardiff, Amber Hiscott's and David Pearl's *Water Towers*, in Callaghan Square, Cardiff, Graham Jones's Poets' Corner window in Westminster Abbey, Martin Donlin's installation at Indianapolis Airport, Alex Beleschenko's screen at Ewenny Priory, and Chris Bird-Jones's memorial to the quarrymen's strike in Capel Bethania, Bethesda.

Swansea itself has been slow to make much of the talents of its stained-glass artists. David Pearl's 1987 project for the revamped Grand Theatre was the first major glass work ever to be commissioned by the local authority. It was followed nearly a decade later by Amber Hiscott's glass-leaf sculpture, which forms the centrepiece of Castle Square. St Mary's Church has several windows by alumni, among them Rodney Bender, Catrin Jones and Lisa Birkl.

"Given Swansea's pre-eminence in stained glass, what we do here is largely hidden to most Swansea people," the school's Chris Bird-Jones said, as she showed me round the building in the spring of 2010. She hoped that the anniversary celebrations spread over that year would raise the school's profile locally.

From the outside, there are few indications as to what goes on within this handsome Italian-classical, redbrick building – until you notice various stained-glass exercise panels propped on interior window ledges. Ambitious plans for the take-over of the old Central Library include a huge glass display frontage at the western end of the building, which will make an unmistakeable statement about the school's existence and artistic intent. Let's hope, though, that in all the upheaval and 'rationalisation', Howard Martin's cap remains securely enshrined on the back of that office door. The place would not be itself without it.

notes

1. Bailey, Rob and Hurst, Ed, *Rude World: the 100 Rudest Place Names*, 2006.
2. From Adrian Mitchell's and Ralph Steadman's *Who Killed Dylan Thomas?*, Tŷ Llên Publications, 1998.
3. I am indebted to Richard Porch (see the bibliography) for this information.
4. This was the goldsmith Alban Leyshon, something of a surrealist, who was wont to make 'creative gestures'.
5. The quotation is a word short of being accurate: the poem actually begins "Now as I was young and easy …" The steel ribbons are evocative of the poem's last line, "Though I sang in my chains like the sea".
6. This is an enthusiasm shared by Susan Morgan who has compiled a superb book-length collection of photographs of Swansea's overlooked architectural grace-notes – for which sadly, so far, she has been unable to find a publisher.
7. The others are to be seen in the Civic Centre (on the seafront) and in the refectory at Swansea University.
8. Roteley seems to have been the owner of the hovel in which, shortly after Roteley's death, the 'father of the novel in Wales', Thomas Jeffrey Llywelyn Prichard (1790-1862) met his grim end. See *Real Swansea*.

9. The others were behind what's now Swansea Museum and in Wellington Street, between Tesco and the Quadrant car park.

10. Named, in 1995, after the bardic Reverend in Dylan Thomas's *Under Milk Wood*, the Eli Jenkins was formerly Hock's wine bar; previously, it had been The Criterion and before that the Plymouth Inn.

11. Griffiths also had a branch in Union Street.

12. There was another in Oxford Street.

13. Founded in Bath in 1848, Duck, Son & Pinker had branches in Clifton, Swindon, Hereford, Bristol, Bedminster and Swansea. The last Duck, Son & Pinker, the Bath shop, closed in 2011.

14. The deed was done, alas, in the days of Duck, Son & Pinker.

15. 'Good afternoon – how are you?'

16. The old language.

17. He called it 'a shambles'.

18. Michele Di Marco, Francesco D'Ambrosio, Ferdinando Pompa, Francesco Rabaiotti, Luigi Rabaiotti, Luigi Rossi and Antonio Zanetti.

19. 'Fully fluent in Welsh'.

20. Where once Belli's fish and chip shop stood. The Milkwood Jam closed in 2011.

21. *Putto*: Italian for 'small boy' or 'small child'.

22. Named after the pugnacious Welsh captain in Shakespeare's *Henry V*.

23. Or Princes Street as it was earlier known.

24. Formerly the Black Cat, and before that Ray's Café.

25. Formerly known as Mysydd Street.

26. The others were the Music Hall in De la Beche Street (1864; renamed the Albert Music Hall in 1881), the Star in Wind Street (1873; on the site of La Tasca), the Swansea Pavilion Music Hall in High Street (1888; today's 'at risk' Palace), and the Empire in Oxford Street (1900).

27. With seating for 3,000, the Plaza (1931-1965) was Wales's largest cinema; the Oceana nightclub stands there today.

28. The site, 24-27 St Helen's Road, was home to Eddershaw's, the furniture store, for forty years after the Second World War. The business, founded in 1835, had been bombed out of its High Street premises during the 1941 blitz. When Eddershaw's moved to the Swansea Enterprise Park in 1989, the property was bought by the Apostolic Church.

29. Published as *Swansea City Centre Heritage Trail* in 2007.

30. After its rest home days, the building became student flats.

31. One of the 'Proverbs of Hell' from Blake's *Marriage of Heaven and Hell* (1790).

32. c. April 2010. By 2011, the Elysium Artspace had moved again, to 31 Craddock Street; in 2012, the Elysium added 15 artists' studios to its provision, at 2 Mansel Street.

33. By June 2010, Bunnies had moved to the more romantic setting of premises above the Gigi Ristorante Italiano (subsequently the Palace of India and then Tantalizer) at 22 St Helen's Road.

34. Literally, 'washing place'.

35. Whitten Brown also lived at Overland Court, on the western end of Overland Road, Mumbles, where a plaque commemorates his residence.

36. The Tawe Delta Blues Club closed in December 2007, after a seven-year run, but it reopened in 2011 at The Club (formerly The Dyffryn), Morriston.

37. Clive John died in 2011 after a long struggle with emphysema.

38. The Opposition's watering holes were little better on the equality front: the Labour Club in Wind Street maintained a men-only rule until the 1980s.

39. Originally known as Brooklands.

40. The (Welsh) language.

41. The campaign's website is www.spanglefish.com/SwanseaAlbertHallReborn

42. De la Beche Road in Sketty was laid down in about 1863.

43. For an 'inside job' on Swansea jail, see *Real Swansea*.

44. Named after the lord of Gower's orchard, which grew hereabouts.

45. Ten years earlier, Wales's first weekly newspaper in English, *The Cambrian*, had been launched in Swansea.

46. Swansea-born Samuel Clearstone Gamwell, author of the *Official Guide and Handbook to Swansea and its District* (1880), was editor of *The Cambrian* and, as 'Pierre Claire' (a witty Gallicization of his middle name), a prolific versifier on local subjects.

47. In Lee Dorsey's 'Ride your pony', with its chorus line 'Now shoot! [bang] Shoot! [bang] Shoot! [bang]'.

48. The Welsh government's *Health, Social Care and Well Being*.

49. It was the first film to be given an 'X' rating by the British Board of Film Censors.

50. In 2011, the School's parent body, Swansea Metropolitan University, announced plans to turn the library into an £8m International Institute of Sustainable Design.

51. The episodes *Silence in the Library* and *Forest of the Dead* were filmed in the library.

52. The reference library's reading room is 26m (88 ft) in diameter, and its glass-domed apex is 7.6m (25 ft) high in the centre.

53. The volcano's eruption in 2010 caused the closure of airspace over much of Europe, following concerns that ash ejected from the volcano could damage aircraft engines.

54. For some of the show's references you had to be in the local know. It was in a cave at Paviland, Gower, in 1823, that the (then) earliest human bone finds in these islands were made. Some fossilised human bones stained with red ochre (or okra, as our actor pronounced it) were unearthed by Dean William Buckland, who wrongly concluded both that they were the bones of a young woman and that they were about 2000 years old. 'The Red Lady of Paviland' turned out to be a young man from nearly 30,000 years ago.

55. I am indebted to my friend Chris Bird-Jones, director of the school's MA programme, for invaluable help and advice in compiling this section.

56. The Royal College's stained-glass course was discontinued in the early 1970s.

57. S. Hall and J. Kraegel, 'Swansea: light years ahead', *Glass Art*, vol. 16, no. 4, May/June 2001.

58. Grant Murray and his wife Margaret (Maggie) lived at 17 Richmond Road in the Uplands, from where he painted a number of impressive views of Swansea Bay. Next door, at number 15, there lives today the distinguished Canadian portraitist Gordon Stuart.

59. The business was continued in Humphrey Street until 2000, by Jaroslav Mykisa and Llewellyn Thomas, whose father, the solicitor Stuart Thomas, had been Celtic Studios' company secretary.

SOUTH

ADELAIDE STREET

Three large, but very different, buildings dominate Adelaide Street, which is diagonally opposite the bottom of Wind Street: Morgan's Hotel (urban Swansea's only five-star hotel), the offices of the *South Wales Evening Post* and the Exchange Buildings. The demolition in 2005 of the Powell Dyffryn House office block[1] and the utilitarian 1950s Unifloc building on the western side of Adelaide Street has opened up the row attractively to Quay Parade's continuation, Victoria Road, which curves westward to become Oystermouth Road. By mid 2006, the site had been transformed into the widely welcomed Museum Green, which shows off to best advantage the old Museum and provides design continuity with the new National Waterfront Museum. It may not, as yet, have any seats – but it's got balls: for leaning against.

Those semi-derelict buildings may have been swept away, but memory lingers of the homeless people who sometimes found shelter in those wrecks, and in particular of the 31-year-old man whose body was discovered in January 1998 after a fire there.

When the buildings were demolished, there were suggestions that the comparably banal *Evening Post* building should also fall to the wreckers' ball. The *Post*, founded in 1930 as the *South Wales Daily Post* and descended indirectly from Wales's first weekly newspaper, *The Cambrian* (1804-1930), began the twenty-first century with three editions, but now it's down to one, which no doubt simplifies its new printing arrangements. South West Wales Publications, whose parent company is the Northcliffe Media group, used to print the *Post* – and other papers, including *The Llanelli Star* – on the Adelaide Street premises. But in 2005, printing was transferred to Staverton in Gloucestershire, with the loss of 67 print jobs in Swansea. It remains, nevertheless, the largest selling newspaper in Wales, its circulation at the end of 2006 reaching 55,616, although this had fallen to 40,999 by early 2011.

Next door to the *Post* was the site of the Countess of Huntingdon's Gothic-style Calvinistic chapel (1787-89) which stood until 1875 and gave Adelaide Street its earlier name of Chapel Street. It was succeeded in 1878 by the Swansea Metal Exchange which, according to W.C. Rogers, "must have been the ugliest building ever". This was replaced by the present Exchange Buildings, designed by Charles Tamlin Ruthen and opened in 1915 as a commercial headquarters worthy of Swansea's status as one of the metallurgical centres of the world; it was rebuilt after bombing in 1941. Note the frontage's *cubic* Ionic capitals, defying the tradition that the Ionic order is derived from nature. The Exchange was dissolved in 1959, but the Swansea Chamber of Commerce continued to use the building as its headquarters for some years, and the upper storeys were converted into flats in the 1990s. In 2007, the empty lower part of the building, with its ship-like wooden panelling, was transformed into the interior of *The Titanic* for a *Dr Who* Christmas special, 'Voyage of the Damned' – written, of course, by Swansea-born Russell T. Davies – which Kylie Minogue, playing the role of a waitress, came to Swansea to film.

The Exchange Building's basement was famous to Swansea youth in the 1970s and 80s as Pandora's Box, later Circles and later again the Marine Nitespot. Discos, punch-ups, live bands, groupies: Sid Vicious and the Sex Pistols expectorated here, Edgar Broughton exorcised his demons, John Cooper Clarke spouted forth, and local heroes such as Man, Alcatraz and the Flying Aces strutted their stuff. One hot, seductive evening in 1974 I gave my first ever Swansea poetry reading at Dora's, as one of *Three Young Anglo-Welsh Poets*[2] (Duncan Bush and Tony Curtis were the others). I thought I'd arrived; I hadn't even set out.

Notable past residents of Adelaide Street include William Jernegan (1751-1836), the principal architect of Regency Swansea, and James Harris (1810-87),[3] a leading member of Swansea's renowned school of marine artists, whose paintings, on the rare occasions these days that they come onto the market, have been known to fetch upwards of £50,000. The street's connection with local painters was renewed in May, 2010 when Nick Holly, renowned for his Swansea scenes with their matchstick-style people – and known, like the Hafod's Jack Jones (1922-93) before him, as the Welsh Lowry – opened the Nick Holly Studio Gallery in the heart of the Exchange Buildings. A showcase for Holly's own work, the gallery also displays paintings, sculpture, photography and glass by a wide range of Welsh artists – along with a yellow New York cab, which Holly has adapted as a reception desk.

James Harris would have been a neighbour, in the 1840s, to one of nineteenth-century Swansea's more flamboyant characters, Baron Doctor Spolasco (c.1790-1858), a Mephistophelean mountebank self-touted in *The Cambrian* as "the most successful Practitioner of Medicine and Surgery in the World!!!" Spolasco

lived from 1838 to 1845 in Adelaide Palace, a Georgian townhouse and later hotel (The Adelaide, destroyed in the 1941 blitz) on what is now the *Evening Post* site.[4] Born plain John Smith in the Manchester area, he was neither a baron nor a doctor, but he managed to con thousands into buying his useless potions, which were little more than chalk dust. In spite of violent altercations with patients who saw through his quackery, and several brushes with the law – including a manslaughter charge – he managed, through canny self-promotion, to make himself a popular public figure. Here's an eye-witness account of his triumphal arrival in Swansea in 1838:

> His advent ... savoured of the ridiculous; yet it was in the nature of a Royal progress.
>
> A large, elegant yellow carriage with certainly four, if not six horses, in splendid trappings, with postillions in brilliant colours and cockades, a black manservant in gorgeous livery and shoulder-knot, yellow silk breeches and white stockings, sitting alone in solemn dignity immovable on the centre of the box seat, the 'Baron' inside, bowing left and right, midst the roaring swell of cheering that beset him on all hands.

And in New York, about ten years after his departure from Swansea, the Baron caught the discerning eye of none other than Walt Whitman, who penned this character sketch:

> Somebody in an open barouche, driving daintily. He looks like a doll; is it alive? We'll cross the street and so get close to him .... Fantastic hat ...; blue coat and shiny brass buttons; patent leathers; shirt-frill; gold specs; bright red cheeks, and singularly definite jetty black eyebrows, moustache, and imperial. You .... saw, when you stood at his wheel, not only the twinkling diamond ring and breast-pin, but the heavy, slabby red paint; and even the substratum of grizzly gray under that jetty dye; and upon our word there's a hair of the same straggling out under the jaunty oiled wig! How straight he sits, and how he simpers, and how he fingers the reins with a delicate white little finger stuck out, as if a mere touch were all – as if his whole hand might govern a team of elephants! The Baron Spolasco, with no end of medical diplomas from all sorts of universities across the ocean, who cures everything immediately; you may consult him confidentially, or by letter, if you choose. It would be worth money to see that old gentleman – they say he is nearly eighty – undress himself! Clothes, wig, calves, stays, moustache, teeth, complexion – what a bald, bare, wizened, shrivelled old granny he would be!

The Baron was used to having things his own way. Ordered, in 1839, to block up an entrance to the rear of his property which he'd created to allow access to a stable, "He taught his horse ... to walk up his doorsteps, several in number, in Adelaide Street, and to pass along the hall and passage just three feet wide, and so to the stables behind."

Spolasco's sojourn in Swansea, together with his survival of a shipwreck off the Irish coast and his death in New York, is commemorated in a set of carved stone panels in an archway at Patagonia Walk in the Maritime Quarter. Quoted there is an extract from some lines he composed in praise of himself, which were "Written and sung on the occasion of his being presented with a Gold Snuff Box, value Fifty Guineas, at a Public Dinner given to him by his Friends and Patients, at the Castle Inn, Swansea, on Monday, the 8th day of June, 1840":

> I pledge unto Spolasco's name
> A name in which we glory;

His splendid cures and healing fame
Recorded are in story
Be mindful of Spolasco's skill
Ye patrons of his merit
Save him from all impending ill
And a relentless spirit.

Spolasco was evidently as dodgy a 'poet' as he was a 'doctor'. And doubtless the old fraudster was already planning to flog that snuff box.

VICTORIA ROAD UNDERPASS

The Victoria Road pedestrian underpass between Wind Street and Somerset Place was closed in July 2011, pumped full of concrete and replaced by an "intelligent puffin pedestrian crossing" – to create, claimed the council, "better links between the city centre and the waterfront".

They seem to have thought the subway had become a dangerous place. Awash sometimes with vomit and urine, it could certainly be a squalid route between the Maritime Quarter and the city centre.

> mighty gob-mouths
> giggly with booze –
> their baby-bottom heads

And there'd often be an unofficial toll to pay – to sickly looking wraiths sitting cross-legged on damp cardboard, begging for 'spare change'. But it got you swiftly from A to B, without having to take your chances with one of the busiest thoroughfares in Swansea. For a few years, the authorities tried to brighten its grimy tiles with some colourful panels by local school-kids responding to the poetry of Dylan Thomas; but their frames weakened and the pictures were removed, leaving subterranean creativity, once again, to the spiders.

The underpass was built in 1966. The road was cut into initially with pneumatic drills, then a crane-drawn bucket grab gouged out the trench in which the underpass – an 80-metre rectangular tube – was constructed.

It was called for, at the time, because of the large numbers of people working in places such as docks offices and the 'bottom tech'[6] (the Old Guildhall, now the Dylan Thomas Centre). Those numbers later declined, but since work started on SA1 there's been a resurgence: the council removed the underpass just as increasing numbers of people living and working in the new dockside settlement could have found it invaluable. Seedy as the old underpass may have been, it took only thirty or so seconds to cross beneath Victoria Road. Now, thanks to the 'intelligent puffin', it can take many minutes for pedestrians to cross the road; some, growing impatient, cross it on red, risking life and limb. The car, as usual in Swansea, wins again.

THE NATIONAL WATERFRONT MUSEUM

As sheds go, this one's about as impressive as they come: a curving series of four interlocked steel, glass and slate boxes connected by a glazed internal 'street' to the two-storey former banana warehouse which, from 1974 to 2004, served as Swansea's Industrial and Maritime Museum. The £35m National Waterfront Museum[7] – widely perceived as part of the consolation prize[8] for the city's failure to attract the National Assembly to Swansea – is a sophisticated work of contemporary architecture. With its shops and cafés, audio-visual exhibits and hi-tech interactive displays – and cocking a slightly provocative snook at the solidly traditional Swansea Museum across the way – it's a museum for people who don't take to museums. Most have been beguiled by its airy and welcoming ambience, but many have complained that unlike Cardiff's Welsh Industrial and Maritime Museum (1977-1998), which it replaced, it is overly 'virtual', containing too few actual things; others have suggested that a more honest name for the place would be the South Wales Waterfront Museum, as it has little to offer on the story of the Welsh coast as a whole.

On one of the approaches from Oystermouth Road, you'll find yourself walking on fossilized slices of a 370-million-year-old river bed, in the form of Pennant sandstone paving from Gwrhyd Quarry near Rhiwfawr in the Upper Swansea Valley. Laid down in Carboniferous times when Wales was part of a tropical delta not far from the equator, this ineffably ancient sandstone throws into almost comic relief the two hundred or so years of recent human activity (a mere tremor of a gnat's wing in the life of the planet) which are the focus of this museum. Stone, albeit in a composite form, has also been used on the approaches to trace the curving geometries – accurate in both gauge and orientation – of the railway lines which ran in and out of the old Victoria Station (sited roughly where today's Leisure Centre stands). The gentle curve described by those dovetailing glass boxes is itself influenced by the arcing trajectory of a siding.

At this juncture, the first-time visitor is likely to be wondering where exactly the advertised waterfront might be, there being no riverbank or seashore in sight. Although the sea is only a short distance away, the view south to Swansea Bay is blocked by housing – which there was talk of demolishing, to give the museum a fittingly marine outlook. But that was never a serious proposition, and the 'waterfront' of the museum's title refers to the South Dock (1859) which was refurbished in the 1980s as a marina, its north-eastern quay providing mooring space for the museum's collection of historic vessels.

Opened in October 2005 by First Minister Rhodri Morgan and rugby legend Gareth Edwards, and employing about 50 people, the National Waterfront Museum celebrates the fact (some would say the opinion) that Wales in general and Swansea in particular[9] was the cradle of the Industrial Revolution (c.1750-c.1850).[10] On the first floor of the old warehouse – approached by a staircase punched through the 1901 building's red-brick wall – there's an interactive exhibit based on the 1851 census which, being the first to show that agricultural workers had been outnumbered by indus-trial workers, is the basis of the 'first industrial nation' claim. As suggested by its design – the work of Wilkinson Eyre of London, the first internationally renowned architects to have bestowed a build-ing on Swansea[11] – the museum purports to be as much about the present and the future as the past.

"It's interesting that 'industry' now embraces things like music," says my guide for the afternoon, Hannah Lawson, the museum's venue-hire officer. A few weeks earlier, we'd both attended the opening of the Waterfront's music gallery, with live performances in the warehouse by Swansea's own Spencer Davis, representing rock's older guard, and my daughter Angharad's folk band Calan. Later in the year (2010), the museum would host the Garnant-born musician John Cale's 2009 Venice Biennale installation.

"Considering how industry used to be is in itself, now, a focal

point for the modern economy, which is based on tourism and service industries," says Hannah. "Whereas my great-grandfather went down the mine, I make my living by coming to a museum that tells people about going down the mine to work."

Hannah has worked at the Waterfront since 2006. I asked her if the incessant recorded birdsong, associated with the interactive Swansea panorama, got on staff's nerves. "The birdsong's o.k. and so too are the choral things in the warehouse gallery, but what drives us nuts is the squeaking of the paternosters." These are the irregular Ferris wheels in the main industrial hall which keep a range of fascinating artefacts constantly rotating.

If things are what you want, then this is the hall for you. Hanging from the roof is Robin Goch, the tiny red monoplane built by Horace Watkins (1884-1976) of Cardiff, who claimed to have made brief hops in it in 1910, making him possibly the first person in Wales to achieve heavier-than-air flight.[12] Beneath it, a ten-tonne coal truck rears strangely at a 45° angle as if to trumpet perhaps the most popular exhibit in the entire museum, Chris Perry's 1980s working replica of the Penydarren engine, the first steam locomotive in the world to pull a load along rails. It was built by the Cornish inventor Richard Trevithick (1771-1833) for the Penydarren Ironworks in Merthyr Tydfil. In 1804, the engine – travelling at about 8 k.p.h. – hauled 10 tonnes of iron and about 70 passengers

14 km along the tramroad from Merthyr to Abercynon. Although the journey, interrupted by stops for the removal of boulders and overhanging branches, took over four hours, it initiated a worldwide revolution in transport.

Three times a year, the engine – three tonnes empty, seven tonnes when full of water – is towed outside and fired up for a short chug. This is often Hannah's job, and it's not without its dangers. "As the driver," she explains, "I stand in a tender that's coupled to the engine, operating the two levers that drive it, and standing very close to the great drive wheel, which could knock your head clean off. And yes, the engine could explode if you didn't know what you were doing. Ideally, it should be fired on steam coal, but we can't get steam coal any more. So we use anything we can. We even used somebody's wooden shed the other day. When you pull the lever to get the engine to move, you never know whether it's going to go backwards or forwards – so you have to be quick off the mark to stop it, if it starts going backwards when you want it to go forwards, and vice versa, as it could easily overshoot the short track.' On one occasion, a wheel on the tender rolled over Hannah's foot – which, although severely bruised, was saved by her boot's metal toe-cap. 'My great-grandfather had a similar industrial accident, and lost everything but his big toe.'

It's the fans of the old Industrial and Maritime Museums who tend to complain loudest about the Waterfront's relative paucity of 'things'. "Overseas visitors are the most positive about the museum," says Hannah. "They think it's brilliant, with all these things about Wales and industry they never knew about. And then you get someone who lives half a mile away who thinks the place is rubbish, and why can't they have the motorbikes and the woollen mill. Change is shocking to some people. They need time to adjust, but they tend to come round."

Architects had more say than historians in the building's design and lay-out: they wanted to reach out – with 36 interactive displays using the latest in computer technology – to a younger, play-station generation. But there's no denying the appeal of the architecture itself, especially the exuberant sweep of the rear elevation's slate cladding, which borders a generous wedge of lawn between the new building and the old. Three slate types from north Wales were used: 'heather red' and 'heather blue' from the Penrhyn Quarry, and 'dark blue grey' from Cwrt y Bugail Quarry, Blaenau Ffestiniog. Over 1,000 sq m of slate, 40 mm thick, were set in about 50 concrete-backed panels, weighing up to 19 tonnes each. Older by far than the Pennant sandstone out front, the slate used to dress this most modern of buildings began as mud and silt on an ocean bed 500 million years ago, in the Cambrian period, before immense pressure and heat, over an unimaginable period of time, transformed it into stone.

With so much glass walling of the museum's atrium and northern frontage, it's hardly the most environmentally friendly of structures. It has to be kept at a constant temperature – which is monitored directly from headquarters in Cathays Park, Cardiff. As an outstation of the National Museum Wales/Amgueddfa Cymru, it's not as Swansea-centric as the Swansea Industrial and Maritime Museum used to be, but its Swansea references remain plentiful, from virtual reconstructions of historic Wind Street to a model of the 1854 steamer *Zeta* (from which the holy Catherine derives her middle name). The old warehouse, with its warm wooden flooring, stripped-back elegance and delightful decorative features, still has a distinctive Swansea flavour. Here, when the display cases are slid back on rollers to the peripheries, banquets may be held, or wedding receptions, concerts and corporate events. It's part of the local bustle created by the museum as a whole, which, in the absence of an entry fee, has to generate revenue from other sources. By 2010, the museum was attracting well over a quarter of a million visitors a year, and every Christmas season scores of thousands flock to the Waterfront's Winterland festival, with its 44-metre giant Ferris wheel, funfair and ice-skating rink.

Visitors are welcome to wander in through any of the museum's four main doors, and to stay for as long as they like. It's a notably relaxed and hospitable atmosphere. Not least among its attractions are its friendly staff, many of whom have a tale to tell themselves – such as, for instance, white-bearded Alun Jones, who followed the museum here from Cardiff. Alun, one of the museum's dozen or so Welsh-speakers, taught Steve Jones of the Sex Pistols at art school in London, where he also did light shows for Pink Floyd. Surprises, official and unofficial, abound at the National Waterfront Museum.

THE TOWER

That weary word 'iconic' was being slapped on it even before the first sod was cut, but since it was 'topped out' on 12 September 2008 as Wales's tallest building, the Meridian Tower[13] has turned

many foes into fans and staked a persuasive claim to the title of Swansea icon.

Not that it'll be Wales's tallest building for much longer. At 29 storeys and 107 metres high, it's almost twice the height of Swansea's one-time tallest building, the British Telecom tower (63 metres) in the Strand, and it has left Cardiff's swankiest erections, the Capital Tower (formerly the Pearl Building; 80 metres) and BT's Stadium House (78 metres), looking distinctly inadequate. But if style and substance are what count in Swansea, size evidently matters in the capital. In the near future, Cardiff will snatch back the crown from Swansea when Wyndham Hotels open their 32-storeys, 127-metres high tower on the Cardiff Bay waterfront. But with the Wyndham's 'sky bar' being on the 24th floor, the elegant Meridian Tower will still be able to claim that its 28th-storey restaurant is the highest in Wales (discounting, of course, low buildings in high places such as Snowdon).

The last building to be completed in the 291-apartment Meridian Quay complex between the South Dock marina and the seafront, the Tower, with its 123 flats, is a residential development, not a hotel. It was a canny move on the developers' part to top it off with two floors of function room, bar and restaurant, thereby giving the public access to what might otherwise be perceived as a view-hogging, shadow-casting fastness for the rich: £600,000 or £700,000 for an apartment near the top; £1m for the flat that occupies the whole of floor 26. But you don't have to be rich to enjoy a meal or simply a pint or a coffee in S.A. Brain & Co.'s Tower-top eatery.

Breathtaking, stunning, spectacular: the clichés, as ever, can't do justice to the views. Staff have observed customers, as they step from the lift into that reeling panorama, welling with tears. No one seems to mind if you wander among the tables to take in the full 360 degrees' worth: Exmoor and Ilfracombe to the south, and then, in a clockwise direction, Mumbles lighthouse and headland, a sliver of Cefn Bryn just visible beyond Clyne, Mount Pleasant's magnificent terraces, Townhill and Mayhill seemingly at eye-level, the Lower Swansea Valley with a radiantly white Liberty Stadium, the louring scarp of Carreg y Fan in Carmarthenshire, fire-blackened Kilvey partially occluding the Brecon Beacons, Swansea docks, the belching stacks of Port Talbot, and, beyond Porthcawl, the limestone cliffs of the Glamorgan Heritage Coast. Immediately to the Tower's north: the sprawl and bluster of the city itself, strangely silenced by thick plate glass and chatter, clatter and muzak. To the south: the promenade with some ants on bikes and jogger ants and boozer ants dipping into the pampas grass for a stealthy waz; and beyond humanity's minuscule agitations, the blue, ineffable wonder of the sea – our reason, in many ways, for being here.

> through the haze
> across the bay – new-mown,
> a field in the sky

The Tower had a rocky start and was loved, initially, by few. It would be grossly out of scale. It would steal the sun from other properties in the marina. It would be the first in a giant's pincushion of seafront skyscrapers, turning Swansea into Benidorm. It would cause traffic chaos and wreck the infrastructure. It would be a nightmare.

Work began in June 2006, and something resembling an armless Transformer robot began to shoulder its ungainly way into the skyline, each of the huge cranes that were coaxing it skyward sporting, at various times, the operator's national flag: the Irish tricolour, Scotland's Saltire, Wales's Draig Goch, England's cross of St

George. As it neared completion, eight months behind schedule, the builders walked out, taking the scaffolding with them. They returned, though, after a couple of months and finished the job – sort of. The celebs turned out in force – Cerys Matthews, Spencer Davis, Stuart Cable, Kevin Johns, Lee Trundle, Ryan Jones – for a glitzy opening bash in November 2009. But trouble hung doggedly around. The cheap-n-chintzy-looking Penthouse restaurant lurched from crisis to crisis. "It was so bad," a friend of mine remarked, "that it was good – an unmissable experience." The chef walked out because the kitchen was a building site; suppliers, contractors and staff complained of non-payment; the owner was declared bankrupt and in April 2010 the Penthouse closed. Redesigned by its new owners, the restaurant re-opened as the Grape and Olive[14] in November 2010, and business – with a distinctive Welsh-Mediterranean flavour – seems to have flourished ever since.

For maritime views and situation, Swansea has few competitors, but its two new seafront developments – the South Dock marina and SA1 – have almost nothing of the populous vitality of Cardiff Bay. Perhaps the Tower and its six associated Meridian Quay apartment blocks, in league with the National Waterfront Museum at the opposite end of the South Dock, will contribute to the revitalisation of a marina which has lately seemed tired and soulless.

Ray Tilley, of the Meridian Quay Residents' Association, lives on the 25th floor with his wife Viv. He has no doubt that the Tower is perking the area up. "A very good community spirit has developed here in a very short space of time," he told me. "There are people milling in the foyer, coming and going. The restaurant is used as a local hostelry, and on New Year's Eve no end of people from the area celebrate in the Tower. With the Marriott nearby, a general store with offy and deli right alongside us, and the Meridian café bar, there's a genuine community feel to the place."

Ray, who was landlord of the Coach House in Wind Street in the pub's musical heyday, now manages the Money Shop in The Kingsway. "I have a car parked in the garage down below," he said, "but it never sees the light of day. I can walk wherever I need to go. Can't imagine living anywhere else now. As I drive towards Swansea on the motorway, I love it when, around Port Talbot, the Tower comes into view. It's a 'welcome home' sign."

The high life doesn't bother Ray. But as you queue for too long in the restaurant for a lift that's much too small, there are invariably edgy jokes about lightning, hurricanes or fire alarms. And someone usually asks if anyone else has seen that clip on YouTube of a plane, 9/11 style, ploughing into Wales's tallest building.

ST HELEN'S

St Helens or St Helen's? A recent lord mayor of Swansea, Councillor Ioan Richard, nearly lost his life in The Battle of the St Helen's Apostophe. The 'maverick' Independent, as the press like to pigeonhole the member for Mawr, decided on a restoration of the apostrophe to signposts pointing to the famous St Helen's cricket and rugby ground (St Helen's is also a city ward, sandwiched between Brynmill and Sandfields). Getting nowhere with 'the relevant authorities', Ioan resolved on a solo campaign and marched to a signpost near the university, armed with a step ladder, an apostrophe of his own making – and an *Evening Post* photographer.

"The sign was very high," he told me, "and I had to stand not on the last step of the ladder but on the bar. As I was placing the apostrophe on the sign, I very nearly tipped over into the path of a heavy lorry. The photographer got very excited and said it would have made a tremendous, worldwide scoop if I'd fallen beneath that lorry."

Spared bigger headlines than he'd bargained for, Ioan eventually won his battle. St Helen's it is, at least as far as road signage is concerned. But when the name appears on and around the clubhouse itself apostrophic indecision prevails.

Who was St Helen?

Some have suggested it's a corruption of the first name of Alianora de Mowbray who, in 1332, gave a church and some land here to St David's hospital (now the Cross Keys pub); benefactors in those days were often known as saints. Or perhaps she was Elen Luyddog (Elen of the Hosts), the wife of Macsen Wledig (Magnus Maximus). Or she could have been the legendary Elen (Helena), daughter of the fifth-century Coel Hen, the last commander of the Roman army in northern Britain (and the Old King Cole of medieval fantasy). This Elen was the mother of Cystennin (Constantine), who became the first Christian Emperor, ruling in both Rome and Constantinople.

Whoever she was, she gave her name to the most celebrated of all the old wells of Swansea. It was situated in a wood behind a mansion known as St Helen's House, which had been built over the crypt of an Augustinian nunnery dedicated to St Helena, in what is now Victoria Park. This seems to be the well described by Daniel Defoe in his *Tour through the Whole Island of Great Britain* (1724-27). Its waters, he wrote, were reputed to be "of great efficacy in fluxes and Haemorrhages of all sorts. Consumptions if not too far gone, palsies rheumatisms, dropsies and other distempers are said to fall before these styptick and restorative waters." Invalids would flock to partake of the 'styptick waters' until the mid nineteenth century when St Helen's House was demolished and the installation of a sewer put paid to the well. Somewhere beneath Victoria Park there's a filled in and once famous hole measuring roughly 6 m deep and 1.5 m wide.

> the daffs that brightened
> her memorial bench ... long dead
> in their colostomy bag

St Helen's Fields was the original name of Victoria Park. Perhaps one day, given some republican gumption, the name will be restored. Opened in 1887 and named after 'the great white mother' in celebration of her jubilee, the park was about three times its present size and had its main entrance at the junction of St Helen's Crescent and St Helen's Road. Tens of thousands would crowd in for major spectaculars such as Barnum and Bailey's Greatest Show on Earth and Buffalo Bill's Wild West Show. Although much reduced in size, thanks to the Guildhall's encroachment in the 1930s, it remains a fitting monument to a local visionary whose statue stands in front of the Patti Pavilion and who deserves to be better remembered: William Thomas o Lan (1816-1909), "the Champion Pioneer of Open Spaces" who fought to keep much of St Helen's area free from what he called "the hand of the destroying angel, THE BUILDER", so that the beauties of nature could be enjoyed by the "sons of toil" as well as "the lords of soil". People's open spaces all over Swansea – Parc Llewelyn, the Rec, Cwmdonkin, Brynmill, Brynmelyn, Dyfatty – owe their existence largely to the inspiration and energies of this alderman from Lan House, Morriston. With 52 public parks, Swansea has the largest inner-city forestry of any city in the world.

Of vastly greater renown than St Helen's forgotten well is the sandy sports ground that bears her name, site of some of the greatest moments in sporting history since it opened in 1873: Welsh

rugby's first home international, against England, in 1882; Glamorgan's first game as a county cricket club in 1888; the All Whites, fired by Haydn Tanner and Willy Davies, beating the mighty All Blacks in 1935, and then the national side also trouncing the New Zealanders; Glamorgan defeating the South Africans in 1951 and the Australians in 1964 and 1968, thanks to brilliant local cricketers such as Gilbert Parkhouse, Jim Pressdee and Don Shepherd (who would otherwise be found serving ice creams at his family's shop in Parkmill). There's some indefinable magic in the seaside air here, as Gary Sobers discovered in 1968 when he became the first player in the world to hit six sixes in one over. Then there was the fractious 1969 anti-apartheid demo, with a youthful and idealistic Peter Hain in the vanguard.

Such were the glory days. With the county cricket centre of gravity shifting to Cardiff in 1996 and the Ospreys decamping to the Liberty Stadium in 2005 (although the Whites still play here), the crowds are not what they were. That same year, St Helen's was visited by that "destroying angel, the builder": the old 3,500-seat grandstand over the Mumbles Road pavement was replaced by a generally derided 1,200-seater 'tin shed'. Saved from the bulldozer, though, was the arched, sandstone doorway through which players of the calibre of Dewi Bebb, Mervyn Davies, Richard Moriarty and Robert Jones often passed on their way to becoming household names in rugby folklore.

Some familiar features stay much the same. County cricket generally returns to St Helen's for a short season every year, during which those tireless fund raisers, the St Helen's Balconiers, dust off the counter at the open-fronted Fred's Bar, one of the best-loved watering holes on the county circuit. And the view of the bay from the pavilion remains as captivating as when it inspired the renowned cricket commentator John Arlott (1941-92) – with Dylan Thomas reputedly at his side – to pen his poem 'Cricket at Swansea (Glamorgan in the Field)', which hymns the 'temper' of Glamorgan's game, "intense as an Eisteddfod anthem / It burns down the day like a flame."[15]

THE SWANSEA BAY POLE

One of the more prominent of the many puzzling objects to be found in Swansea Bay is a mysterious pole about a kilometre west of the West Pier and 500 or so metres south of the Civic Centre.

Visible at all states of the tide, it's topped with an orange-painted metal grid, and exposed near its base at low tide is a chunky platform on which you'll often find a couple of cormorants posing like open umbrellas. Many have tried to guess its purpose. An outlet for gases from the sewage system? A beacon for shipping? An essential fixture for pole-dancing mermaids?

No one I asked at either the sewage works or the ports authority had heard of the pole. The answer came eventually from Swansea Museum's maritime specialist, Dave Hoskin. "It's a marker pole for the end of a concrete pipe which brings run-off water down from Townhill," he told me. "It was built in the mid 1970s to relieve the Sandfields, which until then used to be flooded whenever heavy rainfall coincided with a high tide – because there was nowhere for the run-off water to go. The pole is a marker for boats, so that they avoid hitting the pipe. It's colloquially known by sailors as 'the outfall'."

On the western edge of the Sandfields there's a plaque (c.1965) mounted on the outer wall of the Crown Court yard in St Helen's Road, which recalls (with its superfluous comma) that the

> LEVEL OF THE
> GREAT TIDE
> 29th JANUARY 1846,
> WAS 1 METRE
> BELOW THIS LINE.

– which would suggest that during that memorable inundation people were wading up to their calves in icy seawater – not that there would yet have been a significant population in this part of town. Floods caused by the year's highest tides[16] continued to menace this low-lying tract long after the Sandfields area was developed, particularly if a spring tide coincided with a heavy cloudburst. Until well into the later twentieth century, many houses in the Sandfields kept a stone-slab or brick threshold across their doorways, to guard

against flooding. Thanks to the Townhill outfall with its enigmatic pole, those threshold defences have gradually disappeared.

It's been a while since the Severn Sea last took a wander round central Swansea, but climate-change trends suggest that one day soon it might be back.

TRACKWAYS

What is Swansea's oldest road? The 'Vicus Piscatorum' of medieval renown, later known as Fisher Street (roughly in the region of lower Princess Way), before it was obliterated by the Luftwaffe? Or Pentregethin Road, the old Swansea to Carmarthen road, which the Normans called Hakkydeweye? Neither. To find the oldest known thoroughfare in Swansea we need to go back thousands rather than hundreds of years, slip on some wellies and take to the oleaginous no-man's-land of Swansea Bay.

It's a sultry and intermittently drizzly Monday in August, and I'm squelching around on the Brynmill foreshore with two archaeologists from the Glamorgan-Gwent Archaeological Trust, Ellie Graham and Andy Sherman. They've kindly agreed to show me not one but three ancient trackways that have recently come to light, thanks to the partial erosion of their clay and peat cover. I'm feeling slightly guilty that there's surely nothing new for them in this site visit. But it soon becomes clear as we home in on the trackways – which they've already carefully documented and logged on the global positioning system (GPS) that's guiding us towards them – that for an archaeologist there's no such thing as a predictable visit to Swansea Bay.

"It's absolutely mind-boggling what's out here and how old some of the features are," says Ellie. "When you come out here you never know what you're going to find – there's always something new."

"It's a dynamic environment with stuff washing out of it all the time," says Andy, explaining that there are four main peat shelves in the bay – Oystermouth, Blackpill, upper Brynmill and lower Brynmill – which are sandwiched between layers of blue-grey alluvial clay. On top of the clay rests a thin layer of constantly shifting sand or mud, and it's when the tide begins nibbling away at the topmost layer of clay, exposing the peat, that some of the most exciting finds are made.

"There are four to five thousand years of archaeology dotted across the bay. Digging out on the bay is really exciting. You read about these exciting sites in magazines, and think wouldn't it be great if the city you live in also had such things – but in fact it does! Swansea is such a modern city, and so much of it was destroyed in the war, that it's wonderful to be able to stretch the history of the city back so far. This puts us in the same category as London or Dover, because we do have early archaeology around us here.

"Back in Palaeolithic times the bay was all dry land – people living here, hunting, making ritual deposits. By the Bronze Age, it had become largely fresh-water fenland with some drier areas, on which people could have built huts and lived, although we've found no evidence of that so far."

The first of today's new finds are what I'm all too ready to dismiss as a couple of railway sleepers. But then we notice some knobbly metal extrusions and huge iron nails. Ellie probes some rectangular recesses with her fingers. Ship's timbers, is the tentative verdict, possibly from the eighteenth century. As Ellie then makes a sketch of these relics, we're approached by three wide-eyed lads, aged about ten, who ask if we are explorers. "Yes, in a way we are," replies Andy, who explains roughly what we're up to, "temporal explorers." The boys, who tell us they're from London and in Swansea for a week-long evangelical jamboree taking place in a tented village on the Rec, want to know where the sea has gone – its edge being just visible in the mist about a kilometre away – and seem intrigued to learn that these strange tidal comings and goings are largely the work of the moon.

There seems to be one category of find for which Ellie and Andy cannot raise much enthusiasm: stake-net fish traps. From prehistoric times until the mid twentieth century, fish were caught in Swansea Bay using nets (or wattle, earlier) strung between stakes to a height of about two metres.[18] The stubby remains of these posts protrude a few inches above the mud all over the bay, and our archaeologists, it seems, have had enough of them. "These things just don't stop coming," says Ellie. "The numbers are terrifying – how can you record them all? You start being quite excited by them, but by the time you reach your three hundredth you begin to get just a little bit disillusioned."

But not every stubby protrusion is part of a stake-net trap. Sticking out of the upper Brynmill peat shelf about 130 metres south of Brynmill Lane are half a dozen stubs which do not describe the usual line associated with a fish trap. A building? A boat? A wharf? Andy's keen to start digging soon. With material in the upper Brynmill shelf – which dates from Iron Age (c.700 BC-AD 50) and Roman times – being out of water for longer than that in the lower, it tends to be in a poorer state of preservation and quicker to decay.

Stretching from this point for about 200 metres in the direction of the Brynmill Stream outfall pipe is the first of our old roads, an Iron Age trackway which washed out of the peat shelf in 1993. Today, sadly, it's covered in sand and there's nothing to be seen, although I'm assured by GPS reckoning, as I head towards the pipe, that I am walking exactly on its route.

The second trackway is further down the beach in the lower Brynmill peat shelf, which accreted during the Bronze Age (c.2300-700 BC). A short section of hurdle trackway, having eroded out of the marine clay, was discovered in 2009 by Brian Price of Swansea Metal Detecting Club. The hurdle panel was woven from branches of oak and alder, and a simple oak peg had secured the hurdle in place. It was covered in a layer of brushwood to provide a level walking-surface. (The wheel had probably not yet reached these shores.)

There are few beachscape features to orient us towards this second site, so we're dependent on the GPS to get us there. If those

London lads were struck with wonderment at the mystery of the tides, I am like a kid anticipating his first circus at the thought of seeing – and even touching – a structure which radiocarbon dating experts in Florida have determined was assembled by human hand some 4,000 years ago, in the early Bronze Age.

Andy explains, as we plouter through the sludge, that with a short section of trackway such as this, it's difficult to gauge its length, alignment, and starting and finishing points. "Is it just here and there, over particularly marshy terrain, or is it more road-like, taking you from A to B? It's like a jigsaw puzzle with half the pieces missing and no picture to guide you."

"Here we are," says Ellie, as we reach a patch of sand. "This is it."

But 'it', again, is invisible, entirely obscured by the tide's latest rearrangement of the sand. It's as if, approaching the big-top, I've been told the circus has been cancelled.

"Sorry," she says, assuring me that nevertheless we are standing on Swansea's oldest trackway (*above*), separated from it only by a few grains of sand.

But all is not lost. There's another show down the road, featuring the second-oldest thoroughfare in Swansea, which has been radiocarbon dated to 1040-910 BC. We might just be third time lucky.

On the four-kilometre walk along the promenade to Oystermouth, we discuss the dilemmas and techniques of preservation. Once something as delicate as a trackway has been exposed it may take only months, days or even hours to destroy what has lain undisturbed for thousands of years. "So as things become exposed," says Andy, "we have to decide 'Does the sea get them or do we?'."

Parts of the trackways have already been 'lifted', as they say – a term that seems to resonate with the slightly transgressive nature of the deed. "When you take wood into an aerobic environment from an anaerobic environment it causes problems," says Andy. "Oxygen molecules have been replaced by water molecules, so as soon as the wood dries up, everything twists and warps out of shape. You can store an object in water, but this can cause problems. Or you can replace the water in the cells with a water-soluble plastic. It may then hold its shape. It's an evolving science, and we are at the forefront here in Wales."

The section of trackway we're hoping to see at Oystermouth – only a stone's throw from where a Bronze-Age sword was discovered in 1979 – had probably been exposed for about two years before it was discovered by John Player, another member of Swansea Metal Detecting Club, in the summer of 2009. Andy describes it as more like a boardwalk than the Brynmill trackway, as if made of lengths of 2x4 laid out next to each other. Two sections, apparently of a single trackway, have been found, one – now covered in sand – about 75 metres from the promenade, and the other – the one we're looking for – about 200 metres from the promenade. Ominously, the GPS unit in Ellie's hands seems to be failing, as we dither round and round among foreshore rocks thickly festooned with bladderwrack, with no trackway to be seen. Ellie abandons the GPS and fixes instead on "the lilac house" as our direction finder, the trackway being at a 90-degree angle to the promenade, directly in front of number 448 Mumbles Road.

And here – roll drums, clash cymbals – here it is: emerging from a clay 'clearing' among the rocks is an unmistakeable length of waterlogged timber, its surface slightly frayed by the action of the tides. Looking more closely, there are other, shorter lengths looming out of the mud and running parallel with the bigger timber. We are standing, no doubt about it, on Swansea's second-oldest road, which I can see is about three metres wide and oriented towards Port Talbot. There's probably more of it to be discovered further

down the foreshore. I reach down to run my hand along the sodden wood and to finger the loose end of one of the formerly pliable laths which had been used to weave the structure together. Such are the preservative powers of peat and clay, that we see the trackway almost as it was when it went out of use.

"Although the two Bronze Age trackways are separated by only about a thousand years," says Andy, "it's interesting to see the development between the two. Their builders had the same needs and faced the same difficulties, yet their solutions are slightly different. Were the builders of the Brynmill trackway ancestors of those who built this one, or entirely different, or people who had moved out of the bay area and had then moved back?"

Mission triumphantly accomplished, we trudge back towards the promenade, pausing to examine an ancient tree stump, disguised by bladderwrack, a few metres from the steps up to the Dunns. This has yet to be scientifically dated, but Andy reckons that, like the submerged forest at Borth, Cardigan Bay it's likely to be early

Bronze Age. It's not impossible, then, that the materials used to construct the 3,000-year-old trackway – which is only about 300 metres distant – could have come if not from this tree then from others nearby, some of which have also left traces in the mud.

It's apt that we should conclude our walk, which has been largely about transportation routes, with the discovery in the lee of the sea wall of what is probably a sleeper – comprising two parallel staves bonded together by concrete – from an early version of the Mumbles railway. In a thousand years, perhaps, the sleeper might be considered worth 'lifting' but it's apparently far too recent a relic to pique the curiosity of twenty-first-century humankind.

Six months later, I returned to the site of the Oystermouth track-way to observe the exposure and, eventually, the lifting of parts of what turned out to be a surprisingly substantial structure. Three Trust archaeologists, supported by a dozen volunteers, spent six days exposing and logging two 3x3-metre sections of trackway – along with a small 'sondage' or shallow pit between them, to confirm that they were part of a unified whole. It was one of the most moving experiences of my life to see emerging from the sulphurous, dark-brown peat – for the first time in three thousand years – this purposeful Bronze Age thoroughfare. Each of the two main exposures consisted of about twenty 'roundwood' branches, possibly of alder, yoked tightly together and anchored by stakes driven thirty centimetres into the ground and by the occasional tree stump incorporated into the structure. Where 'potholes' had developed, Bronze Age roadmen had repaired them with wads of brushwood. In one of the sections, there were two sleeper-like slabs, possibly of oak, which looked as if they had been worked, originally, for a different purpose, possibly as part of a house, before being recycled as trackway in-fill. On these and some of the roundwood branches, incisions made by tools were clearly visible.[20]

Kneeling in the mud, scraping delicately with their aluminium trowels at those timbers assembled by Bronze-Age hands thousands of years ago, many an awe-struck digger wondered during 'lifting' week what the trackway's builders would have made of our curious antics. "They'd probably think we were mad," was the general view. I'm not so sure. Throughout that week, I had pressing on my mind those haunting words from Harold Pinter's *No Man's Land*, which the playwright asked to be quoted at his funeral in 2008: "And so I say to you, tender the dead as you would yourself be tendered, in what you would describe as your life." Bronze Age folk – with their individuated burials, funerary beakers, urned cremations, and grave goods such as the magnificent gold mantle unearthed at Mold – were surely cardinal ancestor keepers. Perhaps they'd recognize in our genuflections in the sludge of Swansea Bay a fond straining by twenty-first century man and woman to tender the Bronze-Age dead.

notes

1. Built as Letricheux Buildings in 1914.
2. Published by the Welsh Arts Council in 1974.
3. Not to be confused with his similarly celebrated marine artist son, also named James (1847-1925). Many of their works are exhibited at the Glynn Vivian Art Gallery.
4. Since the *Evening Post* moved to Adelaide Street in 1968, some members of staff claim to have experienced strange paranormal happenings: lift doors opening and closing, a woman in green wandering around, and baby foot prints. Similarly, there have been reports of the sound of air-raid alarms in the city centre and at the docks where workers claim to have smelled burning oil and heard the dull thud of explosives.
5. From Walt Whitman's 'Street Yarn', first published in the magazine *Life Illustrated* (16 August, 1856) and reprinted in the collection *New York Dissected*, eds. E. Holloway and R. Adimari (Rufus Rockwell Wilson, 1936).
6. The lower campus of Swansea College of Further Education (now Gower College Swansea).

7. It's worth £240m according to the Swansea edition of Monopoly.

8. Cardiff's other peace offering was the £11m Olympic-standard Wales National Pool which opened off Sketty Lane in 2003.

9. Residents of places such as Merthyr Tydfil and Coalbrookdale in Shropshire would doubtless contest the Swansea claim.

10. According to United Nations criteria, Wales was the world's first industrial nation by 1851.

11. Wilkinson Eyre also designed the Sail Bridge (2003) over the Tawe.

12. However, William Frost's alleged flight at Saundersfoot in 1896, if it took place, would negate such a claim.

13. Of the word 'meridian's various meanings, perhaps the intended one in this context is "pertaining to the period of greatest elevation or splendour".

14. Brains have another Grape and Olive in Allensbank Road, Cardiff.

15. A framed version of the poem used to hang in the Westbourne pub in Brynymor Road.

16. Equinoctial spring tides rise to about 9.5 metres.

17. The seafront Recreation Ground in Brynmill.

18. They were also caught in V-shaped fish weirs: see *Real Swansea*.

19. The Beta Analytic Radiocarbon Laboratory in Florida dated a sample from the trackway to between 2140 and 1930 BC.

20. An analysis of the finds published by the Glamorgan-Gwent Archaeological Trust later in 2012 concluded: "The Oystermouth trackway ... is extremely rare in Britain as an example of a corduroy road of this date and constructional type ... "

NORTH

PENLLERGARE

It's one of the four lost gardens of Wales,[1] a private paradise created over 150 year ago by the horticulturist, astronomer and pioneering photographer John Dillwyn Llewelyn (1810-82) – and the only one of those gardens yet to be secured against the ravages of neglect, which it has suffered since the 1930s.

This huge country park, 2.4 km long and .8 km wide, and wedged between the M4, the A483 and the hard-pressed estates of Blaenymaes, Port Mead, Penplas and Penlan, may be a Grade II listed landscape of national significance, and no one who has enjoyed a walk in this steep-sided valley could fail to be charmed by its ramshackle delights. But relatively few Swansea people know of its existence and successive local authorities have lacked the will or the resources to reverse its dereliction.

This 'secret and magical place', a model of the (late) Picturesque, nevertheless has its fervent admirers, chief among them members of the Penllergare Trust which was formed in 2000 to restore Penllergare to something approaching its former splendour. The product of a passionate marriage of art and nature, Penllergare has seemed for many decades sadly unloved. It has an unenviable reputation as Swansea's premier dogging venue; many a stolen or unwanted car has ended up torched in its wooded dells; trail bikers and quad bikers regularly tear up its turf; arsonists enjoy burning its trees and firing its bracken; gun owners use its wildlife for target practice; in 2007, mysterious bark-slicing vandals, motives unknown, removed bark from dozens of its trees.

Officialdom has hardly set a better example. In 1961, the Territorial Army were called in to blow up Penllergare House, the Llywelyn family seat, to make room in due course for the hideously utilitarian civic centre (and car park) of the former Lliw Valley Borough Council (now used as offices by Swansea City Council). The park's northern reaches have been 'top sliced' by two major roads running side by side, the M4 and the A48, built on a towering embankment over the Llan gorge. And on the park's western edge, the property developers Bellway Homes were allowed in the 1990s to build an estate of the sort of identikit, cul-de-sac housing you see all over Britain, in return for the funds to turn Penllergare into a country park – a promise which Bellway has yet to fulfil.

The name of that Bellway estate is Parc Penllergaer. Why the divergent spelling? 'Penllergare', although incorrect Welsh, is what the Llewelyn family chose to call their estate (which can be traced back, well beyond them, to the early sixteenth century, when it was owned by the Prices, reputed descendants of Maenarch ap Dyffryn, the eleventh-century king of Brycheiniog); the spelling was in use by the early 1800s and it appears thus on the seal of the estate office. The estate predates the neighbouring village of Penllergaer, which was originally a hamlet known as Cors Einon, becoming Penllergaer in the late nineteenth century, as it developed into a coal-mining village.[2] Although the correct spelling of the name is 'Penlle'rgaer', meaning 'the headland with a fort', the unapostrophised version, 'Penllergaer', has become the established form on signs, maps and documents, other than with reference to the 'Penllergare' estate.

An overcast Saturday afternoon in May brings together, in the car park of the council offices, members and friends of the Penllergare Trust for a tour of the park. We begin at the nearby 'equatorial' observatory (1851), which managed to survive the attentions of the Territorial Army, and has since been refurbished (1980s). The oldest surviving observatory in Wales, it was built in 1851 by John Dillwyn Llewelyn (JDL), whose family owned Swansea's Cambrian Pottery and who had been left his maternal grandfather's Penllergare estate

in 1817, eventually coming into his inheritance at the age of 21; he also inherited the Ynysygerwn estate in the Neath Valley. John was the son of Lewis Weston Dillwyn (1778-1855), and it had been a condition of his inheritance that he add Llewelyn to his name. As a man of independent means he had the time and resources to devote himself to science and invention – his father described Penllergare as an 'Inn of Science' – and to developing the gardens of his estate.

His passion for astronomy dovetailed with that for the new art of photography. The first cousin of John's wife Emma was Henry Fox Talbot (1800-1877), of Lacock, Margam and Penrice, who is generally regarded as the father of photography, and who spent a considerable time at Penllergare, where he is believed to have developed photography's negative-positive method. Fox Talbot stimulated in his entire Welsh family an obsession with photography, and many of them made historic contributions to the art. It was in this observatory – a stone rotunda building capped by a wooden, copper-clad drum that revolved on metal rollers – that John and his daughter Thereza took one of the first photographs of the moon (1857-8), with Thereza enabling John to track the passage of the moon by pushing the telescope slowly and steadily round. John's mother, Mary Dillwyn (1816-1906), was the first in Britain to capture a smile on film – the smiler being John's cousin, William Mansel Llewelyn. The first known photograph of a snow scene was taken at Penllergare, and the family were the first to exhibit a photograph of breaking waves.

We diverge initially from the tour's circuit to inspect the huge culvert, at the northern end of the park, which channels the Afon Llan beneath the six lanes of the A48 and the M4. This 274-metres-long tunnel is big enough itself to take a lane of traffic, and there are plans to sling a ropewalk from its roof, so that you can walk through, beneath the roads, to Penllergaer Forest on the other side.

Fifty years ago, the Llan – which rises at Tor Clawdd near Mynydd y Gwair – was so polluted by coal mines and steelworks that it was virtually devoid of life. Today, it has returned to the relatively unpolluted state of former times, when the Llywelyns fished its waters and hunted its banks for otters – although otters, making a robust recovery elsewhere in Wales, having come close to extinction, have yet to re-establish themselves at Penllergare. If and when they do, they could succeed in displacing the alien mink which flourishes here.

We pause on the edge of the first of the park's two lakes. This one, largely silted up, was 'moved' by JDL from further down the valley, so that the mansion might enjoy a view over water, as well as availing itself of a ready supply of fish.

Climbing some steps towards the site of the mansion, which have been barred at both ends to foil scramble bikers, we come to a Japanese red cedar with a strange, U-shaped bend in one of its branches. Nearby, there are a 350-year-old oak and a 1000-year-old yew. Jennie Eyers, the trust's community and education coordinator, points to the extraordinary variety of flora and fauna in this valley woodland which dates back to at least 1600 and has its own micro-climate, slightly warmer than its surroundings. Among its native trees is the rare and endangered black poplar. The park's owners could afford to import a wide range of exotic trees and plants, among them sequoia, which can live for up to 3,000 years, Japanese larch, azaleas, Himalayan balsam and rhododendron – the last two having become, as elsewhere, troublesome rogues, proliferating superabundantly and stifling other growth. At least 63 bird species have been recorded at Penllergare, of which over 40 nest here.

On the way down the valley, we take the high road, a carriageway (1830s) especially designed to unite the whole estate, providing a grand approach to Penllergare House and reaching nearly 2.5 kms down to Cadle Mill. Although – with archways, bridges and embankments – it was a considerable feat of engineering, JDL was content to leave its construction largely in the hands of his father, while he and Emma decamped for their honeymoon.

To our right, is JDL's walled kitchen garden, within which he built the world's first landscaped orchid house (1836), with hot waterfall – which could be reconstructed, should the opportunity arise, from extant drawings.

Next we pass, again on our right, a Pennant sandstone quarry which supplied all the estate's building and landscaping stone. We view it from a bridge which JDL instructed his father should be at least the width of two carriages. When the quarry's work was done, JDL built a summer house above it, carefully engineering the views to take in the estate's most salient features.

The steep-sided valley soon broadens, as the woodland gardens become bracken-clogged, derelict parkland – and Blaenymaes, Port Mead and Penplas come into view. We pause at an ivy-covered pile of stones at the wood's edge, which is all that remains of Upper Lodge, one of three dotted along the driveway, and the home of the chauffeur. Beyond that 300-house Bellway intrusion atop the slope to our right, there's a ridge covered in bluebells known as Graig Neddfwch which marks the site of the mansion which was the hub of a long-forgotten neighbouring estate, Nydfwch, the ancestral home since late medieval times of the Matthews family. In 1750, they married into the Prices next door, and Nydfwch was absorbed into Penllergare. Nydfwch House, a two-storey structure with ten rooms, was demolished in the 1820s; only its footings remain.

Suddenly the peace of the valley is shattered by half a dozen youths blattering past us on scrambler bikes, in defiance of notices forbidding the use of all motor vehicles, on pain of confiscation. "Another form of wild life," mutters Jennie Eyers, as she and other trust members take photographs of the culprits, abiding by their policy of avoiding direct confrontation with biking youth.

We return up the valley by the low road, a track running roughly parallel with the grand carriageway. It skirts the 8.1-ha Lower Lake (1837) and brings us to a grove of yew trees which were planted by JDL on the ruins of an old mill – whose footings and mill stone have recently been discovered. "Victorians loved anything mysterious, Gothic," says Jennie. "So he used the old mill to create a feature, giving ladies in the carriages looking down from above a slight frisson, which might have them reaching for the smelling salts."

We are standing some 40 metres below the quarry bridge we had earlier crossed. The slope is scarred by an over-engineered storm-drainage channel from the housing estate. Its construction unearthed bits and pieces of the old quarry railway (1831), including a chunk of plateway and two different kinds of (broken) dram wheel. The trust's Keith Clements retrieves them from the bushes where they have been hidden from prying vandal eyes, and demonstrates how the wheel – its spokes and rim knobbly with rust – would have moved on the plateway.

Although we're less than 4 km from the city centre and only 250 metres from the motorway – and near, by now, the end of our tour – all we can hear here are birdsong, and water cascading from the Upper Lake over the dam which JDL built, with stone from the quarry, to look like a natural waterfall. With steps to enable salmon and sewin to pass, a service tunnel, and gear for opening the sluice gates (still operational), it's a substantial piece of engineering.

Given such tranquil, captivating surroundings, I wonder how the Penllergare family could have parted from such an Eden. When JDL's son John Talbot Dillwyn Llywelyn died in 1927 Penllergare was inherited by his son, Charles Dillwyn Venables Llewelyn, of Llysdinam, Radnorshire, who left the house and the estate in the care of his butler. During the Second World War, Penllergare was requisitioned and occupied by American troops, who used the woods for battle practice and badly vandalised the mansion. The estate was eventually acquired by Glamorgan County Council, but then repurchased by JDL's Llysdinam descendants, who leased it for that Bellway development and the 'country park' which it has yet fully to become.

In his mansion above the Wye, just outside Newbridge-on-Wye, JDL's great-great-grandson, Sir John Michael Dillwyn-Venables-Llewelyn (1938), has a memento close to hand of his forebear's Picturesque, romantic but much slighted paradise: a bedroom transported intact from Penllergare House.

In 2010, the Penllergare Trust was awarded a £2.3m Heritage Lottery Fund grant to restore the garden and woods to their former glory.

LLANGYFELACH

To the thousands who pass through this village on their way to and from Morriston Hospital or junction 46 of the M4, Llangyfelach may seem little more than an unremarkable road through bland suburbia. But it was once a place of high Celtic culture, intense spirituality, festive excess – and perhaps a proto-capital of Wales, whose magic may still cast a spell if it can work its way through the fog of amnesia that has descended on the place.

The village is a waning shadow of what it was. The Welsh language, spoken by the entire community less than a century ago, is now as lost in Barratt-land as the odd fragments of hedgerow that are all that's left of its built-over farms. Vanished almost without trace are its half-dozen coalmines. Its five pubs have been reduced to one, the Plough and Harrow on the cherry-treed green, opposite the village's one shop and a unisex hairdresser. Of the few who've heard of Llangyfelach's once famous holy wells, Ffynon Ddewi and Ffynon y Fil Feibion,[3] no one can tell you where they are.

Finding a guide who really knows the village is not easy. My imaginary companion on any visit to Llangyfelach is invariably another treasure of the parish unknown to most of a younger gener-ation, the painter Evan Walters (1893-1951). In his day, he was a local and sometime national hero, but his reputation was damaged by conservative critics alarmed at his 'dangerous versatility'[4] and his

wayward experiments in form and subject matter; it wasn't until the early years of the present century that he began to be reappraised as one of the great painters of twentieth-century Wales.

I call for him, as it were, at his birthplace, the Welcome Inn on Mynydd-bâch Common, where his mother was the publican (his father was a carpenter). The present pub, towards the end of a driveway which passes a partially overgrown cemetery on the left and a scrubby triangle of common on the right, is not the original inn where Evan Walters and his four siblings were born; built around the 1720s as a coaching house, that Welcome Inn was demolished in 1926. The inn this lunchtime – known to locals as the Welci – is doing a brisk trade, but the ultra-classical Capel Mynydd-bâch (established in 1762 as Swansea's first Congregational chapel; rebuilt 1866) just beyond the pub seems at the end of the road in every sense, and is up for sale, along with its narrow-gutted, 'modern' manse. Founded at a time of persecution of Nonconformists, when their places of worship had to be built five miles outside the town's boundaries, this historic chapel's role in the development of Nonconformity makes it internationally important. Among the thousands buried in its nearly two-hectare graveyard are the poet Daniel James (Gwyrosydd; 1847-1920), who wrote the words to the hymn 'Calon Lân', and the renowned architect John

Humphrey (1819-88), designer of the rebuilt Mynydd-bâch, whose masterpiece was Tabernacl in Morriston.[5]

We're in the depths of urban-cowboy territory here. On the common, where a couple of tethered ponies droop forlornly, the miners used to race their greyhounds, and the teenaged artist – who, at the age of two, had begun to draw with chalk on the kitchen floor – found himself in demand as a painter of colliers' greyhounds, for a shilling a piece. His earliest known painting is of 'Silver and Patches' (1909), two greyhounds in a betting race on this common. Another early painting, made in about 1911, when he was a student at Swansea School of Art, is of Cefngyfelach colliery,[6] which was only about 200 metres away from the pub. He painted some of the most affecting portraits of coalminers in the history of art; most of the individuals seem to have been workers at Tir-dwncyn colliery, a kilometre or so further to the north-west.

After leaving the pub, the family lived at Morfydd House, 1120 Llangyfelach Road, a sizeable detached property at the back of which the artist, although living for long periods in London, kept a studio for the rest of his life, painting portraits and views of his native *bro*.[7] In the *parlwr* of Morfydd House, he painted a multi-coloured frieze and ceiling of interlaced Celtic motifs, which, as his longstanding partner Erna Meinel remarked, eventually "fell to the Philistines" and no longer exists.

Llangyfelach's then predominantly agricultural character is celebrated lovingly in paintings such as 'Landscape with Farm' (1938). Although it takes up a tiny portion of the canvas, the paint-ing's central presence – in competition with the whitewashed gable of a cottage – is the top of the ancient church tower.

The one thing that most passers-by notice about Llangyfelach is that bell tower, which stands about thirty metres uphill of the actual church. It's one of only three in Wales to be thus detached.[8] Much restored and repaired over the centuries, the tower dates from the twelfth century. It finally parted company with its already dilapi-dated church as the result of a storm in 1804, which toppled the east wall of the tower and sent it crashing into the nave. Too poor at that time to rebuild the church, the parishioners decamped for their services to the nearby tithe barn, where the church stored the dues-in-kind, especially wool and cheese, which were collected annually from its parishioners. After various adaptations and extensions, the barn became the replacement church, much of it reconstructed with stone from the abandoned building.

The separation of church and tower has given rise to various stories and sayings, such as the folk verse:

> Mae Llangyfelach hynod
> Yn ddigon hawdd ei 'nabod:
> Mae'r eglwys draw, a'r clochdy fry.
> Pa fodd y bu'r anghydfod?[9]

The 'mystery' of this separation is 'explained' in a popular local legend. During the construction of the church, progress was constantly frustrated by the devil's nightly theft of building materials. One night, the priest kept watch and caught the devil stealing away the entire tower. Assailed by a holy invocation from the priest and the sign of the cross, the devil was frightened into dropping the tower – where it stands to this day.

Known much further afield than Llangyfelach, at least to those who enjoy traditional music, is the old folk song 'Ffarwél i Langyfelach lon',[10] concerning a lad who was press-ganged into fighting in England's imperial wars and who fantasises about a return to Llangyfelach and a "merch fach lân / Sydd yn gweddio nos a dydd / Am i'w hannwyl gariad gael dod yn rhydd."[11] Long before that hopeful young soldier's time, Llangyfelach was a meeting point for Welsh archers on their way to fight England's battles against the French in the fifteenth century.

Llangyfelach's origins reach much further back than the twelfth century. If it's true that, in accordance with the church's dedication to both St Cyfelach and St David, the church was founded by the somewhat chimerical Cyfelach, an early saint of the Celtic Church, and then re-established by St David (d.?589) in the late sixth century, Llangyfelach can claim to be one of the earliest Christian settlements in Wales. According to Rhigyfarch's Life of David (c.1094), the saint "founded a monastery in Gower, at a place called Llangyfelach" – which, it's implied, he may have regarded even more highly than St David's. During a pilgrimage to the Holy Land, David was consecrated Archbishop by the Patriarch of Jerusalem, who presented him with four gifts: a bell, a staff, a cloak woven with gold, and an altar – all of which were kept at Llangyfelach. After David's death, the altar – which was famously associated with miracles – was draped with animal skins, as it was considered too holy for mere humankind to gaze on directly.

This made Llangyfelach, for centuries, an important place of pilgrimage, especially around the time of the church's mabsant,[12] March 1, when tens of thousands would flock to its famous two-day fair, the biggest in Wales. The first day was the horse and cattle fair and the hiring fair, when the farmers would contract labourers for the coming year. The second day was the fig and flannel fair, when all manner of food, drink, domestic goods and agricultural wares would be offered for sale. Held originally in the churchyard, with tombstones in later years used as counters, the fair for many country people – who laboured year round from dark unto dark – was a feast of misrule and desperate hedonism; five ballads were written about its amorous ambience. Such revelry, with the church tower being used as a temporary gaol, was fundamentally at odds with the ascetic ways of the church's patron saint, and in 1815 the fair was banished from the churchyard to the fields of Pen-y-pant Farm opposite, where it continued until 1869.

Although there was indeed a saint (as well as an eighth-century bishop) called Cyfelach, historians have lately cast doubt on the church's founding by an individual of that name, suggesting instead that Cyfelach could be an understandable corruption of *cyfeillion*, meaning 'friends' or 'brothers'. If so, the *cyfeillion* would have been the monks who accompanied St David and who established their *clas* (monastic settlement) just up the road from Llangyfelach at what is still known as the Clase.

Like most Swansea churches, Llangyfelach is locked most of the time. So I have made arrangements with the church warden, Terry Phillips, to have a look inside. A retired primary school teacher, who was baptised in this church in 1931, Terry is obviously proud of the place, although saddened by the dwindling of its congregation: around 45 for the Sunday morning Eucharist, and half a dozen for evensong. With its pristine white walls, timbered ceiling, carpeted aisle and ornate rood screen (1916) by W.D. Caröe, the church is in attractively good shape, in spite of the huge and mostly overgrown graveyard which surrounds it. Terry has 'modern' ideas about church usage, and would like to see the stiff-backed pews at the rear of the church replaced by comfortable chairs for concerts and meetings – rather as the old tithe barn, where farm implements were stored during the winter, served secular as well as spiritual needs. It's an idea that finds little favour with the more conservative churchgoers, says Terry, who is rather afraid that, given the rate of decline, the present (excellent) vicar, the Rev Robert Davies-Hannen, could well be the last in a line of over 30 vicars of Llangyfelach that reaches back to 1066 and the incumbency of one Aggerw.

There are three things in particular I've come to see in the church. One is mounted on the northern wall at the rear, although it was found when excavating the floor of the present nave in 1913: a ninth-century slab incised with a Celtic-style wheel cross and the words CRUX XPI (The Cross of Christ). Llangyfelach's major significance as a religious site is further affirmed by the second, glorious object: a slotted base for a churchyard Celtic cross, probably from the tenth century, which lay for centuries in the lee of the tower but which was brought inside the church a couple of years ago, to protect it from further erosion. Of the actual cross-and-shaft, which may have been about three metres high, no remnant nor record remains, but judging by the intricate plait and key patterns on four sides of this sandstone boulder, it must have been a work of exquisite Celtic craftsmanship.

Such artistry would certainly have fired the imagination of Evan Walters, whose Celtic motifs in Morfydd House could well have been inspired by the church's ancient stones. As a boy, he sang in the church choir and whenever he was back home in later life he'd attend Sunday services here, invariably in a seat near the door. A painting by Evan Walters is my third object, his 'Holy Communion

in Pentonville Prison' (1937). Walters donated it to the church as a memorial to his parents, after his father's death in 1946 (his mother died in 1942). The long years of his parents' decline, which he spent mostly in Llangyfelach looking after them, led eventually to a breakdown in his own health.

In the church's chancel, Terry points out the realm of another stone conspicuous by its absence – a blank oval, about a metre high, once occupied by some bigwig's memorial plaque. Terry was present when it fell from the wall and smashed down, missing by only seconds the Rev Ryland Evans – 'a small man' – who had just left his seat, right beneath the plaque, to administer communion.

A hundred or so years ago, one of Terry's warden predecessors would have been able to point confidently to another inscribed stone, serving as a lintel above the door to the tower. We'd have seen a ringed cross framed in a rectangle. The slab would once have stood upright and is probably a monument from the ninth century. Observers have been complaining for at least a century about the gradual erosion of the slab's markings. By now, sadly, the erosion seems to be complete. As far as my eyes – and Terry's – can make out, there is no longer a trace of what observers such as Evan Walters, and generations for a thousand years before us, would have seen on this stone.

The formerly huge size of the parish, covering much of the ancient Welshry of the lordship of Gower; the potent relics the church once hosted; the presence of inscribed stones whose crafting could have been commissioned only by a well-endowed and influential monastic body; such features hint at some huge but as yet ungraspable significance. Time has erased so much here that these intriguing bits and pieces paint as spectral and insubstantial a picture as the minimal names and dates on the thousands of gravestones that clutter the four-acre churchyard.

It wasn't until the late seventeenth century that headstones started to be used to mark burial places, if families could afford to pay for them. Sometimes their brief inscriptions hint at a heartbreaking narrative. To your right, as you enter the churchyard, there's a headstone listing the painfully short lives of Richard and Hannah Rees's eleven children: they died, all eleven of them, between 1867 and 1885, most of them as babies or toddlers; one made it to the age of fourteen.

In contrast with the swanky monuments of local industrialists, there are several graves marked with mysterious coffin-shaped objects made of iron, which bear no inscription. Iron seems to have been sufficiently plentiful during the industrial era for these 'coffins' to be used as grave markers, to 'book' a burial place. Or so some say; no one seems sure what these strange things are.

In 1893, the churchyard was closed to all new burials, which is why there's no point in looking here for Evan Walters' grave. He's to be found – with his parents and sister, who died aged three – across the road in the cemetery to the rear of Bethel Presbyterian chapel (1809).

The painter's last years were difficult. Those who had lionised him in the 1920s deserted him as the artist stubbornly pursued his continuous revolution. His final exhibition in London, in 1950, resulted in only a few sales, and a friend who paid him a visit at the exhibition recorded the poignant scene of the artist asleep on the settle in an empty gallery. In spite of the exhibition's failure to re-establish his reputation, Walters would no doubt have been looking forward to a major exhibition of his work being planned at the Glynn Vivian; but he died in his London studio of a heart attack, aged 58, and the anticipated homecoming of the most successful artist that Swansea, at that time, had ever produced became the 1952 memorial exhibition.

His one, constant champion, until her death in 1977, was Erna Meinel. She wanted him to be buried in Hampstead, where they had lived together, but Walters' patron Winifred Coombe Tennant (1874-1956) intervened, with the family's support, and Erna's plan was dropped. She did not attend the funeral, but she was instrumental in getting a death-mask made, which is kept in the basement at the Glynn Vivian Art Gallery.

His grave at Llangyfelach – alongside one of those mysterious iron coffins, and with bluebells around his feet in springtime – has a beautifully carved slate headstone. It concludes with the words, "Breuddwydio am lawenydd / a dihuno i'w gael" (To dream of joy, and through death to achieve it).

THE CLASE

Death and taxes. Drink, drugs, fights, burglaries. Chronic unemployment and social hardship. Urban cowboys running as wild as their horses. The Clase, as they say, has a reputation.

It's unarguably among the most deprived areas of Swansea and Wales. But those who have lived in the Clase tend to paint a different picture. My friends the guitarist Brian Breeze and his wife Maybellene, for instance, who lived in the Clase for nearly twenty years before moving to a much tamer Cockett in the late 1980s, describe a wild yet rather wonderful place with an exceptional community spirit. "It was a lovely, lovely place to live," Maybe told me on a return visit. "We were as happy here as anywhere we've lived. It was such fun."

Wedged between Morriston and Llangyfelach, the Clase (rather than simply Clase) grew from the 1950s onwards as a working-class estate, many of its residents being housed in apartment blocks which have since been demolished in favour of detached housing (of notably banal design) and open spaces. The name of this relatively recent settlement is ancient, and it's echoed elsewhere in the neighbourhood in names such as Clase Farm, Clasemont and Clase Road. It stems from Welsh, the term *clas* being used to describe a major native church of pre-Norman Wales. Y Clas was the territory that belonged to the monastic community at Llangyfelach, which was established – or re-established – by St David himself. And the Clase is still – with Penderry, Mawr and Rhwng-dwy-Glydach – one of the four 'parcels' constituting the extensive parish of Llangyfelach.

For hundreds of years after St David's time, the Celtic Church would have been a commanding presence in people's lives. A very different institution lords it over the Clase these days: the 16-storey "Stalin-era blockhouse" of the Driver and Vehicle Licensing Agency (DVLA; 1974) whose 6,000 employees collect £5.7bn of vehicle excise duty a year from Britain's 44 million drivers and their 36 million vehicles. Swansea's biggest employer after the local authority,[13] 'the MOT' (Ministry of Transport), as it was originally known, was built on farmland off Clasemont Road. It was a (somewhat delayed) response by the British political establishment to the rise of Plaid Cymru: toss the Taffs a few jobs, and perhaps they'll desist from this nationalist nonsense. The delay was attributed, in part, to certain ungrateful Taffs wafting building materials from the rear of the site almost as quickly as they were checked in at the front. There were stories about police finding houses in Llangyfelach being constructed with stolen materials, and council-house tenants in the Clase with exactly the same taste in wallpaper as the Ministry of Transport.

The eighth floor is devoted entirely to heating and air-conditioning. The system has to be efficient, as the tower's windows are designed not to open. Just as well, perhaps. I've never met a DVLA employee who's been conspicuously happy in their work.

"It was very, very monotonous," I was told by the poet and writer Rhys Owain Williams, who once had a part-time job there. "A very good wage for very little work – £7.40 an hour (then) – although there's always the concern that you'll receive a letter-bomb in the post. Everyone in Morriston seems to have worked there. It's difficult to get in unless you know someone – they can tell you the best wording for the application form and the best approach for the interview. But it takes a long time to get in. It was six months before I got an interview and then a year and a half before I got the job. They prefer to employ people on temporary, short-term contracts, and will try to avoid giving them permanent contracts. They can finish you whenever they want, and then you have to wait for another short-term contract to come up."

Given the monotony of the job (aside from the occasional bomb scare[14]), some find inventive ways of passing the time, such as the young woman who was suspended in 2005 for the movie snaps of her sex life that were downloaded onto the phones of 300 colleagues.

This oppressively ugly building can be seen – and is meant to be seen – for miles. Jan Morris has described it, with kite-eyed accuracy, as the "modern equivalent of a Norman castle – an incubus of British imperial authority in occupied territory."[15]

In the Clase, as elsewhere, "nothing can be said to be certain except death and taxes",[16] and sure enough, immediately next door to the road-tax behemoth is its twin in inevitability, Morriston cemetery and crematorium, where up to twelve bodies a day are reduced to ashes.[17]

But the Clase spirit seems undiminished by mortality's smoke signals gusting relentlessly from the crematorium stacks. Anyone who has lived in the Clase brims over with tales of native wit, resourcefulness and an almost tribal solidarity.

It's a sunny August morning, and Brian, Maybe and I are standing on the grassed-over site of their first home here, the long-demolished, five-storey Longview Court apartment block (after twelve years here, they moved round the corner to a semi-detached house in Beacons View Road, also long-demolished). Overlooking the grassy roundabout at the eastern end of Rheidol Avenue – with the pub, the bookies and the shops opposite, the bus stop in front and the Police Station across the road – the Breezes, in their balconied maisonette, were at the heart of Clase life.

Brian has parked his car more or less where he used to park the bandwagon – full of musical equipment and invariably unlocked.

Nothing was ever stolen from it, although the local 'boys', who enjoyed having a well-known rock musician living in their midst, did once remark to Brian, "You are lucky, gwboi, that we knows ew."

The Longview crew were a tight-knit community. Sitting out on their balconies in the summer, drinking cider and enjoying impromptu parties, they'd call it Candlelight Court. "We were all young," says Maybe. "None of us had any money. None of us felt we had to explain ourselves. We had everything on the doorstep, and whatever you wanted – babysitting, a shoulder to cry on, help with benefits – would be yours, you wouldn't even have to ask for it. We knew everyone coming and going. When the t.v. detector vans called, we'd start a chain of a certain kind of knock on our doors, throughout the whole of the flats, and by the time the detector men came to your door, you'd have unplugged the t.v. and hidden the cables, and you'd say it hadn't worked for years, you just used it for your ornaments. The same sort of routine with the gas and electricity. It always felt safe here and you never worried about the children. All the mothers and all the fathers knew each other. You were from the Clase and you were safe. We had a wonderful time in Clase and I missed it awfully after we left – for years."

They had their own rules and regulations, without need of police, and enforced them. The women in particular took exception to the way the bin-men would torment a younger member of their team. On one occasion, the men tied up this boy and dumped him in one of the wheely bins. One of the Longview 'justiciars' went for the ringleader with a bamboo cane, gave him a thorough whipping, and told him never to treat the boy like that again. "And, at least when the rubbish cart visited those flats, they never did," says Maybe.

"People here were good at looking after the old and vulnerable. Often you'd see people walking down the road on a Sunday with two plates of food, taking dinners to the elderly."

For many years, the focal point of social life was the Wildfowler pub (now Faiza's Indian takeaway) – popularly known, given its lively ambience, as the Flying Chair. Brian remembers when the singer, raconteur and Man-band MC and roadie Vyvyan 'Spiv' Morris (1949-2011) and his then wife Sue were installed as the new publicans.[18]

"The time they took it over, it had a very bad reputation," Brian recalls. "One of the barmen came through from the bar into the lounge saying there was a very odd woman sitting up on the bar, a busty blonde in a skin-tight red dress propositioning every male in sight and refusing to leave. One of the locals complained that the newspapers that were usually there on the counter for customers to read were missing, whereupon the blonde reached into her left bra cup and pulled out a wad of newspaper. 'Do you want the *Sun*, lovely?' she said, 'Or ...,' as she reached into her right cup, '... the *Daily Mirror*?' It was Spiv, the new landlord. Some of the regulars began commenting that the lunatics had taken over the asylum.

"Spiv had a way of defusing potential trouble by responding in eccentric, unexpected ways. 'Yes, sir,' he'd say in the poshest of posh accents to some lumpenprole who had grunted angrily for attention at the bar, 'what would you like?' 'Pintafuckinlager, o course.' 'And would you care for a potato with it?' He'd disarm aggression in this way – they'd be too confused to fight."

If a fight broke out in front of the Flying Chair, it was good news for children living nearby, who'd wait until the fracas had subsided and then move in to gather up spilled coins, cigarettes and lighters. The Breezes' daughters, Emma and Donna, who have since worked in some tough environments, have often remarked to their parents, "Thank god we were brought up in Clase – we can deal with anything."

There was hardly any crime in the early days, according to Maybe, "although sad things did happen, of course, and there were, as ever, some ruthless and dangerous characters." She mentions, for instance, one Johnny Jawbreaker, an enforcer whose speciality was rearranging mouths and breaking legs to order: "I've seen his guns." Fortunately, such heavies tended to revere the community's successful musicians, and the bands would often employ them as bouncers. "It wasn't until about the late 1970s that crime got worse, as a result of drugs and the council moving in problem families and criminals who'd just come out of jail."

Then, as now, Clase people had a passion for horses, which can change hands these days for as little as £5. Some of them roam around the streets, plundering gardens and bin bags; many are staked out on the numerous grassy plots that dot the area. There are said to be about 200 'urban horses' in Swansea, some of them well cared for, but others mistreated or cruelly neglected.

The urban cowboy is mostly a bareback rider, a saddle being an expensive and cumbersome item. With a minimal and often bit-less bridle, he may lack equestrian finesse, but he can usually manage to stay aboard when speed and manoeuvrability demand. Brian remembers a robbery at the post office across the way. "The alarm

bells were going and there was a man on a horse, galloping away. They regularly did their robberies on horseback, which seemed to be a method entirely beyond the capabilities of the police. 'There was nothing we could do,' they'd say. 'He made his getaway on a horse.'"

Modern Clase declares itself to passing traffic down on Llangyfelach Road with two prominent buildings: the ten-storey Rheidol Court tower, re-clad in eye-catching white and green panels in 1994-95, and, on a plateau behind it, the sprawling Clase Social Club. Hidden among firs, oaks and chestnuts beyond the club is the similarly sprawling Treetops Country Club built, extension by extension, around the late nineteenth-century Clase House, which once stood in isolation surrounded by fields. It was lucky to survive the war, when a thousand-pound bomb fell nearby: the blast, by chance, blew in the opposite direction. With its copse of mature trees, its hill-top position, its neighbouring trackway – in the lee of the water tower – banked with fragments of ancient walling, this site hums with as yet unexplored significance.

MORRISTON

Creationists may be discomfited by Darwinian findings that less than 2% of human DNA distinguishes us from chimpanzees, but I'm rambling around Morriston with a son of the town who's proud to be known as a Monkey. One of the last babies to be born (in 1987) in Morriston Hospital, the poet and psychogeographer Rhys Owain Williams spent his first eighteen years in Morriston and still considers himself to be a Monkey first, a Swansea Jack second.

"Fuck off back to Monkey town and play with your nuts," was the supposed insult hurled by a Pontardawe Inn centre-forward, miffed that Rhys's Morriston team had beaten the boys from Y Gwachel for the first time in three seasons.

"For this unenlightened fellow, calling a Morristonian a 'Monkey' was obviously intended to cause offence," says Rhys. "But in fact the opposite is true."

Morristonians may have been known for generations as Monkeys, but few these days remember why. Some ascribe it to the so-called Monkey Parade when, sixty or more years ago, the town's young bloods used to step out after chapel in their Sunday best and parade back and forth along Woodfield Street, the town's main thoroughfare, wolf-whistling and cat-calling to local females

similarly lurking with flirtatious intent. A comparable post-chapel parade took place on Swansea's seafront, where youngsters prowled between Singleton Park and the (long gone) Swansea Bay station, opposite St Helen's rugby and cricket ground. So, the regular Sunday saunter between Morriston Cross and St John's – 'the church in the middle of the road' – became known as the (Morriston) Monkey Parade to distinguish it from its equivalent on what is now the promenade.

But, as Rhys observes, the neatly alliterative Monkey moniker has an earlier origin: the former proliferation in Morriston's better-to-do streets of a member of the conifer genus, *Araucaria araucana*, native only to Chile and west-central Argentina and known more familiarly as the monkey-puzzle tree. It acquired that name, the story goes, when a nineteenth-century stroller in Pencarrow gardens in Cornwall was moved to exclaim of a fine specimen, "It would puzzle a monkey to climb that!" (Puzzlement, says Rhys, would instantly give way to painful injury, because the tree bears needle-sharp pointed leaves which were developed in order to stop dinosaurs eating them before the tree could grow beyond their reach.)

As we climb Clyndu Street in the south-west part of town, passing abandoned houses blighted by a 1988 landslide at the junction with Pentremalwed Road, Rhys suggests that Morriston's first cuttings of *Araucaria araucana* arrived from Chile (where it's the national tree) with cargoes of the copper ore on which the wealth of Swansea – with Morriston at the region's industrial heart – was founded. As elsewhere in Valleys communities, the monkey-puzzle tree, planted as an ornamental feature in the gardens of white-collar and managerial types, came to be seen as a status symbol.

What are our chances of finding a monkey-puzzle tree in today's Morriston? Slim, Rhys reckons, although his father has heard rumours of at least one survivor, over Cwm-Bath way. We resolve to keep a keen lookout. With almost 17,000 residents, Morriston is the biggest of the city of Swansea's seventeen communities, so there could still be an *Araucaria araucana* shaking its unruly, reptilian mop-top in some overlooked backstreet.

There's no point in expecting anything from an obvious place such as the centrally situated Crown Street whose small front gardens once boasted several monkey-puzzlers, and where the supposed last was felled in the early 1980s. But it's worth pausing at the top of this street to take in below us the layout of Morris Town[20] – Treforys in Welsh – which is of historic importance as Wales's first planned industrial settlement. When in 1768 the copper master John Morris (1745-1819) inherited the properties of his Shropshire-born father, Robert Morris, he decided to construct on the western bank of the Tawe a model settlement to house his employees.

His architect and planner was the Congregationalist minister William Edwards (1719-89), best known for his famous 'New Bridge' (1756) in Pontypridd, which was the longest single-arched structure in the world at the time. He provided Morriston too with a distinguished river crossing, the single-span Wychtree Bridge (1778),[21] with two cylinders in each of its spandrels.[22] It was demolished in 1959 and replaced by a succession of inelegant girder-works which, until the M4 was built, carried all the main London to west Wales traffic.

The 35-hectare settlement was built between 1790 and 1796 on a grid-iron plan, with the parish church of St John's at the intersection of the two main roads, Sheep Street (now Woodfield Street) and what is now Morfydd Street – originally called Edward Street, or familiarly Hewl Neti (from Ned or Edward), after the town's fondly remembered designer. In providing his workers with a plot for a house and vegetable garden, and sufficient land nearby to graze a cow, John Morris was motivated as much by self-interest as by philanthropy. Copper smelting was a highly skilled craft, often handed down from father to son, and, in the competitive conditions of the Lower Swansea Valley, the captains of industry knew the importance of keeping their workers loyal to the firm.

It's thought that only two of Morris Town's original houses remain, but the street plan survives, as does Morriston's sense of itself as a town apart from its big sister by the sea. Not much smaller by now, in population terms, than Carmarthen, it was intended from the outset as its own total community, with shops, a market, churches and chapels, pubs, and easy access to its residents' main places of work – with, these days, the role of the old coal, brass, copper, steel, tinplate, zinc and chemical undertakings being super-seded by that of the Driver and Vehicle Licensing Agency on the north-west edge of town. It's easy too, with the M4 on Morriston's doorstep, to commute to work in Carmarthen, Cardiff or Newport – and to return to a community which still feels culturally distinc-tive. Morriston has the highest number of Welsh speakers of Swansea's districts: in the 1970s, about 40% spoke Welsh, although that had declined by 2001 to about 25%. The first Welsh learner ever to win the chair at the National Eisteddfod – at Rhyl in 1985 – was Morriston's Robat Powell, and in 2010, at the Ebbw Vale National, Robat was one of the adjudicators who awarded the chair to Morriston-born Tudur Hallam. Then there are institutions such as its choirs, chief among them the world-famous Morriston Orpheus, formed in 1935, and the popular summer carnival, once the biggest in Wales.

Our view from the top of Crown Street is dominated, like most views of Morriston, by the soaring spire of the Congregational chapel, Tabernacl,[23] the renowned 'cathedral of Welsh Nonconformity' which, seating 1,450, has long claimed to be the largest chapel in Wales. Designed by the chapel deacon and self-made architect John Humphrey – whose only training had been as a carpenter – it was built, between 1870 and 1872, in an idiosyn-cratic yet assured mixture of classical and Italian Renaissance styles. "The chapel seems to stand out as one great redeeming feature in the whole of that huge manufacturing district," wrote *The Cambrian* when it opened. "It is an oasis in a desert, an object worthy of admiration in the midst of unsightly works and manufac-tories of every size and description." And still it stands out in these

post-industrial times against the banal retail sheds that have replaced those "works and manufactories".

Asda is one of those sheds. Local Welsh-speakers were somewhat bemused in November 2008 when a spectacularly mistranslated sign appeared at the junction of Clase Road and Pant-y-Blawd Road. Purporting to bar Asda-bound lorries from the area, it read in English "No entry for heavy goods vehicles. Residential site only". The Welsh, however, communicated a rather different message: "Nid wyf yn y swyddfa ar hyn o bryd. Anfonwch unrhyw waith i'w gyfieithu" (I am not in the office at the moment. Send any work to be translated). It seems that highways officers of Swansea Council, having emailed the translation unit to ask for a Welsh version of the English – and understanding, evidently, not a word of the language of heaven – adopted somebody's 'out of office' reply as the text for their sign.

Although Morfydd Street, Crown Street and Slate Street are bisected at equal intervals by Woodfield Street, it's not only for reasons of topography that the portions on rising ground to the west of that central artery are known as Upper Morriston, Rhys explains: "The people who lived in the upper halves of these streets tended to be managers and foremen and their families, the bosses, while those who lived in the lower halves of the same streets, in Lower Morriston, were the workers – no monkey-puzzle trees for them."

Morriston boasts an exceptional number of chapels, some abandoned and decaying, others converted into housing, such as Capel Carmel (1898), where Parry Road joins Vicarage Road, which has recently become flats. We turn near here into Morriston Park, formed in 1912 from Morris's Clasemont estate. Here John Morris built his Palladian mansion, Clasemont Hall (1775), as part of a carefully planned and aesthetically pleasing landscape, the view from this ridge embracing the castellated block of flats he built for his workers on a crag overlooking Landore (the ruin known today as Morris Castle), the town he was developing alongside the Tawe, and the cupolas and rotundas of his smelting works in the valley below. It was a picturesque fantasy wrecked all too soon by the smoke and noxious fumes gusting up from those very works. Like other industrialists who settled too close to the source of their wealth, the Morrises were smoked out of their mansion in the early nineteenth century. Clasemont was demolished and, according to local legend, its stones were transported in a single night by hundreds of carts to sylvan Swansea west, where the Morrises built Sketty Park,[14] a poor imitation of their once idyllic Morriston seat.

All that remains of Clasemont Hall are its grassed-over footings, above a broad slope in the northern reaches of the park where Rhys remembers games of rugby and football on anything but a level playing field. There are four or five distinct 'oases', each planted with a dozen birches, and fringed this morning with daffodils about to bloom: these mark the foundations of the mansion's central block, its two flanking wings and various outhouses.

Leaving the park, we join Clasemont Road opposite the entrance to the 18-hole Morriston Golf Club which is famous for its association with those keen club-wielders Catherine Zeta-Jones and Michael Douglas (Catherine's father, 'Dai Hollywood', is a member here) and for another significant Morriston industry: funerals. With funeral parties debouching from Morriston crem, just up the road, every half hour or so, there's an unfailing demand for venues to hold a wake, much to the enrichment of local hostelries. I've nibbled many a funereal sausage roll in Morriston Golf Club – where, indeed, the wake for Catherine's grandmother, 91-year-old Zeta Jones, was held in August 2008.

Distracted by thoughts of the holy Catherine as we wander down Clasemont Road, we seem to have forgotten about the numinous but omni-absent Araucaria araucana – when all of a sudden, I'm pretty damn sure, towering two houses high above the junction with Vicarage Road is the very object of our quest. "It can't be," says Rhys. It can. "Surely not," says Rhys, "I can't understand how my father could have missed that tree – he lives on this road." By the time we reach the walled garden of a handsome residence called Penbryn, at 155 Vicarage Road, there can be no further doubt: a monkey-puzzle tree it is, possibly the last in Morriston. I'm tempted to hug its scaly trunk in celebration, except that I could soon find myself a bloody wreck in Morriston Hospital's notoriously overworked A&E department.

But if Rhys's father has managed to overlook this resplendent specimen, what of the one that, rumour has it, might be lurking in nearby Penrice Street? We head south along Vicarage Road, which is regarded as one of Morriston's two posh streets (the other is Pentrepoeth Road). The underwhelming 1970s-style vicarage, where the two roads meet, does little to burnish the street's aspirational renown, but other houses strive, sometimes a little desperately, to strike the requisite affluent note – with, for instance, a triumphal flourish of spiked and curlicued wrought-iron gates that dwarf the modest property they defend. The owners should have planted a monkey-puzzle tree.

Penrice Street, with its unadopted surface, has fewer pretensions – and no trees, it seems, of any kind. We nose down back alleys on both sides of the street to check the rear gardens – not that any self-respecting conspicuous consumer would seclude an *Araucaria araucana* in the realm of *tŷ bach* and vegetable patch. We're about to give up when Rhys notices, protruding at eaves level above the brow of the road's steep lower half, a sprig of evergreen. Probably an overgrown Christmas tree. But as we approach, a young monkey-puzzle tree declares itself unmistakably outside number 12, on the verge of out-growing its small front garden.

In spite of a notice warning me to 'Beware of the Cats' (it should perhaps have read 'Beware of the tree'), I ring the bell and a young woman in dressing gown and slippers shuffles to the door. I explain our surely bizarre interest in her tree, and she says it was planted by her father. She's not surely exactly when, so she calls him on her

mobile and passes the phone to me. Chris Clarke tells me he planted the tree 24 years ago and that yes, indeed, he does know about the Morriston Monkey nickname – in fact, it's why he planted the tree.

"I'm not from Morriston," he says, "but when we moved here from Cardiff I decided I wanted to do something to try to fit in with the Morriston community. I'd heard about the old monkey-puzzle trees and how they led to Morriston people being called Monkeys, so I decided to plant one in my garden, to suggest our identification with our new home."

It would have been around 1987 when he planted the tree, only a few years after the supposed last monkey-puzzle was felled in Crown Street. Familiarity with the origins of the nickname would have been generally keener then than now.

A sense of specifically Morriston identity is similarly bedimmed in Woodfield Street, which we wander down after a pie and pint in the Red Lion in Sway Road (soon to become yet another Wetherspoon pub).

"To retrace the Monkey Parade today," says Rhys, "is to see first-hand what the age of huge supermarkets and out-of-town shopping has done to Britain's local independently-run shops." The shoe

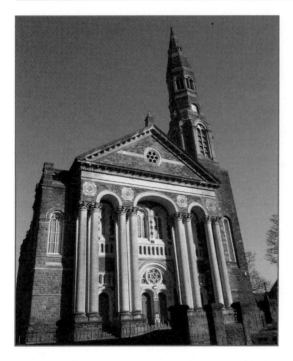

shop owned by the popular footballer Len Allchurch[25] is now a
Domino's Pizza take-away. Alun and Ann Rees's Allison Jayne
fashion and bridal store has become part of the Subway fast-food
chain. Long gone are Haydn Morgan the greengrocer, Greep the
ironmonger, Jupp the TV store, Hunts the baker, Led Davies the
bikes, and many more. Hair dressers, charity shops, kebab joints,
and Indian and Chinese take-aways abound, as do empty premises
– I count at least twenty. One of the relatively few businesses in local
hands is Morriston Computers at 91a Woodfield Street. This is one
of perhaps only two buildings which remain from the foundation of
Morris Town in the late eighteenth century; the other is at 35
Morfydd Street.

  If the mainly Victorian and Edwardian character of the buildings
on the west side of Woodfield Street has managed to survive the
imposition of corporate frontages, the same cannot be said of the
east side, where the plate glass and concrete horizontals of supermarkets rule. But they are dwarfed, in every respect, by Tabernacl,
the glory of Morriston, its four pairs of Bath-stone columns
seeming this afternoon to out-glow the early spring sunlight itself.

It's a sight that might encourage even an atheist to believe – if only in the redeeming power of architecture.

CWMRHYDYCEIRW

"Croeso i Gwmrhydyceirw / Welcome to Cwmrhydyceirw" reads the sign at the entrance to the disused quarry. But, as Rhys Owain Williams and I discovered when we first came here, the casual visitor is far from welcome. We were ordered off the site by a shaven-head security man, who told us we'd need official permission – although we did manage to sneak in a ramble round the north-eastern rim of the quarry and the extensive remains of Cemex UK's ready-mix plant, which closed in 2008.

Cwmrhydyceirw Quarry is sensitive. There's nothing happening here at the moment, but between 1985 and 1991 it was a fly-infested, stinking dump for domestic waste, filter cake waste, sludges, oils and incinerator residues. The neighbours weren't happy. And now that permission has been given for dumping to resume, many are again none too cheery, in spite of assurances that this time there'll be no household rubbish, no hazardous waste, just soil, rubble and inert commercial waste.

Having eventually received official permission, Rhys and I are met at the quarry, one sunny April morning, by Antonio Montinaro, the geologist who's in charge of operations here for the quarry's Italian owners, SI Green of Milan.[26]

Cwmrhydyceirw Quarry, from whose Pennant sandstone much of Morriston was built, seems to me huge. You could drop the Liberty Stadium into it and still have room to spare. But to Antonio, it's small. "If you want to see a big quarry," he says, "you should go to Pontardawe."

Antonio is from Lecce in the 'heel' of Italy. He lives in the Maritime Quarter, loves the beaches of Gower and finds Wind Street alarming. In addition to an office in the Enterprise Park, he has an on-site portakabin.

"What we are doing here is not so much landfill as remediation," says Antonio, explaining that stringent conditions have been imposed by the Environment Agency. The 90,000 cubic metres of old waste lying 15 metres deep on a leaky polyethylene membrane on the north side of the quarry floor will have to be shifted to the south side, where a heavy-duty membrane has already been laid to receive the waste. The cleared area will have to be re-lined, to protect water courses from further contamination, before the old waste is returned to the north side. Only then may landfill operations resume.

The intention is to fill the quarry right to the brim, with 810,000 cubic metres of new waste. "Then it will be an open space – with trees, maybe, for a park or for an extension of Morriston golf course." How long will it take? "Five or six years," he says. "I'll be Welsh by then."

I ask if we can wander down into the quarry. "Not allowed," he says, "Health and safety."

It doesn't look to me particularly unsafe, apart from a sickly green pond which it would probably be unwise to fall into. In fact, with its sandstone cliffs sketched with greening saplings and glowing a golden brown in the spring sunlight, the quarry this morning has a rugged beauty which I can't see a landfill park improving on.

Quarrying was well under way here by the mid nineteenth century, but in 1979 it ceased. Perhaps the most famous block of blue Pennant sandstone to have come from Cwmrhydyceirw is the fitting memorial to Dylan Thomas in the water garden at Cwmdonkin Park. Dylan's friends, the poet Vernon Watkins and the sculptor Ron Cour (1914-79), came here on 1 August, 1963 to choose a suitable stone, on which Ron inscribed the last three lines of 'Fern Hill'. Ron's wife, the painter Glenys Cour (1924) and their daughter Jane were with them that day.

"Vernon was fascinated by how tiny the quarrymen looked on the towering rock faces," Glenys told me. "It took all morning to find the right stone, and then, as we were leaving, Vernon announced 'Roethke died today' – not that I had heard of Roethke[27] at the time."

The quarry inspired two lyric poems. "Never shall time be stilled in the quarry of Cwmrhydyceirw," Vernon wrote in 'Cwmrhydyceirw Elegiacs', "Not while the boulder recoils under the force of the fuse." And in 'At Cwmrhydyceirw Quarry' – "this gigantic theatre", as he describes the place – he addresses both the death of Dylan, via "This stone, soon in his childhood's park to lie", and that of the American poet: "But who had guessed, in the hush of many graves / Riven by love, it was Roethke's turn to die?"[28]

Some have remarked on the 'amateurish' appearance of Ron Cour's inscription – but this was intended. "Ron wanted it to look completely informal," said Glenys, "as if Dylan had scratched it on the stone himself."

Oh as I was young and easy in the mercy of his means
time held me green and dying
though I sang in my chains like the sea

DYLAN THOMAS

Cwmrhydyceirw is a place of big holes. As you turn in towards the quarry from the northern end of Vicarage Road, you cross a railway cutting, so deep and narrow that even some locals are unaware of its existence, although its four tracks are silvery with constant wear. The railway emerges from a tunnel beneath the Vicarage Road/Chemical Road junction and runs for about 80 metres before disappearing into the kilometre-long Llangyfelach Tunnel. This is the 16-km Swansea district line which was built by the Great Western Railway in 1912, to shorten the route between London and Fishguard Harbour. The last mainline railway to have been built in Wales, it was intended to realise Isambard Kingdom Brunel's (1806-1859) dream of seamless travel from New York to London (and vice versa), enabling passengers crossing the Atlantic to disembark at Fishguard and catch the boat train, reaching London a day earlier than by continuing to Liverpool. The express from Fishguard to London took under five hours, stopping only at Cardiff. (The First World War finished Fishguard as a transatlantic terminal; its harbour since then has served only the Irish ferries.) The line diverges from the main south Wales line at Cwrt Sart junction, Britton Ferry and runs to the Morlais junction near Pontarddulais, where it joins the Heart of Wales line, eventually

rejoining the main south Wales line at Llanelli. Few Swansea people
have cause to use the line, which is why it's so little known. It's used
solely for freight trains, apart from a daily passenger service
between Cardiff and Fishguard Harbour, which bypasses Neath
and Swansea.

A bigger, noisier hole is the M4 motorway which began
hereabouts, on a foundation of broken-up slag heaps, as the
Morriston by-pass in 1972. It cuts Cwmrhydyceirw in two, with
Morriston Hospital and Rhys's old *alma mater*, Morriston
Comprehensive School, to the north of the divide.

Less than 100 metres south of that frenzied artery is the site of
the distinctly more tranquil thoroughfare that put the 'rhyd' (ford)
in Cwmrhydyceirw – which translates as 'the valley of the stags'
ford'. In Heol Maes Eglwys, Rhys points through the hedge to a
glint of stream beside the primary school, which he believes to be
the site of the ford. But what of those stags? The name, originally,
had nothing to do with deer. It was Cwmrhydy*cwrw*, 'the valley of
the beery ford' – so called, it's believed, because a combination of
foot-muddied water and white-churned bubbles gave the impression to users of the ford that they were wading through ale. 'Beer'
became 'deer' around 1870, at the behest, it's believed, of zealous
temperance supporters, chief among them the ministers of new
chapels embarrassed to have 'beer' as part of their address.

On the other side of the road is the Deers Leap. A somewhat
identikit hostelry belonging to the Sizzling chain of pubs, it nevertheless cocks a satisfying snook at the ghosts of killjoys past by
applying the determinedly teetotal name of Deers Leap to the title
of a boozer – which probably attracts a bigger congregation of a
Sunday than all the local chapels combined.

THE HAFOD

"They say that when you go back to the place of your childhood,
things get smaller, but for me they don't," says Felicity Kilpatrick,
who was born in the Hafod in 1960. "This place gets bigger. It's
fresh, bright and airy – you can smell the sea air."

She could almost be describing the Hafod[29] eulogised in a poem
of 1737, which contrasts bizarrely with the Hafod familiar to later
generations as part of the most polluted industrial environment in
western Europe:

Thy verdant fields, which wide extended lie,
For ever please, for ever charm the eye:
Thy shady groves afford a safe retreat
From falling show'rs, and summer's scorching heat:
Thy stately oaks to heav'n aspiring rise
And with their utmost tops salute the skies ... [30]

The Hafod this cloudless spring morning does indeed 'charm the
eye', although not in the sense intended by Anon. For after a
dismaying 35% of its houses were declared, at the turn of the
century, unfit for habitation, the Hafod has benefited from a multi-
million-pound renovation programme which has transformed its
terraced streets, returning them to the architectural coherence – and
beauty – of something approximating their original appearance,
when they were laid down in grid form by the copper master John
Henry Vivian, from the late 1830s onwards, as a self-contained
township for his workers: he wanted to "get and keep the best men
at Swansea". Morris Town, over half a century earlier, may have
been the first such township; the east bank of the Tawe also saw the
establishment, sometime between 1799 and 1813, of the much
smaller Grenfelltown (today's Pentrechwyth), for the workers of
Upper and Middle Bank copper works; but Trevivian or
Vivianstown, as the new settlement at Hafod was initially called,
with many of its streets named after Vivian family members, was the
most fully realised of Swansea's copper workers' townships. Indeed,
there's probably no better example anywhere in the world, and this
morning the Hafod Renewal Area looks the part, with its re-
rendered or exquisitely re-pointed Pennant sandstone walls, new
doors and windows, long and gently arced 'slate' roof ridges,
regimented two-tone chimneys, and fanciful pediments (lending a
touch of Renaissance elegance to most front doors). The place
exudes a sense of pride and purpose.

The same cannot be claimed, alas, of the internationally important but shamefully neglected industrial remains on the township's
eastern flank, most conspicuously the Hafod Works' (1810-1924)
two engine houses (early 1860s and 1910 respectively), two nearby
smokestacks, and the Morfa Works' (1835-1980) late nineteenth-
century electrical powerhouse, which later became the canteen of
the amalgamated Hafod and Morfa works.[31]

It was in this works, known by then as ICI Landore, that Felicity's
father, J. Ramsay Kilpatrick (1929-2007), began his working life,

aged 14, in 1943. The memoir he wrote towards the end of his life
in collaboration with Felicity, *Down the Memory Lanes of My Hafod*
(2008), is an absorbing account of his community and the work
that sustained it.

Felicity has driven over from Brecon, where she teaches at Christ
College. We meet in the Landore park-n-ride in the shadow of the
old canteen building, now roofless, charred by fire, vandalised and
graffitied. She points out, alongside the canteen, the slope down
which the men would have walked into the Morfa Works, with a
'Great Wall' to their right that separated the two competing
concerns.

"When I asked Dad how the two works were amalgamated, he
said 'They just knocked down the wall'," says Felicity. "What the
amalgamation couldn't demolish was the rivalry between the two
workforces: they worked in teams and they still didn't speak to each
other."

The entrance to the Hafod Works – which by 1842 was the
largest copper works in the world – is harder to find. Just off the
new bus lane that runs up past Landore Social Club (the old works
office) towards Neath Road, there's what looks like a paved
pathway cutting through the grass towards the works' ruins. This is
in fact the bridge over the Swansea Canal that leads to the works

entrance, although the canal has been filled in, obscuring all but the walkway of the bridge.

"When Dad came here for the first time in forty years," says Felicity, "he couldn't get his bearings at all, such had been the changes."

The continuing neglect of the Lower Swansea Valley's industrial heritage has caused considerable anxiety, both locally and internationally, for many years. When in 2010 Swansea Council unveiled plans for a Hafod by-pass, to be driven straight through the old copper-smelting quarter, that anxiety turned into despair. Fortunately, a team of concerned historians at Swansea University, led by Professor Huw Bowen, succeeded in negotiating a memorandum of understanding with the council under which they would oversee a sensitive and resourceful regeneration. If Swansea is to succeed in claiming World Heritage status – probably the only means of securing the millions needed to restore and promote its crumbling industrial heritage – the exemplary restoration of Trevivian will surely advance the cause.

As we wander uphill and beneath the railway bridge towards Neath Road, Felicity explains that her family lived in the Hafod from the 1840s onwards, mainly in Aberdyberthi Street. "But when my great-grandmother had the temerity to move round the corner to Gerald Street, it must have seemed like moving to a different world. The Hafod was that territorial."

It wasn't until she worked with her father on the writing of *My Hafod* that her fascination with the township took root. She's now a passionate advocate of the Hafod and delights in giving talks about the area. "When I give talks to rural and urban audiences, they say there's surely an element of rose-tinted glasses in all this. But when I talk to people from similar industrial communities, such as Brynhyfryd, they say yes, it was exactly like that. It really is true that you didn't lock your doors in the Hafod."

The first terraces we come to, in Neath Road, are the township's oldest. Their exceptionally long gardens – for growing vegetables and keeping chickens or a pig – are divided by walls capped with half-moon slag blocks. As the township expanded westwards, on a triangular site wedged between Cwm Bwrlais and Neath Road (about half the size of Morriston), the gardens got smaller, but every house was still provided with a standpipe, *tŷ bach* and coal-hole out the back.

"People make a thing about these houses being small," says

Felicity, "but they are bigger than plenty of Barratt houses and were certainly something extraordinary for their time."

Trevivian would have been the envy of those living across the Cwm in the grossly overcrowded Irish quarter of Greenhill, with its 'beggars' hotels', its chaotic hovels with mud floors, its unpaved and unlighted streets awash with human filth, and its frightening diseases.

"Anyone who doubts the Vivian family should take a walk around the streets of Trevivian – all of three cars wide – on a sunny day. I'm interested in exploring the idea of the clouds that were left by the industry, the ones that still cloud our views and our understanding of the place."

We pause at the northern end of the 600-metres long Aberdyberthi Street, the Hafod's backbone, to consider the Great Tip. Until its removal in 1973, to clear a site for Pentrehafod Comprehensive School (1976), this mountain of clinker and copper slag, rearing sixty metres high between the northern end of the township and the 'Swansea loop' railway link, was considered the biggest slag tip in Wales. In the 1930s – before the construction of Pentre-Mawr Road which would act as a barrier against the southern sprawl of the tip – it even lapped against the houses at the top of Aberdyberthi Street and slumped into the road. Some of it was removed during the war, as hardcore for the aerodrome that was constructed, in some desperation, on Fairwood Common, and much of it, later, was used to fill the ravine of Nant Rhyd-y-Filais at Landore.

The tip looms large in many of the Lowry-like paintings of the self-taught local artist Jack Jones (1922-93) who liked to describe himself as "the Leonardo of the slag heap", and it haunts the imagination of many older Hafod people, as both the backdrop to their lives and, in childhood, a spectacular playground. It was a hiding place and look-out; somewhere to sneak off to for a quiet fag; fires could be lit from the old timber supports of the cable system that once carried the waste up from the works; there were valleys, caves, cliffs, tunnels, battlegrounds galore; there was a polluted marsh as suctorious as quicksand. "It was to us children of the iron and copper works, railways and docks as was mother Earth to the heroes of legend," writes Haydn Williams in his Hafod memoir *Angels in Hobnail Boots*. "The Great Tip was the centre of the universe. It was an all-embracing, vibrant living entity, which had a soul and personality of its own. It held the same primitive magic as did the sun for Neolithic man."

We turn left at the top of Vivian Street into Odo Street, named after Odo Richard Vivian (1875-1934) who became the third Lord Swansea. Laid out in 1879-80, and the final stage in the development of the township, its most important feature is the Hafod Copperworks Infants School (1847), later a clothing factory and now a somewhat run-down community centre. By 1893, a remarkable 1,114 children were on the school's roll. An inspector's report of 1859 declared the Vivians' three Hafod schools to be "at the head of the list of the best schools in Wales". They did much to foster a strong sense of community, but they were a disaster for the Welsh language: the Vivians employed teachers from London in their schools, so that within three generations a largely monoglot Welsh-speaking community had been converted into a largely monoglot English-speaking community.

As we chat to Eddie Maddocks, an old workmate of Felicity's father's who lives in the schoolhouse next door, a couple of bareback urban cow-youths in reversed baseball caps clop by on bedraggled ponies, with an arrangement of ropes standing in for bridle and bit – as traditional a feature of the Swansea working-class scene as these two-up, two-down symmetrical terraces.

Although Anglicans themselves, the Vivians established non-sectarian schools and they encouraged their workers to found their own Nonconformist chapels.[32] They nevertheless provided the community with a neo-Gothic Anglican church, St John's (1880), near the southern end of Odo Street, which seems to compete for grandeur with the Roman Catholic cathedral of St Joseph's (1888)[33] across the Cwm. Too large for its congregation, it was an incomplete, scaled-down and simplified version of St Mary's, Truro, the Vivian family's traditional burial place. The half finished parapet on the south side shows clearly where the money ran out. The church's somewhat beleaguered state today is emphasised by the great slabs of Perspex which have been mounted to protect its Perpendicular-style windows from missiles.

If Christianity is on the wane here as elsewhere, the same cannot be said of Islam. The Hafod's growing Asian population, who used 1 Odo Street for weekly prayer meetings, were given permission in 2009 to convert the long disused Brotherhood Hall at the other end of Odo Street into an Islamic community centre.

Although it's the school holidays, the streets are strangely quiet this morning. The Hafod's shops are concentrated these days on Neath Road, but Felicity recalls when all manner of shops could be found among the terraces, sometimes in people's front rooms. Many a sandstone wall is ghostly with the outlines of doors or shop windows that were filled in after a baker's or a grocer's or a pawnbroker's closed.

We turn into Gerald Street – named after Gerald Vivian (1869-1921), the son of JHV's third son, Arthur Pendarves Vivian (1834-1926). Felicity lived at number 46 until the family moved to Dunvant in 1964. "The best part of living in the Hafod," she says, "is that you'd go out of your door and there would be a street full of children. Where are the children today? Indoors with their computers and televisions. My tiny world was between the inside door and the front door, especially when it was raining. We'd play tea parties or dolls there. If it was dry, we'd spill out onto the pavement. You could play safely outside for the whole day because everyone knew who you were. As the sun went over the top of the houses opposite it would get cold and you'd know it was time to go home for tea." She and her friends would confine themselves to certain areas of the street. It would be inconceivable that they'd venture as far afield as Odo Street or Aberdyberthi Street, both of them mere yards away.

The curious name 'Aberdyberthi' has mystified many. The street is named after Aberdyberthi House which stands in pebbledashed detachment on the corner of Aberdyberthi and Morgan Streets. Built in the 1820s for the Hafod Copperworks general manager, it takes its name from Aberdyberthi Farm which once occupied the east bank of the Bwrlais Brook (now culverted beneath Cwm Bwrlais). The name is believed to be composed of *aber*, which can mean a 'joining of waters', and *dybarthu*, signifying the 'point of separation' between the Bwrlais Brook and the leet that flowed from the brook into Greenhill Mill.

Jack Jones – Felicity's father's second cousin – was born into a loving but poverty-stricken household immediately opposite that managerial villa,[34] at a time when seven out of ten men in the Hafod were unemployed. "The poverty should have broken our hearts but in most cases it didn't," he wrote in a three-part series in the *Evening Post*.[35] "We supported each other and were very kind to each other. There was a keen sense of neighbourliness and loyalty. The Hafod, though poor, was regarded as respectable."

The 'illegitimate' son of a married man from Bridgend, Jack and his half-brother Mervyn Matthews were brought up by their mother and grandmother, although – strangely and pointedly – he makes no direct mention of his mother in those articles. It's his beloved grandmother who is idolised as "my mother, my father, and

my guardian angel". Mervyn, who was ten years younger than Jack, grew up believing Jack was his uncle, and it was only as he left for university that he was informed by Jack that he was in fact his brother. In his memoir *Mervyn's Lot*, Mervyn registers the first apparent glimmer of Jack's artistic light. One day in 1947, the two brothers were sent to tar the coalhouse, but Jack proved hopeless at the task, applying the tar in tiny dabs like a French Impressionist. Although he'd had no training and "couldn't draw for love nor money," writes Mervyn, "for some inexplicable reason my Uncle was beginning to take an interest in art."

Jack's untutored, 'naive' paintings reduce his Hafod scenes to sentimental, basic elements: the louring tip, the viaduct with toy-town trains, the Lego-like terraces with their matchstick people. But they had sufficient appeal for him to retire from teaching in London in the mid 1970s and to make a triumphal return to the Hafod – with his French wife Huguette and their son Sean – as a full-time painter. This was when I first encountered Jack: a stocky, neatly bearded man with a ready sense of jollity, invariably sporting a sailor's cap. We'd often meet at openings at the Arts Workshop in Gloucester Place, before repairing to the Queen's Hotel across the road, where he'd relish his pint as keenly as the thought that not only had he returned to Aberdyberthi Street after all these years, he'd actually bought and was now inhabiting the manager's house.

"I have to pinch myself sometimes," I remember him saying

when he invited me back to Aberdyberthi House for a prolonged nightcap. Sitting comfortably in the biggest house in the Hafod, drinking a decent red wine and surrounded by his own paintings and those of famous artist friends such as Kyffin Williams, Jack could hardly believe his good fortune.

But family life was difficult and drink eventually took its toll. After a spell of homelessness, Jack was rescued eventually by Alcoholics Anonymous and Roman Catholicism, and he was able to return to painting during his last seven years.

Pebbledash has been applied to many of the terraces in the renewal area. It's not to everyone's taste. Here and there, you'll find an individualistic bucker of the trend, as in lower Aberdyberthi Street, where – a dozen or so doors along from Jack's former home – there's a proudly white house with bright blue quoins. The biggest exception to the Hafod's regularizing but generally pleasing aesthetic is on Neath Road: the utilitarian pile of the Hafod Renewal Area Office itself. Bureaucracy personified in ugly brick.

notes

1. The others are Middleton Park, Carmarthenshire, now the National Botanic Garden of Wales; Aberglasney, Carmarthenshire, now restored and attracting thousands of visitors; and Hafod, Cardiganshire, currently under the sensitive management of the Hafod Trust in partnership with the Forestry Commission.

2. The adjacent community of Lower Cors Einon eventually dropped the 'Lower' and became simply Gorseinon.

3. St David's Well and the Well of the Thousand Innocents.

4. Goronwy Powell in the *Western Mail*, 5.6.52

5. By mid 2012, when the celebrity artist Rolf Harris visited Mynydd-bâch while making a documentary on Evan Walters, there were hopes that a recently launched restoration project might reverse the chapel's decline.

6. The colliery closed in 1903.

7. Home patch.

8. The others are at Bronllys, Breconshire and Henllys, Denbighshire.

9. "Llangyfelach's a strange place / Easy enough to recognise: / The church in one place, and the belfry in another. / When did this quarrel take place?" Another version of the final line is, "Pa bryd gwan rhai'n gyfarfod?" ("When will the two meet?")

10. "Farewell to gay Llangyfelach".

11. "a pretty young girl / Who prays night and day / For her dear beloved to be set free."

12. A mabsant festival was a celebration associated with the feast day of the patron saint of a parish church.

13. Swansea City Council employs about 12,000 people.

14. There's a specially constructed chamber for bomb squad personnel to examine suspect packages.

15. Jan Morris and Aerofilms, *Wales from the Air/Cymru o'r Awyr*, Ted Smart Publications, 1993.

16. Benjamin Franklin, 1789.

17. There are approximately 2,100 cremations a year at Morriston. In the (less mortal) summer, there may be on average four to six cremations a day.

18. Spiv, also a notably inventive music columnist for the *Evening Post*, later ran the Tenby in Walters Road.

19. Swansea's main maternity provision moved to Singleton Hospital.

20. Often referred to as a town, Morriston was never granted a town charter.

21. Also known as the Forest bridge.

22. The Pontypridd bridge has three cylinders per spandrel.

23. Known originally as New Libanus.

24. Sketty Park was demolished in 1975.

25. Len Allchurch (1933) was a member of the 1958 Welsh World Cup squad and brother of the even more legendary Swansea footballer Ivor Allchurch (1929-97).

26. 'SI' stands for Servizi Industriali. The company, established in 1988, specialises in separation of liquids technology.

27. The American poet Theodore Roethke (1908-63).

28. The poems are published in Vernon Watkins's *Poems for Dylan* (Gomer Press, 2003).

29. A 'hafod', meaning 'summer dwelling', was where, traditionally, cattle were grazed during the summer months, usually on upland pastures, as opposed to the permanent 'hendre' (old dwelling) on lower ground.

30. From Anon's 60-line poem 'On Havod, Near Swansea' in James A. Davies's *A Swansea Anthology*.

31. Amalgamating in 1924, the new company became British Copper Manufacturers. After various changes of owner and name, it ended as Yorkshire Imperial Metals. The works' closure in 1980 brought to an end Swansea's 250-year engagement with copper.

32. Some chapels established by the earlier coal-mining community of Pentre-estyll predated Trevivian. Although *estyll* means 'planks', here it implies strips of land.

33. St Joseph's was made a cathedral in 1987.

34. According to Jack, it was number 54 Aberdyberthi Street; according to his half-brother Mervyn Matthews, in *Mervyn's Lot*, it was number 64.

35. October 7, 14 and 21, 1992.

WEST

SINGLETON PARK

as we breathe out,
scurrying through the park,
the trees breathe in

If there are five defining properties of a city park – tall, mature trees;
the apparent randomness of their planting; undulating terrain; the
impossibility of seeing all boundaries at once; gated entrances –
then Singleton, with its magnificent botanic gardens, amply quali-
fies as a classic urban park.

As the thrustful city restlessly reinvents itself, this 80-hectare
oasis, slung serenely between Sketty and Brynmill, has changed so
little that any stroller from before the Second World War would
surely find the place pleasingly familiar. These rolling acres tilted
gently towards the sea on an underlay of glacial boulder clay were
first consolidated as an estate in the early fourteenth century by
Robertus de Sengeltone who came from Sussex;[1] and Singleton was
the name chosen by the copper magnate John Henry Vivian (1785-
1855), whose family came from Cornwall, for the 'Abbey' he built
in its south-eastern corner (1837) and for the estate that he assidu-
ously reconsolidated from about fifteen small farms and various
cottages that dotted the landscape.

behind the dog man
a-swagger with leash –
a damp chihuahua

If Singleton today, with the eight bells of the Vivian-built church of St Paul's, Sketty pealing out over its greensward, exudes an essentially English if not Anglican air – especially during bell-practice on Tuesday evenings – for centuries almost all the farms and their fields had Welsh names. The Abbey itself was built on the site of Tir y Powell farm. Two neighbouring farms in the north of the park were Gwerneinon and Gwerniddiff. Singleton Hospital's southern car park was the site of Tŷ Gwyn farm, with the hospital itself occupying the site of Tŷ Sirie farm; the western car park was Bryn Miskil farm, its Cae Skibor ('barn field', from 'ysgubor') behind the fire station serving today as Bishop Gore School's playing fields. Only the odd fragment of the fields' outlines remains – the hint of a bank, a hedgerow grown into a line of trees – but the park, for me, is haunted by those old field names: Cae Bach, Cae y'rth Tŷ, Coedcae, Gwaun dan y Berllan, Cae Tŷ Gwrdd, Cae Corner, Cae Pwlla, Cae Newidd, Cae Baker, Cae Kennol, Cae Mawr, Coed Cae, Cae Carn, Cae Bach, Cae Furndu, Cae Issa.[2]

The boundaries of Vivian's estate are still plain to see, particularly the sinuous eastern wall running almost unbroken the entire 900-metre length of Brynmill Lane. Built in the late 1830s of a mixture of glacial boulders and quarry stones, and topped with half-moon blocks of black copper slag from Vivian's Hafod copper works, it was significantly heightened in the 1890s when the terraces of neighbouring Brynmill were being developed – and when the Vivian family evidently took steps to keep the encroaching riff-raff at bay. Set in the newer, upper part of the wall, about 140 metres north of the neo-Gothic Brynmill (or Singleton Park) Lodge, is a crudely inscribed stone (final digit missing) recording the date of elevation as '189()'.

Vivian's interest in agriculture was more serious than that of the typical dilettante gentleman farmer who makes his serious money elsewhere – as a visit to his Home Farm proves. Without copper, of course, there'd be no Abbey, no park, indeed no Swansea as we know it. The Home Farm he built between the late 1830s and the early 1850s, in what is now the south-west corner of the park, shows that in spite of his enthusiasm for *recherché* Tudor design he was driven by an industrialist's ardour to apply scientific principles to

the business of farming.

Used these days as the park's depot and offices, the Home Farm is not, strictly speaking, open to the public, but I have found that anyone showing an interest in the place is made welcome. Built where the de Sengeltones anciently established themselves, it's a spacious and attractive farmstead, comprising three barns, a dovecote, outhouses, cowsheds, animal pens, and – greeting you as you walk up the drive – clear, cold water streaming from a spring sheltered by a capricious stone archway inscribed with JHV's initials. The farmhouse itself incorporates some windows and dressed stone from the 500-year-old Plas Newydd (New Place), the ramshackle mansion that dominated what is now Castle Square until its purchase and demolition by JHV in 1840.

The park workers based at Home Farm are proud of the place, in spite of the overgrown and dilapidated state of some of the buildings. Chatting to a small group of them on a recent visit, it's clear that they welcome long-overdue measures being taken to conserve and celebrate the historic industrial sites of the Lower Swansea Valley, but they regret the continuing neglect of Home Farm. "This place too is part of Swansea's copper heritage, but the people of Swansea know nothing about it," says one of them. "The Vivians' experiments in farming were way ahead of their time. Using spring water to cool the milk, this was the first farm in the world to sell TB-free milk."[3]

Evidence of JHV's innovative approach to agriculture includes tramlines coursing across the yard from the cowshed, for transporting dung. My guide steers me through the cowshed – where the father of renowned Antarctic explorer Edgar Evans (1876-1912) once milked the cows – to the bull pens and workers' cottages which he and his mates, in breaks between jobs, have recently rescued from an impenetrable thicket of brambly vegetation. I've never seen bulls accommodated as palatially as this, with curvaceous 'Gothic' slag blocks topping the stall dividers, and wall-end trimmings of glistening granite. We pass beneath a granite archway to inspect the (far from palatial) workers' cottages with their tiny walled gardens, all gloomily overshadowed by a louring perimeter wall. "There's huge potential in this place," says my guide. "If it was properly restored it could be like St Fagans."

> off-duty nurse,
> mobile-rapt, smiling smugly
> through the park

It was in 1920 that the Council bought the Singleton estate for £100,000, ceding land on its southern rim to the university and, in the 1950s, to the hospital. Although open at all times these days, the park was open to the public, initially, only on Thursdays, Saturdays and Sundays, and the Home Farm continued in agricultural use until 1957. Local historian Bernard Morris, who died aged 79 in 2012, was one of many who remembered "cattle and sheep grazing in the western part of Singleton, and sheep being sometimes driven on the hoof through the streets of Sketty to enjoy a change of grass in Cockett Park, just over a mile away."

The park is dotted with souvenirs of various uses over the decades.

> half a dog-turd
> bejewelled by a feasting
> blowfly

A red-brick shed about 100 metres in from the Park Place entrance takes us back to the Second World War when American troops, with their guns and tanks, camped in the park prior to the Normandy landings. The shed itself is the last of a row of public shelters and welfare huts built for people evacuating the streets of Brynmill. Dug-outs were originally intended as shelters, but the park was so wet that some trial holes filled with water. After heavy rain, the southern reaches of the park can become an almost impassable delta, and a flash flood will turn the Vivian Stream[4] into a boiling torrent overtopping the footbridge at the Park Place entrance – over

which, on calmer days, students stream by the hundred for their nine o'clock lectures. Here, incidentally, we find a classic example of a 'desire line': rather than walking past that shed and along two paved sides of a triangle, the students would cut directly across the grass to the university's eastern gate, wearing a (frequently muddy) path which eventually attained 'official' status when the authorities decided to pave, light and drain it (although it still floods).

> the 'good morning' walker
>> greeting only
> women

One of the park's more puzzling items is a metal water wheel, about 100 metres south of the Gower Road entrance. What was it for? Where's the water? When the Vivian Stream was the Cockett Stream and before it was culverted through much of the park, Henry Hussey Vivian (1821-1894), owner of Parc Wern, the neo-Gothic pile on the north-eastern side of Brynmill Lane,[5] wanted an improved water supply. So, in the late 1850s, he diverted the stream and set up a wheel, with U-shaped buckets, to raise water to a tank at the top of his mansion. This system, if it worked, seems to have been abandoned by the late 1870s. The original, rusting wheel was replaced in the 1980s by a notably dissimilar version.

The gorsedd circle nearby is a reminder of Swansea's associations with the National Eisteddfod. Since the twelve perimeter stones and the central logan stone were set in place in 1925, the proclamation and induction ceremonies of Swansea-based National Eisteddfodau have been staged here, and on three occasions – 1907, 1964 and 1982 – the Eisteddfod itself was held in the park. I recall an unholy fuss in 1982 when the Eisteddfod's then 'no alcohol' rule[6] was deemed to have been violated by a Breton stall-holder who was caught drizzling his *crêpes* with Grand Marnier.

Many were disappointed that the 2006 Swansea Eisteddfod – *Eisteddfod y Pafiliwn Pinc*, when the festival's by now familiar pink pavilion was first unleashed on the world – was held not at Singleton but on the cindery site of the Felindre tinplate works (1956-1989),[7] alongside the M4. But the park is in such demand these days – for rock and classical concerts, fêtes and flower shows, horse and motor shows, battle re-enactments and sporting events – that the Council doubtless feels that it can no longer afford to allow the Eisteddfod to hog the park for the many weeks it needs both to set up camp and then to tear it all down.

> round and round
> the logan stone – a whirling
> gorsedd of leaves

Some of the park's souvenirs remain well hidden. Whenever there's a rock concert in that perfect grassy amphitheatre that sweeps down towards the sea, the police, getting itchy about illegal substances, often conduct spot searches as music lovers enter the leafy arena. Canny dope smokers and pill poppers, growing wise to the ways of PC Plod, tend to bury their drugs in the park a day or two before the concert, and then dig them up – after passing, searched and clean, through the police cordon – if they can remember where they stashed them. I should think a purposeful couple of hours with a trowel among the roots of the magnificent beaches in the western reaches of the park would unearth some interesting finds.

> no dog in sight ...
> but this man, for sure, is out
> walking some hound

THE SWISS COTTAGE

Tucked away in the depths of Singleton Park is Swansea's most exotic building, the much-loved Swiss Cottage, which was badly damaged by fire in 2010.

It's often thought that this playful timber structure, with its fretted woodwork and overhanging eaves and gables, is an import from Switzerland or a copy of the famous Swiss Cottage that gave its name to a district of London (and, indeed, to the practice of 'cottaging'). But it was designed by Peter Frederick Robinson (1776-1858), the London-based architect of Singleton Abbey (and various other buildings around the estate), and built for the Vivians in 1826, as testified by the date painted beneath the front gable. This makes it years older than the London Swiss Cottage (also designed by Robinson), which dates only from the 1840s; it's probably the oldest Swiss cottage in Britain.

By 1827, its first occupant had moved in: the clerk of works engaged on the creation of Singleton Abbey. Soon afterwards, JHV's wife Sarah established a dame school there for 25 boys and girls to receive "individual instruction from an excellent matron in reading, writing and arithmetic, with knitting for the boys and both knitting and sewing for the girls". Subsequently, it was a home for park staff, although it was unoccupied at the time of the fire, and had become a magnet for vandals. (Indeed, the park in recent years has become something of an arsonists' corner: among other buildings destroyed by fire, in 2012, was the refreshments kiosk next door to the cottage.)

The Swiss Cottage's walls bear two thought-provoking inscriptions in German, translated for me by Ruth Jenkins. On the east side:

> We build here solidly
> yet are still alien guests
> and where we are forever
> there we do not build

And on the west side:

> Live [in such a way] that you would like to live again.

Within days of the fire, a 'Save the Swiss Cottage' Facebook campaign was started, in hope that the cottage itself might indeed 'live again'.

SKETTY LANE

Although its name suggests a bucolic byway, Sketty Lane, linking the A4118 Gower Road with the A4067 Mumbles Road, is anything but. While the northern approach – as you turn from Gower Road into Sketty Park Road – may be full of Mediterranean or Swiss lakeland promise, with pine trees framing a crescent of sun-misted water fringed by Mumbles Hill and Exmoor beyond, by the time you've reached this busy dual carriageway its charms are likely to be wearing thin. Yet for many Swansea people, these 800 metres of bustling tarmac have been a boulevard of profound if mixed emotions, thanks to the presence here of the 550-bed Singleton Hospital. Like thousands of others, I've travelled down Sketty Lane joyous after the birth of a child, or speechless after the death of a parent, or relieved after a diagnosis that could have been worse.

Traffic hurtles along it in a more or less straight, no-nonsense line. But until about 1828 – when it was re-routed by John Henry Vivian well away from the environs of the swanky Tudor Gothic pile he was building as Singleton Abbey – it was indeed a deep and circuitous country lane, notorious for wet and muddy conditions, known as Heol y ffessyr. In *The Houses of Singleton*, Bernard Morris describes its route from Sketty Green. According to Bernard, it ran along the line of one of the tarmac paths just inside the western boundary of what remains a somewhat boggy region of Singleton Park. (Note here, where the park meets the road, the remains of an underpass built by Vivian for cattle and sheep to cross to pasture on the other side.) It seems to me, though, that a likelier route would have been slightly to the east of that path, between a still extant alleyway of trees, suggestive of the banks of a lane, and incorporating for some its length a stream. It then took a sharp bend east near the present hospital boiler room (with its tall chimney stack), then another to the south, running a little to the east of the footpath between the hospital and the university, joining the newly constructed Mumbles Road near the entrance to the boating lake.

The modern thoroughfare is topped and tailed by two buildings closely associated with the Sketty industrialists who settled in and

around Singleton Park: the much modified and dazzling white Georgian mansion of Sketty Hall, which began as New Hall in the 1720s, and, at the junction with Mumbles Road, a single-storey lodge known as Tŷ Harry, built around 1830 to house estate workers.

Notable occupants of Sketty Hall have included the butcher and cattle dealer William 'Butcher' Jenkins, the Cambrian Pottery proprietor Lewis Weston Dillwyn (1778-1855), the industrialist and politician Frank Ash Yeo, and – perhaps the most appealing of them all – the supposed black sheep of the Vivian copper dynasty, Richard Glynn Vivian (1835-1910), who loved art and travel more than industry and commerce, and gave Swansea the Glynn Vivian Art Gallery (1911). The upright worthies of his family tend to be memorialised in aloof statues and stiff formal portraits, whereas the bushy-bearded fourth and youngest son is caught in delightfully unbuttoned mode in a photograph of him clutching a pug-like dog and wearing an eye shade surmounted by a Panama hat. When he bought Sketty Hall in 1898, he found it "stiff and dull and prim"

and proceeded to animate it with all manner of grace notes, including a gazebo tower, still in place on the roof, and an Italianate garden stuffed with statues and pedestals imported from a demolished church in Genoa – which make a popular backdrop these days for wedding photographs. Having put the finishing touches to both house and garden, he signed off the work with an ornamental plaque above the main entrance porch, which reads (with the aid of binoculars):

RICHARD GLYNN VIVIAN
DECORAVIT
1902

But in that same year, this connoisseur of art, who had derived the greatest pleasure in life from the use of his eyes, was stricken suddenly with blindness. It's sad too that although he'd laid the foundation stone, in 1909, of the magnificent gallery that bears his name (the biggest in Wales) he died before its completion.

In the late 1930s, Sketty Hall was sold for £20,000 to Swansea Corporation who used it as an Air Raid Precautions h.q. during the Second World War, and built Bishop Gore School on part of its grounds. After the war, my grandfather, the industrialist Captain H.

Leighton Davies, was chiefly responsible for establishing at Sketty Hall a British Iron and Steel Research Association centre concerned mainly with developing coatings for tinplate. They built a huge laboratory workshop to the west of the house, which was subsequently demolished, prior to Swansea College's (now Gower College Swansea) handsome renovation of Sketty Hall in 1993 as a conference centre and catering school. It's renowned for its weddings, banquets, Sunday lunches and themed evenings (St David's Day, James Bond, Medieval, Italian, Murder Mystery, Latin American, Rat Pack, Jazz).

One of the many curios Richard Glynn Vivian imported from foreign parts was a set of gates, between whose pillars the visitor still passes. The left-hand pillar bears the intriguing inscription:

Old Gates.
From a Convent in France
1904.
After Nuns and Monks were Expelled

As to why those monks and nuns were expelled from what sounds like a veritable Eden, history appears to have drawn a veil.

Tŷ Harry, wedged between the boating lake and Mumbles Road, was originally paired with Tŷ Graham on the opposite side of the lane. The lodges – in Sketty industrialists' Gothic style (for the Vivians were in love with the middle ages) – were named after the two eldest Vivian boys, Henry (Harry) Hussey and William Graham.[8] Tŷ Graham, its site lying now beneath the widened roadmouth, seems also to have been known as Gors(e) Fawr Cottage (probably from cors, bog): even today, after heavy rain the neighbouring playing fields can turn swiftly into a series of irregular lakes, bobbing with seagulls. No doubt ancestors of those gulls relished pickings from the rubbish tip that once sprawled over the playing fields, its encroachment forcing the abandonment of Tŷ Graham in the 1930s. Tŷ Harry too, since the 1980s, has stood empty for much of the time.

Much of the west side of Sketty Lane is given over to sport: the Bishop Gore playing fields at the top of the lane, on what used to be Bryn Miskil farm, and, down on the flat, the university playing fields, overlooked by the university's sports village, with its august pavilion (1932) designed by Glendinning Moxham, and the architecturally underwhelming, Olympic-standard Wales National Pool (2003).

"You could say that the WNP has a vanishing aesthetic," muses my friend the novelist Stevie Davies, who swims there regularly. "The impression is of light on the pool – radiance – it makes way for the light, once you are inside. Outside it is nothing."

Sport of a distinctly unofficial kind – Gypsy horse racing – was pursued hereabouts, into the early twentieth century, by the Romanies who camped at Gypsy Green on the western edge of what are now the King George V playing fields (1951). These betting races, along selected lengths of Mumbles Road, would often draw a crowd, although they were held at times calculated to avoid the attentions of the law, such as the early hours of the morning.

The ten-storey hospital, with its sprawling ancillary buildings and huge car parks, dominates Sketty Lane. Most of it was built in a sort of Soviet utilitarian style in the 1960s, but it's still being added to: at the time of writing, the architecturally adventurous Maggie's Cancer Care Centre was under construction a few metres away from where the long-forgotten Heol y ffessyr once passed.

It was cancer that killed my father. When the call came to my workplace in Leamington Spa, I left for Singleton Hospital straight away, passing on to a friend my ticket for that night's Led Zeppelin gig. By the time I reached his bedside, high above Swansea Bay, Dad was barely conscious, informing me politely that he was "Very well, thank you." The world that long December night, as I held his cold hand or swabbed the strange white mould that furred his brow, shrank to an inconsequential blur: the orange street-lamps fringeing the bay, the futile car headlights and irrelevant stars, and beer, poetry, Led Zeppelin and all. Nothing mattered, nothing surely could matter, beyond the racked stertor being endured in that towering box of lights at the sea's edge.

A father is hurried in through the hospital doors; and out through them later wanders a son, clutching a brown paper bag of owner-less belongings. Exits and entrances. Sketty Lane.

BLACKPILL

It's at Blackpill, where there are virtually no sea defences, that sooner or later the islanding of peninsular Gower is likely to start, with a steadily rising Severn Sea pushing its way up the Clyne Valley until it meets with saltwater flooding in, via Gowerton, from the Llwchwr estuary. Swansea – or what might be left of it – would

then have its own mini Menai Strait, with the wooded slopes of Ynys Gŵyr reaching down to the waterside on the opposite bank.

Blackpill (or Blakepulle, according to a charter of *c.*1170) is a translation of the Welsh name for the Clyne stream – up which that inundation will one day flow – that gives the village its name: Dulais, composed of '*du*' (black) and *(g)lais* (stream) – 'pill' being a common word for 'stream' in Gower, as in other parts of south Wales. The so-called Roman bridge over that stream – lately rendered invisible from the highway by the clueless building there of a high, stone parapet – might propose the existence of a Latin name for the village, but the bridge has nothing to do with the Romans, having been built in about 1750.

Apart from the relentlessly busy Mumbles Road (which propels some 36,000 vehicles a day through Blackpill), the scene today seems tranquil: two men fishing with a drag net at the mouth of the river; beach artists making transient sculptures out of sand, driftwood, feathers, shells; young families splashing about at the lido; others sauntering through Clyne Gardens and the Clyne Valley Country Park, which flank the village on either side. But Blackpill was once a centre of industry, with coal being shipped from the sands and, later, from a quay on the foreshore that has since disappeared. The area could have developed like a small-scale Lower

Swansea Valley, had a consortium of industrialists pursued a plan to build furnaces on the banks of the pill; but the project fell through and the local coal mines were worked out by the 1920s, by which time Blackpill had settled into the role of country estate village.

The hub of the estate was Clyne Castle, hidden among the trees about half a kilometre up Mill Lane. Woodlands was the house's original name; then, after rebuilding in 1819, it became Woodlands Castle – nineteenth-century landowners, with their pseudo 'castles' and 'abbeys', taking pains to establish that "the upper classes still held the upper hand". It turned into Clyne Castle when the property was bought by Graham Vivian – of the local coppermaster dynasty. He was responsible – without benefit of architect – not only for refashioning much of it but for designing and building many of the estate's lodges, cottages in Blackpill and the Clyne Chapel (1907) on Mayals Road. It was in the hands of its next owner – Algernon Walker Heneage (1871-1952), who inherited it from his uncle Graham on condition he add 'Vivian' to his name – that the 21-ha estate came to full florescence (he also inherited the Parc-le-Breos estate at Parkmill). Rear Admiral Walker-Heneage-Vivian, as he became after a distinguished wartime career, managed the estate for 31 years, employing a cohort of staff that was out of all proportion to Clyne's relatively modest size: a butler, a governess, pantry boys, cooks, kitchen maids, scullery maids, laundry maids, a dozen housemaids, footmen, two chauffeurs for his three Daimlers, a groom, a carpenter and two assistants, two plumbers, an estate agent, a head-gardener, twelve gardeners, a head keeper, two under-keepers – about fifty workers in all, who lived chiefly in estate cottages or in the terraced housing in the village.

His twin obsessions were shooting pheasants and growing rhododendrons. According to one of his three daughters, Rhoda Campbell, in her book *Water Under the Bridge*, he wasn't much of a father. Disappointed not to have had sons, he seems to have gone out of his way to avoid contact with the girls; they were left nothing in his will but a few hundred pounds each, Uncle Graham having decreed that Clyne must never go to a female descendant. The book is a vivid account of Clyne in its heyday, its sad moments leavened by much humour – such as an account of a voyage to South America in 1933, when, one evening, the children burst into the stateroom their father was sharing with their brassy new stepmother, and could make no sense of the sight that greeted their eyes: "What was going on? Beryl we could hardly see in her bunk as she was squashed underneath my father who was clad in a pyjama top with naked bottom thumping up and down on top of her. We burst into peals of laughter … then someone told us we should not be there at all so we turned and ran!"

The Admiral was the subject of a striking portrait by the Swansea painter Evan Walters. I wrote a poem about it.

Rear Admiral Walker-Heneage-Vivian

It comes down, the eye comes down
past ribbons, medals, tassels, stars
and almighty sleeves
to those fingerly bones
and that democratic cigarette –
and then returns
to the eyes at blue sea and the wreckage
of a smile.

The master, Walters, of *HMS Powerful*
has not got all day: there are

pheasants to be shot, communists to quell,
daughters to be avoided, and, above all,
rhododendrons to raise.

If a fag ain't the sum
of the Admiral's joys,
he will draw small delight
from this dauber's lurid dabs
as imperium's peacock cries its last,

though they're the best, if not all,
that will one day remain.

Towards the end of the Admiral's life, Clyne's upkeep was costing £50,000 a year, and the estate had to be sold eventually to pay off death duties. The Corporation bought the castle, intending it as a judges' lodging or replacement Mansion House (the mayor's official residence in Ffynone). Neither plan was pursued, and the university bought it, in 1953, for £17,500. With two new accommodation blocks built in the grounds, Neuadd Gilbertson and Neuadd Martin, Clyne Castle now exerted a more student-focused influence on Blackpill. For the best part of half a century, there'd be the (not too) early morning exodus from Mill Lane of scores of students heading towards the campus, by foot or bicycle, along the broad pavement of Mumbles Road. They provided the Woodman pub with its core clientele, and their presence no doubt contributed to the success of the village's Clyne Cellar Club which 1960s Swansea youth thought of as their equivalent of Liverpool's Cavern.

When the students went home for the long summer break, the castle would come into its own as a conference and holiday centre. Among holidaymakers to have used Clyne as their base – where they always brought their own cooking utensils, to prepare food according to their faith's strict codes – have been some fifty families of Hassidic Jews from London and Manchester. In their black and white formal clothing, and with their beards, skull caps and broad-brimmed hats, they are an exotic addition to the summer scene. Since the university sold Clyne to a developer, they have had to find alternative accommodation, at Swansea Metropolitan University's Townhill campus. In 2006, the property was converted into seventeen half million pound apartments. Swansea City striker Lee Trundle and his Atomic Kitten, Liz McClarnon, bought one in 2007.

As the name of the café at the lido – the Junction – suggests, Blackpill (earlier known as Bishopston Road) has long had a reputation for various kinds of traffic, motor vehicles today being the most noisily apparent. Road users passing this way once had to pay a toll, as testified until recently by the name Toll Gate House that was attached to the porch of one of the terraced houses opposite the Junction. Hauliers attempting to dodge the toll would take their horses and carts on a wide diversion across the beach, a manoeuvre that sometimes ended up with a rescue party digging them out of the mud. Then there were the truckloads of coal, limestone, bricks and other industrial fare passing through from Clyne and Mumbles, and, later, the LMS trains clanking over the now demolished railway bridge whose parapet boasted the legend, 'Mumbles Road Station / Quickest and shortest route to / Liverpool Manchester & the North'. The station buildings were also demolished, but the platforms are still to be seen, flanking the bike path that passes between them. The most striking piece of railway architecture here is surely unknown to almost everyone who passes over it as they walk, jog or pedal between the platforms: the tall, inverted U-shape of a tunnel – with walkway for horses or pedestrians – which takes the Clyne stream under the old station, just before the stream turns a bend to flow beneath the Roman bridge.

The Junction café itself is the largest surviving relic of the most famous of Swansea's wheeled conveyances, the Mumbles railway. As Richard Porch has remarked, "The classical symmetry of this humble little building [with its five round-headed windows] is a joy to look at …" Designed by borough architect Ernest Morgan, and built in 1927, it was more than simply the half-way halt between Swansea and Mumbles: as the railway's electricity substation, it housed two 500-kw rotary converters that switched 6,000 volts of alternating current into the 650 volts of direct current needed to power the railway's cars. If you look carefully at the brickwork on the north-east corner of this building, you'll see a dusting of sand-coloured camouflage paint left over from the Second World War.

Blackpill's most numerous creatures of passage are not the humans in their cars but the birds.

> we do not see
> til flight tilts them sunward –
> oystercatchers

They gather on the foreshore – oystercatchers, waders, gulls of all sorts – in their thousands, increasing in number as the rising tide forces birds off their mud-flat feeding grounds elsewhere and onto the accommodating foreshore at Blackpill, which has long been recognised as one of Wales's most important estuaries for birds. Then there are seasonal visitors such as dunlin, knot and sanderling, refuelling on their long journeys between their Arctic breeding grounds and their wintering bases in Africa. On one day in 1989, no fewer than 13,000 dunlin were counted here. There's often a bird watcher or two lurking in the bushes with binoculars and tripod, or in the lee of the Birdlife Centre, a brick-built hut beside the lido, revelling in the variety and richness of the birdlife of Blackpill (the poet R.S. Thomas (1913–2000), a keen ornithologist, would invariably pitch up here on visits to Swansea). And when a rare visitor flies in – such as the glaucous gull, or the Mediterranean gull or the ring-billed gull from America or an avocet – the twitchers will turn out in even larger numbers than the twitched.

> black Lab puppy
> dodging the waves; there's time, still,
> to outlive a dog

OYSTERMOUTH CEMETERY

What is it to be, when the fat lady has sung: worms or flames? Some people go through life with their minds made up, especially perhaps those who manage to live 'in a sure and certain hope' of some kind of resurrection. They might want their bones about them when at last the call to rapture comes. Having no such hope myself, and tending to regard both worms and flames as equally abysmal options, I am undecided. If it's to be flames, my final journey will doubtless be to Morriston crem. If worms, I could go 'home', as it were, and lie with my father and his people in Pennard churchyard, next door to what used to be the family farm. Or I could join certain other members of the family (along with one of the most hauntingly beautiful of Welsh women) in what for over thirty years has been my local cemetery, Oystermouth. It boasts, after all, one of the finest hill-top views in Swansea (not that there'd be the eyes to enjoy it), and in 2003 it inaugurated a woodland burial ground, for those with ecological inclinations – the first of its kind in south-west Wales. Worth a look. Time I made up my mind.

Unless you've attended a burial at Oystermouth, you're not likely to know of the existence of this magnificent Victorian necropolis, which covers in total about 12 hectares. Lost among trees above Underhill Park and set well back from Newton Road, its undemonstrative wrought-iron gates – ever open – draw you in to a leafy uphill lane. At its base is the supervisor's house and cemetery office – where this morning the supervisor, Waunarlwydd-born Andy Parsons, is waiting, in dark suit and black tie, to give me an insider's tour of his domain, with its (silent) population the size of Bridgend's.

The supervisor's house, Andy believes, is where the (long abandoned) Callencroft Quarry used to stable its horses. He's found the remains of a well beneath the floorboards, which would have slaked the horses' considerable thirsts. The cemetery's first gravediggers were probably Callencroft quarrymen, their expertise with dynamite proving particularly handy when it came to blasting away any limestone obstructions. Today's team of council employees comprises four diggers and a foreman, who are also involved in general upkeep duties and in tending Underhill Park. Andy himself was foreman for five years, but for the last ten he's been supervisor.

He loves his job, he says, as we wend our way up the sinuous, wooded lane towards the cemetery, the old quarry face dropping

sharply to our left. "It's good to be helping people and supporting them at a difficult time. And this is such a special place. It's wonderfully peaceful. Not morbid at all. It feels like a park feels. People come here to eat their sandwiches and just have a wander around. All the information on these old grave stones – the place is like a history book. And now that the local farms have been built over, it's increasingly important as a haven for wild life. We've got two badger sets, foxes, green woodpeckers that suddenly fly up in front of you."

At the top of the lane, beneath two massive cypress trees, there's the old chapel of rest, now converted into a private house, and, stretching before us, the shallow vale of the oldest part of the cemetery. With its grand boulevard of 26 pairs of yew trees – like dark, sculpted flames – sloping gradually away from us, then rising steeply at the far end, it's like a scene from *Last Year in Marienbad*. Mortality with style. The quintessential valley of the shadow of death.

The earliest grave here, that of Alfred Gasston, who died aged 23, in 1883, is a relatively modest presence, with its tall stone cross and rusting balustrades; an inscription on the footstone reads, 'THE FIRST INTERMENT IN THIS CEMETERY'. Many others, planted largely in the period leading up to 1930, are far swankier affairs, with no expense spared in the statements they seek to make about the status, wealth, piety and individuality of the deceased, with their vast slabs of imported stone, ornate statuary, vaunting obelisks and fulsome inscriptions. Competing to impress their fellow citizens, these self-regarding Victorians and Edwardians seem to have forgotten (camels, eyes of needles, anyone?) what the god they purported to worship had said about the impossibility of a rich man entering the kingdom of heaven.

> not crying
>   – this girl with hand to bowed head –
> but phoning

Beneath a sycamore in the north-west corner is the comparatively minimalist grave – with chilling epitaph – of the cemetery's most visited inhabitant, the composer, pianist and mezzo-soprano Morfydd Llwyn Owen (1891-1918). She's the haunting beauty referred to above.

"There's a steady stream of people coming to visit her grave," says Andy. "And at eisteddfod times they come by the busload."

Her tragically early death, at the age of 26, was a severe loss to Welsh music. In the ten years that she was active creatively – in Cardiff initially and then in London, where she studied at the Royal Academy of Music – she produced some 180 compositions, including chamber music, choral and orchestral works, hymn tunes, piano solos and songs, many of them drawing on Welsh literary and folk sources. She led something of a twin-track life in London, socializing with expatriate Welsh Presbyterians on the one hand, being herself a Christian, and, on the other, mixing in artistic circles with the likes of D.H. Lawrence and Ezra Pound. Her Presbyterian family and friends were aghast when, in 1917, Morfydd married Gowerton-born Dr. Ernest Jones (1879-1958), a pioneer of the new discipline of psychoanalysis, the leading champion in Britain of Freud's ideas – and an atheist. The couple managed little more than eighteen months together, before her death from delayed chloroform poisoning, following an emergency appendectomy at the house they were staying in on holiday, Craig-y-môr.[9] (It's next to the gated compound in Plunch Lane, Thistleboon, which a later beauty, Catherine Zeta-Jones, built for herself and her family). The elegant restraint of her memorial is doubtless attributable to Jones: a shallow trough, overflowing in spring with wild garlic and daffodils, headed by a slim shaft, of the same red sandstone as the trough, surmounted by a stylized Celtic cross. The inscription at the top of the shaft reads simply 'Morfydd Owen / wife of Ernest Jones' (no mention of her musical achievements), followed by three (unexplained) dates, which are those of her birth,[10] marriage and death. The inscription at the base, embodying a sobering truth which the funerary flamboyance of neighbouring tombs labours to deny, is from Goethe's *Faust*: 'Das Unbeschreibliche, hier ist's getan' ('Here, the indescribable is done') – an unflinching reminder of the inexorable demolition, six feet under, of an exceptional human form. Given the date of her burial, in the last desperate months of the First World War, Ernest Jones must have had quite a task finding a stonemason willing to carve an inscription in German, the language of Freud and the leading psychoanalysts.

There are few other graves in the immediate vicinity of Morfydd Llwyn Owen's, because the underlying rock is too close to the surface for a grave to be dug. A bigger grave-free expanse lies to the left of the entrance, where three venerable pines cast their shadows on uninterrupted grass. No sophisticated geological equipment is available to Andy and his team to gauge in advance where the bedrock might impede their operations: they proceed, with spade and bar, by trial and error. A bluff on the opposite, eastern side, where limestone breaks the surface among the graves, would seem an even more difficult place to dig a hole. But here, apparently, explosives were used by the old quarrymen gravediggers to blast out the odd tomb, including the imposing family vault of the tinplate magnate Henry Folland (1878-1926). One-armed Henry Folland, who was born in Waunarlwydd, started work as an office clerk and rose to be a director of the largest tinplate company in Europe. Because of ill health, he spent his winters in Egypt – where eventually he died. He returned from one of these Egyptian sojourns with a white Arabian stallion and a native to ride it; they became part of his household at Llwynderw, Blackpill. After Folland's death and the repatriation of his body, the Egyptian rider would take the stallion to the cemetery every evening, for both horse and rider to pay their solemn respects.

There are no problems with rock in the floor of the valley, where the soil, says Andy, is like butter: the spade almost glides through it. But such yielding soil is not without its dangers, particularly when you're digging a four-coffin, nine-foot grave. "These days," says Andy, "we use aluminium sides and hydraulic rams to shore up the grave, and there's a strict procedure to follow. But in the old days they'd have had to make do with planking. It must have been dodgy at times."

Mechanical diggers cannot be used in the old part of the cemetery: everything has to be done by hand. It takes three days to dig a fresh nine-foot grave, but only a day to dig a reopened one, because the earth has already been disturbed, even if that disturbance was decades ago. Most of the burials in the old part of the cemetery are re-openers. Here lie my great aunts Eira and Eluned, and my great uncle Meurig who, as something of a black sheep, spent most of his life in English exile but came home to be buried, as did later his sweet and kindly widow Mary. Most were lowered into deep graves, already containing various family members, with room still remaining for a relative or two more. Because the graves are so close together, a re-opener burial can be a challenge, not only for the gravediggers, who have to find somewhere temporary to lay heavy stone slabs and deposit large amounts of soil, but also for the undertakers and the mourners. It's often difficult for mourners to get near a reopened grave, and it may even be dangerous – not to mention undignified – when bearers have to clamber with a coffin around or over possibly rickety old tombs, especially if the body in the box is that of, say, a twenty-stone man.

The upkeep of the graves is the responsibility of the relatives of the deceased, and when graves need attention it's often impossible, with these older graves, to find anyone who'll take responsibility for them. This is less the case with the graves which were established, from 1930 onwards, on top of the hill.

The graves most visited here, a group of eight, are those of the crew of the Mumbles lifeboat who were killed in 1947 when they attempted to rescue the crew of the *S.S. Samtampa*, which had been blown by a hurricane onto rocks at Sker Point. All 39 members of the *Samptampa*'s crew also lost their lives.[11] (Six graves in the older part of the cemetery testify to an earlier disaster, in 1903, when the Mumbles lifeboat capsized off the entrance to Port Talbot harbour, and all but one of the crew perished.)

A short distance away lies the footballer Trevor Ford (1923-2003), one of the greatest goal scorers in Welsh soccer history. His infamous shoulder-charging of goalkeepers, legal in football at the time, was characteristic of the abrasive style that brought him 23 goals in 38 appearances for Wales, a record he held jointly with Swansea's Ivor Allchurch (1929-97) for many years.

Andy points out some other notable graves. Near the eastern boundary, there's the grave of Sgt. William Charles Fuller (1885-1974) who was awarded the Victoria Cross for conspicuous gallantry after he rescued a wounded officer, under heavy rifle and machinegun fire, during the retreat from Mons. Nearby, there's the grave of the now largely forgotten but once famous motorcyclist Jack Daniels (1916-48) who started out as a barber in Ben Evans's department store before going into the motorcycle business and winning the 1948 Senior Clubman's TT race on the Isle of Man. When he died in an accident at Fairwood, he was the closest Wales had come to producing a world-class motorcycle racer.

By now, we've reached the row of firs that bristle like a Mohawk across the crown of the hill, the breeze through their needles making low, mournful music.

> at home too
>   a buzzard's cry, the soughing of firs
> remind me of home

Before us lies that spectacular view of Swansea Bay, Mumbles and the pier – which every headstone on this gentle slope is positioned to face, like a blind eye. "When people see this view," says Andy, "they often decide that this is the place for them. Fine. But you can't buy a plot in advance, like in the old days. To be buried here, there's got to be a body or cremated remains. If we had a pre-purchasing policy, all the spaces here would have been snatched up ages ago."

Filling up from the west, this is the most 'active' part of the cemetery. One of the most recent graves here is that of the guitarist Micky Jones (1947-2010) of the Man band – whom Frank Zappa described as "one of the ten best guitarists in the world". The bare earth surrounding Micky's grave, which is covered in still-fresh wreaths and bouquets, has been liberally scattered with sand, in an attempt to tone down the mud churned up by the grave-digging machinery and the feet of mourners. It's as raw as grief itself. The temporary crosses that mark most new burials will be replaced with headstones (mainly polished black granite) when the graves have settled, and the graves themselves grassed over lawn-style, for ease of upkeep.

Such neatness is quite contrary to how the woodland burial ground, a stone's throw away, is meant to appear. The grass is cut

only twice a year, to nurture the flora and fauna, and from a distance it looks like a scrubby field, dotted randomly with trees. In fact, there are already seventy people buried here, although it's only the most recent graves, with a posy or two and a wooden name-roundel, which are noticeable, temporarily.

Natural and simple is the idea here: one burial per grave space; all graves prepared by hand; shrouds of wool or cotton; if there's a coffin, it should be made of cardboard, wicker or wood (not the standard chipboard or MDF); no plastic fittings; no embalming (embalmed bodies can take twenty or more years to decompose, whereas untreated bodies can take half that time to 'skeletonize'); wreaths composed of earth-friendly materials, not wire and plastic; no herbicides or chemicals. There could hardly be a more environmentally friendly way to go. It certainly beats cremation, which consumes huge amounts of energy and can be highly polluting.

"Everything will rot down, so that in years to come, as you wander among the trees, you'll have no idea that there are hundreds of people buried here," says Andy.

It may look like a grassy wilderness, but there's an orderly system in place to enable anyone's grave to be accurately located. "Every few yards, there's a holly tree, and at the base of each tree there's a stone marker. The place is gridded exactly – like the rest of the

cemetery. You know that from that stone marker there's a grave every four feet."

On the way back down to Andy's office, we pause at the Jewish burial ground, which was consecrated in 1975 (or 5736, according to the Hebrew calendar) and is owned and managed by Swansea's Jewish community. It's the successor to the original Jews' cemetery established on Mayhill in 1768, which, after two hundred years, had reached capacity.[12] The spasmodic vandalism suffered by the old and increasingly unkempt cemetery has not been repeated at out-of-the-way Oystermouth, where there's an almost military uniformity to the ranks of about 200 shiny black tablets, each topped with the Star of David, and inscribed in Hebrew and English, often with Hebrew as well as Gregorian dates. I spot one or two familiar names. Nat Burns, for instance, who died in 1995, aged 83: he performed magic tricks at children's parties, and was the making of one of my daughters' birthdays. All the gravestones are facing the same direction – west. Sadly missed by relatives and friends. Shalom.

I ask Andy, as we move on, about his own final plans. "Burial, no doubt about it." At Oystermouth? "Certainly. As cemeteries go, it's got the X-factor. You couldn't hope to find a better place."

It's vital, he believes, to make your wishes known well before you die, by leaving instructions in your will and telling family and friends what you want. "The worst thing is when a person dies suddenly, leaving the family with having to decide whether that person should be cremated or buried. They can end up deeply troubled as to whether in fact they made the right choice."

Back in the office, Andy pulls out the oldest of his ledgers. It opens with a brief record of young Alfred Gasston's burial in March 1883 – logged as burial number 1. Then we consult the current ledger and look up the burial that will take place later today: it will be number 25,561 (there are some 14,000 actual grave spaces). Full sets of these records are held both at the cemetery and in County Hall, as with Swansea's six other public cemeteries.[13] A computerized record has also been kept since 2000, but there's no beating the old ledgers as an informational tool, says Andy.

Two of Swansea's cemeteries, Cwmgelli and Danygraig, have almost run out of space. How much life, as it were, is there left in Oystermouth Cemetery, which grows by around 250 plots a year? Andy reckons that if current demand continues – and it's only a minority these days, 30%, who opt for burial rather than cremation – Oystermouth should be good for another 25 or 30 years. It looks, therefore, as if Andy – who's a long way from retirement age – is going to be 'lucky' to find himself a last resting place here before closing time. My chances, on the other hand, would be rather 'better'.

> hill-top graves –
> their headstones catching
> the last of the light

MUMBLES PIER

When the Swansea edition of Monopoly was launched in 2005, Mumbles Pier was voted favourite of the 33 Swansea landmarks featured on the board game.

To children especially, it's a fairytale place. The pier's continuing popularity, in spite of its pitiful deterioration in recent years, must in many cases have roots in memories of the full-tilt wonderment of childhood visits: the Big Apple, as your car approaches, selling whirligigs, shrimp-nets, buckets and 99s; the vibratory plummet, over ridged concrete, down to the magic-castle-like pier-head buildings; and then the most deliciously terrifying walk of your infant life, over those perilously narrow planks, with the surging ocean – dare you steal a glimpse? – waiting to suck you through the gaps in between. This experience of danger in relative safety, with your left hand in Mam's and your right in Dad's, would seem to me in later life like a foretaste of how we experience tragic drama, sitting comfortably in the dark, with food in our bellies and homes to go to, while unspeakable torments unfold onstage, filling our imagination, yet sparing us direct, ruinous involvement.

Once in a while there would be the additional thrill of a trip by paddle-steamer to Ilfracombe, 28 miles away on the north Devon coast. For this, we'd have to get up especially early, after an excitedly semi-sleepless night, to be sure of finding somewhere comfortable for the grandmother and great aunts to settle for the two-hour crossing. There waiting for us at the end of the pier, like some miraculous appendage, would be one of P.&A. Campbell's elegant steamers, twin white funnels aslant – the *Glen Gower*, perhaps, or the *Bristol Queen* or the *Cardiff Queen*. Campbell's regular, summer-season excursions around the Severn Sea ceased in 1981, to be replaced by intermittent sailings by just two vessels, the screw-driven *Balmoral* and the ineffably graceful *Waverley*, the last sea-going paddle-steamer in the world.

No steamers have called at Mumbles Pier since the early 1980s, owing mainly to the dilapidation of the landing stage. I was on board the *Waverley* on what may have been the last occasion she tied up at Mumbles. The tide was low, exposing the rotted ends of a set of wooden buffer posts which had been positioned to protect the landing stage's iron uprights from chafing by ships. Once or twice as the *Waverley* lay alongside, the fall and rise of the swell resulted in the stabilisation ledge that runs around the vessel's paddle-box dropping below the ends of those rotted posts – and then getting trapped momentarily as the ship rose on the swell, causing her to tilt alarmingly towards the pier, until released again by the fall. It was clearly no longer safe for steamers to dock at Mumbles.

> the seafront flags
> winnowed, by autumn,
> to ragged halves

Since then, the rot has continued. Most of the end section has been fenced off, apart from a passageway giving access to the three-tiered concrete landing stage, the top shelf of which is a popular

fishing platform. There are gaping holes in the pitch-pine decking
of the no-go areas, through which the rusting steel superstructure is
plain to see. Lying on her back among the wreckage, with her feet
on the decaying handrail, is Nansi the 9-ft fibreglass gorilla, from
whose extended arms in happier, vertical times there used to hang
a couple of swings. Nansi, surely the world's only sex-change gorilla
(albeit a plastic one), started out as undeniably a bloke, Norman.
She, or rather he, a popular fixture since the early 1980s, disappeared from the pier one summer's night in 1999. Security cameras
filmed the ape-napping by four balaclava-clad men in military
fatigues, carrying ropes and scaffolding poles. Weeks passed and the
pier's owners gave up hope of ever seeing their gorilla again, the
only clues to his whereabouts being photos sent to the pier owners
from different holiday locations. But one morning, as inexplicably
as the primate had vanished, and shortly after police had received
information that the ape was in a strip club in St Ives, Cornwall, it
reappeared at Mumbles – as a girl gorilla, in sassy red bikini, lipstick
and a stylish black hair-do. Where precisely this transformation took
place and at whose hands remains a mystery. The only one who
knows, grinning fixedly at the sky, utters not a sound.

As voluble, with their clamorous complaining, as Nansi is dumb,
are the dainty kittiwakes that throng the pier. They are the biggest

such colony for miles, having taken up residence here in about 1992, after abandoning their bases, for reasons unknown, on the cliffs near Worms Head and at Common Cliff, midway between Port Eynon and Paviland. They normally like to build their nests – of grass and seaweed – on steep cliffsides, but they appear more than content with the iron, steel and wooden ledges they have found on the pier, and seem quite untroubled by the close proximity of numerous rod-wielding or camera-toting humans.

It has been estimated by the Amusement Equipment Company (AMECO), the family concern which has run the pier since 1934, that over £3m needs to be spent to save it from closure. Twice a day, the pier's metalwork is immersed in salt water, to a depth of up to 12 metres, which lingers perniciously in its joints. The problem rests largely with the steel and wooden superstructure, rather than with the pier's original iron legs, which are said to be as sound as the day they were cast.

The challenge for AMECO is to devise some means of financing these repairs. AMECO have announced plans for a massive £39m privately-funded redevelopment, which would see the pier restored and upgraded as part of an extravagant (some have said greedy) scheme to create a luxury hotel and spa, restaurant, cafés, entertainment centre and boardwalks, in addition to apartments 'with millionaire's views' on the approach-road car park.

Public reaction to the plan has been sharply divided. Many have questioned its scale and others have doubted that in a period of fiscal retrenchment the capital will be found to finance such a scheme. But in June 2011 Swansea Council ignored the advice of its officers and the objections of the Gower Society and Mumbles Community Council, and approved the plans; a month later the pier closed for its two-year, £9.5m restoration programme to begin.[14]

High, and sometimes frustrated, ambitions have been part of the pier's story from the beginning. Although it has always been associated with leisure and tourism, it was originally conceived as an industrial undertaking – as was the associated Mumbles Railway (as it became known). In the late nineteenth century, Sir John Jones Jenkins, chairman of the Rhondda and Swansea Bay Railway Company, wanted to extend the railway to Mumbles Head and construct there a deep-water harbour, featuring a stone pier on which trains would travel. Exports, imports, transatlantic liners: Sir John, who lived at the Grange, West Cross, had extravagant hopes for Mumbles as a trading and industrial port. In 1892, the railway was indeed extended, from its old stopping place at the Dunns (roughly the site of the mini-roundabout outside the White Rose) to Mumbles Head, but the pier that that extension made possible was not the masonry leviathan of Sir John's industrializing dreams. When Lady Jenkins formally declared the £17,000 pier open in 1898, its future as a place of resort and relaxation was assured by the relative delicacy of its structure, built to support light-footed weekenders rather than trucks groaning with coal and limestone.

Escape, rather than hard-headed commerce, was the pier's purpose, although it has always had to pay its way. Orchestras, brass and military bands, concert parties and choirs, afternoon teas, 'gramaphonic records', 'sweetmeat vending machines' and an electric shooting gallery were among early, lucrative attractions. These days, people still come for a cup of tea, in the spacious café with its chandeliers and automated baby-grand played as if by a ghost. You can buy cod and chips at a side window and take them for a wander down the planking, or sit at a picnic table outside the hotel (1899), with a pint from one of its two bars: the Toby, which has a welcoming open fire in the winter, and the Salty, with its sail canopy and rigging décor. The Toby and the Salty remain much as they were when I first drank there in the 1960s, apart from the infliction of television, and the two bars being knocked into one. Most Mondays, 'me and the boys' would bomb down to the Salty in the old man's Austin Cambridge for a warm-up pint before the weekly rock nights at either the Langland Bay Hotel or the Redcliffe at Caswell. And when I landed my first job, as a newspaper reporter in Leamington Spa – which is about as far from the sea you can get in Britain – my first port of call on visits home, straight from the A465, would be the Toby. To sit on the sea wall with a pint of bitter, after that three-hour drive in my dodgy Hillman Imp van, was to experience untrammelled contentment – as long as the wind wasn't blowing from the direction of the lighthouse: at that time, and until 1999 when the high-tech sewage treatment plant opened on Fabian Way, raw sewage from the entire population of Swansea was pumped out at high tide from an outfall some 230 metres beyond the lighthouse island, and the place too often stank.

The dancehall attached to the hotel, known as Cinderella's or Cinder's, used to attract scores of students, local youngsters and coach parties from up the Valleys, many of them attempting that mother of all binges, the Mumbles Mile, which consisted of a drink in every pub between the White Rose and Cinderella's. But Cinder's, like many of those seafront hostelries, closed (in about 2005), as the Mumbles Mile surrendered its boozy crown to Wind Street and The Kingsway. It became a plastic (ice-effect) skating rink.

Next door to the café, there's the money-spinning gaming hall with an upstairs bowling alley, and on the pier itself a scattering of attractions designed to pull the punters through its portals at 50p a head. If Nansi was 'resting', in the run-up to the temporary closure, a red fibreglass dragon did slide duty, and there was a saucy, McGill-style cut-out couple, in whose face-holes you could insert your own for a photograph. You could also have yourself snapped in a mock-up of an electric chair, the least attractive of the pier's supposed attractions. Why not add a guillotine, or a cross for pretend crucifixions?

Of Wales's six remaining iron piers,[15] Mumbles at 7.6 metres wide and 253 metres long (discounting the landing jetty, which was added in the 1950s) is not among the biggest (Llandudno, for instance, is 699 metres long). Unlike, say, Aberystwyth, which had 30 metres lopped off it by a storm in 1866, Mumbles has had a fairly uneventful history. Most of its crises have arisen from the seemingly endless struggle against rust and wet-rot. After the Second World War, during which the pier was requisitioned as part of the war effort, it had to be largely rebuilt, reopening in 1956. It now needs the same kind of dramatic renovation as was necessary after the war.

Drama of a more apparent kind has been the (sometimes tragic) lot of the Mumbles lifeboat. A lifeboat was first established at Mumbles in 1835, and was launched down a stone slipway which still exists today, opposite the rowing club's boathouse, which was originally an early lifeboat station (1883). In 1916, a new slipway, with connecting gangway, was constructed alongside the pier, at the top of which perched the lifeboat, exposed to the elements. It wasn't until 1922 that the boathouse, with its 'iconic' yellow walls and red roof, was added to the slipway. For the better part of two centuries, heroically brave Oystermouth volunteers – "iron men in wooden boats", as the early lifeboatmen were known – have put themselves at risk "for those in peril on the sea", saving hundreds of lives and, on occasion, suffering severe losses themselves, most poignantly in the disasters of 1883, 1903 and 1947, dates etched into the consciousness of many a Mumbles old-timer. Until the advent of pagers and mobile phones, everyone in the village knew when the lifeboat was about to be launched: the lifeboatmen would be summoned to the station by two cannon-like booms, and within minutes – having cycled, driven or sprinted to the pier – they'd be piling aboard the lifeboat, ready for chocks away and that breathtaking plunge down the slipway. Then, for those left on shore, there would follow the anxious wait, with the minutes perhaps turning to hours, to see the lifeboat's safe return.

Some of the lifeboats over the years might seem to have had rather odd names: the *Wolverhampton*, the *Ethel Anne Measures*, the *Babs and Agnes Robertson*, the *Peterborough Beer Festival*. But these simply honour the generosity of institutions, areas or individuals who have raised the funds for the RNLI to purchase a boat. The Tamar-class lifeboat which Mumbles is scheduled to acquire will be too big for the existing boatshed, which is why a new one, at the end of the refurbished pier, is a key element of the redevelopment plans.

Drama of a different sort, almost entirely unsuspected by the pier's visitors, lurks beneath them. The clean lines of railing and planking give way below to a dank and eerie realm of barnacle-encrusted stanchions and cross-bars, from which there hang, swaying in the breeze, tangles of rope and fishing tackle, which have built up over the years and decades, many of them heavy with agglomerations of mussels. Once or twice a year, in early afternoon, the tide goes out far enough to expose – for no more than a matter of minutes – a remarkable world of marine wildlife: sponges, giant starfish, sea slugs, cowries, whelks, dead man's fingers, anemones, all manner of fish and crabs. These creatures have made themselves at home among a vast clutter of human debris, most of it deliberately dumped – rubble, chunks of masonry, old grates, jars and glass bottles, some embossed with names of long-forgotten local firms – which marine life has nevertheless put to productive use.

Of the many coins which have been found on the sea bed, turned blue-green with verdigris, pennies tend to predominate, suggesting that people have thrown them into the sea for luck. I think of how the luck ran out for Brighton's magnificent West Pier, rotting photogenically into the English Channel beneath clouds of starlings. Mumbles Pier now waits for more than a few good-luck pennies to come its way, to ensure the survival of its magic in the twenty-first century.

Pier Hotel

He sits outside, because of the kids,
drinking beer on the first of spring.

The boys lark with pebbles and a can;
his daughter does tricks on the handrail.

He says 'Don't, Jane …', forgetting trees
he'd conquered, the wall-tops he'd walked.

They reel on the beach, they throw and chase,
tipsy with the day, the day and themselves.

He buys himself another pint; it helps
remind him how it is to be drunk.

MUMBLES LIGHTHOUSE

The booming foghorn at Mumbles – once known as Jasper's Baby after Jasper Williams, one of the old lighthouse keepers – was the perfect, reassuring accompaniment to childhood nights when a mist loured or a storm raged: all is and will be well, it seemed to 'Om' through the dark, as you pulled the eiderdown up around your ears and shipwrecked dreamily into sleep. Its modern replacement, an officious, high-pitched hooter akin to a car horn, may cast its warning note wider, giving three beeps every 60 seconds, but it lacks the cosy romance of Jasper's big old Baby.

Night or day, no matter the weather, Mumbles lighthouse, atop its tidal island, is the unavoidably present guardian of Swansea Bay. Although the lighthouse itself is not open to the public, the island is worth a visit.

The only time to cross to the island is at low water, making sure you head back before the incoming tide. Many who have been neglectful of the tide have found themselves stranded on the island or, worse, have attempted to wade or swim back to the mainland, against potentially lethal currents. You'll need stout shoes because the going's rough after you leave the sandy little beach just below the Pier Hotel. When gun emplacements were built on the island during the Second World War – still there today, albeit gun-less – a causeway was constructed from this beach, past the middle island and across to the concrete steps leading up to the lighthouse, for building materials, supplies and ammunition to be transported to the island. Throughout its length, it had earthenware pipes to allow seawater to pass through, thereby reducing the destructive pressure

of the currents. After the war, the causeway was removed with explosives, apart from a fragment at the Pier Hotel end and a longer section in the lee of the middle island. Bits and pieces of it, including chunks of earthenware, lengths of piping and power cable, and even (from an earlier link) a set of railway points, are still to be seen among the pebbles and barnacled rocks you have to stumble over to reach the lighthouse. The reason for the causeway's removal seems to have been that its presence radically altered the currents in Swansea Bay, causing the sand to shift and, when the tides receded, to form a huge lagoon on Swansea beach, about 250 metres wide, between the cenotaph and the Brynmill Stream outfall (south of the university). Within months of the causeway's demolition, the beach had returned to its former contours – and local children had lost a spectacular swimming pool.[16]

For over 200 years the island has been dominated by its lighthouse. Until 1791, when the Harbour Act decreed that a 'Light at or near *The Mumbles* [is] to be kept constantly burning in the night from one hour after sunset to one hour before sun rising throughout the year', ships were at the mercy of two main hazards as they set sail from or sought the safe anchorage of Swansea Bay: the Cherrystone Rock, a reef south-east of the island, and the Mixon Shoal, a notorious sandbank to the south. There was also the need to distinguish Mumbles Head from other promontories. In 1760, the captain of the *Caesar*, which was stealing away some 90 press-ganged Swansea men[17] to fight in the Seven Years' War, was moved by worsening conditions in the Severn Sea to turn back into what he believed was Swansea Bay. But he'd mistaken Pwlldu Head for Mumbles Head, with disastrous consequences: the ship ran onto the rocks and every one of its human cargo, imprisoned below decks, was drowned. They are buried in a mass grave on Pwlldu Head, an area known to this day as Graves End.

The Swansea Harbour Trust's first, and over-hasty, attempt to build a lighthouse, in 1791, resulted in failure. The half-built structure collapsed and they called in the leading Swansea architect of the day, William Jernegan to bail them out. On the octagonal lighthouse's pier-facing wall, there's the coat of arms of Trinity House – 'TRINITAS IN UNITATE' – which took over the management of the lighthouse in 1975. Above it, difficult to decipher because fogged by whitewash, there's a relief which reads:

> 'MDCC.XCIII.
> W. JERNEGAN. *Arch*'.

The Roman numerals signify 1793, the year in which the building was completed. It was lit originally by two open coal fires in braziers, one half way up the 17-metre tower and one on top – an arrangement still reflected in the two-tier structure of the lighthouse. This was to distinguish it from Flat Holm lighthouse, which had one light, and St Ann's Head which had two, on separate towers. Those costly and ineffective coal lights were replaced in 1798 by an enclosed oil lamp, fuelled initially by spermaceti oil from the head of the sperm whale – said to be "very brilliant across the channel" – and later by paraffin. In 1969, the light was electrified and in 1995 it was converted to solar power, with solar module arrays being mounted on the roof of the fort which partly surrounds the lighthouse. The light-source itself is tiny – a two-and-a-half inch halogen bulb, with a lens around it to focus the light, which, emitting four flashes every ten seconds, has a range of 16 nautical miles (c.30 km). There's a cluster of six of these, so that if one fails there are up to five spare bulbs that can be resorted to.

In 1977, the glass and cast-iron lantern which had encased the light for generations suddenly disappeared, apparently in the interests of heightened visibility. The naked appearance of the seemingly decapitated lighthouse was startling. It wasn't until 1987, when a lantern from a retired light vessel was helicoptered into place, that the lighthouse recovered some semblance of architectural proportion. The brilliant white lighthouse is itself a beacon which can be seen for over 25 km in all directions. Every five years Trinity House workers spend two weeks on the island cleaning the tower with a high-pressure water jet before applying a fresh coat of paint.

For much of the time before its automation in 1934, the lighthouse had to have a resident keeper on the island, the costs of his wages and the upkeep of the lighthouse being met by a levy on all ships which 'passed the light' – initially at the rate of a farthing per ton of goods carried. The first of several dwellings on the island was built in 1795, and by 1881, when the island community was at its most numerous, there were fourteen people living there, comprising two keepers and their families, in separate households, and, in the barracks which had been built in association with the 1860 fortifications, a sergeant and gunners of the Royal Artillery who manned the battery, along with their families.

The most renowned of the lighthouse families were the Aces. They became famous throughout the music halls of Britain after the influential *Daily Telegraph* theatre critic and occasional, sentimental versifier Clement Scott (1841-1904) published his interminable tear-jerker 'The Women of Mumbles Head'. Based on the 1883 disaster in which four lifeboatmen and a sailor lost their lives, its heroines are the daughters of lighthouse keeper Abraham Ace, Margaret and Jesse, who hauled from the sea with their chain of plaid shawls two crewmen of the lifeboat *Wolverhampton*, which had capsized while rescuing men from the barque *Admiral Prinz Adalbert* of Danzig. My grandmother and her two sisters, along with most other Swansea schoolchildren of their generation, were made to learn the poem by heart. Well into old age, they could still reel off formidable chunks of it. One of them would start the ball rolling:

> Bring, novelists, your notebook! Bring, dramatists, your pen!
> And I'll tell you a simple story of what women do for men …

And away they'd go, passing the baton of the stirring narrative – fudging the odd line, skipping the odd verse – until one of them would be left to deliver the resounding conclusion:

> Well, many a heart beat stronger, and many a tear was shed,
> And many a glass was tossed right off to the Women of Mumbles
> Head![18]

By the 1920s, the automation of the lighthouse was sufficiently sophisticated for there to be no further need for a resident keeper. The houses fell into disrepair, and in the 1960s they were demolished, apart from a wall or two. Their bricks, many of them stamped 'Graig Brick Co/Morriston', are scattered around the island; those tumbled into the sound have been smoothed into large red pebbles.

Much remains of the fortifications and gun emplacements that were hastily constructed on the island at various times of international tension, from the French Revolutionary and Napoleonic Wars onwards. In 1978, the sea near the Head yielded up a dramatic souvenir of nineteenth-century defensive intent, namely a massive cannon which had been mounted on the island. The gun has been given shining pride of place outside Swansea Sub-Aqua Club in the Maritime Quarter.

It has sometimes been suggested that although Guglielmo Marconi is normally credited with transmitting the first wireless

signals over open sea – between Lavernock Point near Penarth and Flat Holm, in 1897 – the island at Mumbles Head has a prior claim. This is largely wishful thinking, but there's no denying that the island deserves a place in the history of underwater cable telegraphy. In the summer of 1844, the industrialist and botanist Lewis Weston Dillwyn of Sketty Hall and his son the photographer John Dillwyn Llewelyn, both keen amateur scientists, collaborated with the distinguished English scientist Charles Wheatstone (1802-1875) in trials which Dillwyn describes in his diary: 'Went with Wheatstone & John to the Island where the Lighthouse stands & from a Boat we made many experiments in the passage of the Electric Current through Sea Water.' Submerging a length of insulated wire, they signalled through it from a boat anchored in Swansea Bay to the lighthouse. The experiment was a crucial step towards the laying of the first successful transatlantic telegraph cable in the mid 1860s.

> clatterous thunder,
> thunderous rain – drowning out
> the foghorn

CASWELL VALLEY

"If you go down to the woods today …" My eldest daughter, who lives with her mother and sister on the eastern rim of Caswell Valley, is taking me on one of her favourite walks, and has promised me "a big surprise".

Caswell is famous throughout Britain for its beach, which in 2007 was declared by the *Guardian* one of Britain's ten 'rockpool hotspots'. But the seaside, this May afternoon, is not our destination. Few of the thousands who flock to swim or sunbathe at Caswell frequent the 19-ha Bishop's Wood Nature Reserve that borders the eastern approach to the bay and reaches nearly a kilometre inland, and even fewer, Angharad is sure, will have seen the strange and intriguing thing she is taking me to see.

Summerland Lane at the northern end of Caswell Avenue transports us within minutes from well-heeled suburbia to low-budget, eco-conscious shack-land. The asphalt dwindles to a pot-holed track which in turn gives way – no cars, no streetlights – to a narrow path, slippery after recent rain, which twists and turns down the eastern flank of the valley, beneath tree cover so dense in summer that relatively little direct sunlight filters through to the splendidly anarchic cluster of wooden dwellings collectively known as Owensfield. The shacks – or chalets, as some owners prefer – are resourceful assertions of their occupants' 'alternative' lifestyles. No mains electricity. Wood-burning stoves. Wind-chimes, windmills and whirligigs. Wandering around here at night – torchlight, wood-smoke, bongos, patchouli – is like drifting on ganga through a medieval forest village.

It's often assumed that the huts of Owensfield, along with those of Holts Field at the northern end of the valley, were thrown up as emergency accommodation for people bombed out of their homes by the Luftwaffe in 1941. Some no doubt sought shelter here during the war, but most of these attractively individualistic dwellings were already well established, having been built by their owners in the inter-war years as holiday chalets. They soon became occupied on a permanent basis, symbolising, in the words of a council document, "the ordinary Swansea City dwellers' desire to obtain access to the perceived benefits of fresh air and the peace and tranquillity of the countryside and coast", and they offer a valuable insight into a way of life which has almost disappeared.

As the path – which has lately, it seems, been a stream – approaches the valley bottom we pass through a cathedral of towering beeches; on the forest floor, thick with beech-mast, there are stones arranged for a communal fire, and a large wooden model of a spider. Bishop's Wood is a classic example, relatively rare in Britain, of a limestone woodland. Part of it is classified as ancient woodland, which means it has been wooded since at least the seventeenth century, as testified by the 1673 survey of the ecclesiastical manor of Bishopston. The 'bishops' remembered in both Bishopston and Bishop's Wood are the medieval bishops of Llandaff, to whom Bishopston formerly belonged. Among this nature reserve's many curiosities, recorded nowhere else in Wales, is the meat-coloured Latticed Stinkhorn or Red Cage fungus which smells of rotting flesh, in order to attract flies and other insects to help disperse its spores.

With the name Caswell probably meaning 'cress stream', from the Old English word 'cerse', you'd expect to find said stream meandering along the valley bottom, but for most of the valley's length the stream, like many streams in limestone country, flows underground, until it spills from a culvert onto the beach.

The stream's absence from the point at which our path joins the main valley path has made possible the construction here of a remarkable timber roundhouse. Designed and built by the Llŷn-

based storyteller and woodcraftsman Dafydd Davies-Hughes, and inspired by a study of a medieval cathedral spire, it's made from green hard woods harvested locally and has a living green roof of grass and wild flowers, with a hole in its centre for smoke to escape from the stone fireplace beneath. Its dark and cosy interior make it an atmospheric venue for storytelling sessions and musical assemblies, or for taking shelter with a few sandwiches during a downpour.

We clamber up the western side of the valley to where the woodland meets the fields of Herberts Lodge Farm. "Getting close now," says Angharad. There are fragments of abandoned homesteads here and there among the trees: a snatch of garden hedge gone wild, a brick pillar or two, scatterings of slates, bottles, crockery. Someone, perhaps a year ago, has made a start on a daub-and-wattle, Celtic-style hut; the wattle walling is a good four feet high, but the builder seems to have run out of puff with the daub.

"Ah! Here we are," she says.

Immediately beside the barely used path, there's more overgrown domestic hedging, some low fragments of wall and a metre-deep end-section of what looks like an Anderson shelter, curved panels of rusting galvanised steel arching over a brick wall. Pulled across the wall's empty window space is a garish orange curtain. This end section describes a room that is otherwise bereft of walls or roof, apart from straggly hedge and overhead foliage. Nevertheless, it's neatly appointed with an electric fire beneath the window, a dresser decorated with bits of mostly broken dishes, and a single bed made up with pillow and blanket, all sodden after days of rain. Some boots and shoes are lined up alongside the fire, and wild garlic grows from beneath the bed.

"Magical, isn't it?" says Angharad. "When I was here a week ago, the dresser was leaning on the bed, perhaps blown over by the strong winds we've had lately, and the china was scattered over it – but someone since then has been and replaced everything carefully."

But who? This fantasy installation doesn't have the feel of a children's den. There's something calculating, weird, adult about it.

And there's more. In a neighbouring 'hedge room' there's a chess board, made of black and white ceramic tiles set in a square of concrete placed on boulder uprights. Round the corner, there's a fridge amply stocked with beer bottles and a can of Stella, all empty. In a nearby alcove, there's a table laid for four, with red and white check oilcloth and place mats with broken plates. Curiouser and curiouser …

Angharad scribbles a note greeting the maker of this 'house' and asking who he, she or they might be, using a cup to pinion her message to the dresser.

Following the path back down to the floor of the valley, we come to the ruined walls and teetering eastern gable – much undermined by tree growth – of the medieval chapel of St Peter's, which has been in existence since the early twelfth century, if not earlier. It's believed to have been in ruin since at least the seventeenth century when Isaac Hamon, Bishopston blacksmith and steward of the manor, mentioned its conditon in the detailed account of Gower he prepared for the polymath Edward Lhuyd (?1660-1709), Keeper of the Ashmolean Museum in Oxford, as a contribution towards Lhuyd's survey of Wales. Hamon describes the site as "a desolate place between hilles and woodes … but it is open to the morning sunne". The chapel, dedicated to the virgin Mary, was associated with a priest's cell and, according to Hamon, with not one but two holy wells. The waters of the smaller, dedicated to St John – of which there seems to be no trace today – were said to be "good for the eyes". The bigger, St Peter's, a few metres north of the chapel and fringed in May with wild garlic, is still delightfully present, if lacking by now the stonework surrounds that Hamon describes. St Peter's well, he writes, "is very firm walled & stone benches and pavement belonging to it, it never friezeth it continueth the stream, be the weather wet or dry, the water is drying and good to wash old sores scabs etc."

A stream from the well flows into a rectangular tank from which a green hosepipe snakes in the direction of the abundant Holts Field allotments. They spread across much of the valley floor here, some of them fenced Celtic-style against marauding foxes, rabbits and badgers. There's as much variety and inventiveness about these gardens as there is in the size, shape and colour of the 27 dwellings that constitute the Holts Field community of some 50 or so people, scattered higgledy-piggledy among the bushes and trees on the surrounding slope – many of those dwellings, if you look closely, with worked stone recycled from the chapel as steps or garden enhancements. No two of them alike, the chalets are built of light materials, mostly timber, with bricks employed for chimneys and foundation plinths.

As we amble towards the settlement in bright sunlight, the sound of bongos and guitar drifts down from somewhere on the slope. Exuding a sense of peace and plenty (you can almost hear those

vegetables growing), this is the very opposite of "a desolate place". But for all its evident tranquillity, there has been, for decades, a troublesome serpent in Holts Field's Eden – in the form of Elitestone, a development company which in 1988 bought the land on which the chalets stand, with the intention of sweeping them away and replacing them with executive mansions. Elitestone – whose director is Tim Jones, the father of rugby hero Alun Wyn Jones – has been as determined to get rid of the Holtsfielders as the Holtsfielders have been determined to stay, and a complicated legal battle has raged for years, involving petitions, sit-ins, court cases, a march from Holts Field to the House of Lords, and considerable press interest. The *Guardian* columnist George Monbiot, writing in *Red Pepper* in December 1995, cited the Holts Field case as "an extreme example" of how land use in Britain will always work against the people until we demand control over the decisions which govern it. "The residents have no legal means of preventing [the chalets'] demolition," Monbiot observed. "As they have no foundations they are viewed by the law as mobile homes, so the land beneath them can be used as its owner sees fit .... the principles at work here intrude, in one way or another, into all our lives." The struggle continues.

With most of the chalets being accessible by foot only, Holtsfielders with vehicles have to park where they can on the fringes of the settlement, around the northern approach from Manselfied Road, Murton. Hippy-ish jalopies are in evidence here, but so too are gas-guzzling four-by-fours – an ominous taste of things to come, if Elitestone gets its way.

Although Angharad occasionally called by that spectral house in the woods, she received no reply to her message, which mouldered there for weeks in the damp summer weather. She later found out it was the project of an art student living in Holts Field. Today, nothing remains of it, except the chunk of Anderson shelter which evidently inspired it, and the chess board.

WAUNARLWYDD

Feint-hearts linguistically challenged by this splendid place name with its rolling middle 'r' usually flunk it with a wanly retiring 'One-ahl-with' or, even feebler, a disdainful 'One-eyelid'. You'd think they'd get matters right at the rugby club, but a gable-end plaque there has the village's name misspelled as 'Waunarlydd'. 'Waun', they tend fondly to call the team, in any case, not bothering much about the subsequent syllables. But the full name carries a significant burden of history, taking us back to Norman times when the lord of Gower declared his entitlement to a large tract of meadowland (the Portmead) north-west of the boundary of Swansea borough. A sixteenth-century lawsuit led to the division of Portmead, with the lord of Gower being permitted to retain the portion known to this day as Waun-ar(g)lwydd (the meadow of the lord).

For hundreds of years, from post-Roman to early medieval times, it was part of an unstable buffer zone between, initially, warring indigenous tribes, then between the native Welsh and waves of land-grabbing Danes, Irish and Normans. Swords surely rang in many a mother's head around here. But it's a kind and sunny October day as I cycle into Waunarlwydd from the direction of Gowerton, choosing to fork left off the busy Gowerton–Swansea main road. I pedal against the gentle gradient of the old Swansea Road that takes me through the sleepy Saturday morning heart of what is still identifiably a village, although it's separated by only a few fields from the urban sprawl of Swansea. Wedged between the bracken-rusted heights of the Graig to the south and the Afon Llan to the north, Waunarlwydd has the feel, this brittle, golden morning, of a place apart, which is how most of its inhabitants like it. They don't want it to become Swansea, although it's been edging in that direction, metaphorically if not literally, for a couple of decades.

"When I was a kid, Waunarlwydd felt safe," says my former writing student Hannah Lawson, whose family – the Georges – have lived here for generations. Her great-great-uncle, after whom Heol Will George is named, was the first Waunarlwydd person to become mayor of Swansea. "You could always go into a pub and find someone you knew. But in the last ten or fifteen years, there's been a real atmosphere shift. New council estates, with problem families shifted out here. Cars getting pinched. Everything getting vandalised. Always having to lock things up. It used to be a place of traditional working-class values. People weren't well off, but they were honest, with a good sense of community spirit. People now are more likely to lock themselves inside and feel a bit intimidated."

Hannah lives next door to her parents in a terraced house on Swansea Road, which is among the oldest housing in the village. Waunarlwydd was built on coal, in every sense, and most of the older houses were constructed for miners, with thick, sound-proofed walls. Many, like Hannah's, have unusually long rear gardens, which enabled the miners to be self-sufficient in vegetables, often with surpluses which their womenfolk would carry to Swansea in characteristic large baskets, to sell from door to door. Coal-mining ceased here decades ago, and few now have heard of Waunarlwydd's (once) most famous resident collier (and *eisteddfodwr*), Cwmafan-born William Abraham (Mabon; 1842-1922) who worked at a colliery on Graig y Bwldan known as Caergynydd (subsequently The Elms), and who later became first president of the South Wales Miners' Federation (and MP for the Rhondda).

The main employer in Waunarlwydd in recent times has been ALCOA (the Aluminium Company of America). But in 2007, ALCOA closed the plant, with the loss of nearly 300 jobs, leaving the Dallas-based Titanium Metals Corporation (Timet) as the village's chief employer. With a bar-rolling capacity of four million pounds a year – largely for jet-engine fan-blades and medical applications – Timet Waunarlwydd is one of the biggest suppliers of titanium bar in the world. The village's three old people's homes are also significant employers.

And there are three pubs. Hannah and I begin our wander through Waunarlwydd outside the 'modern' red-brick Village Inn which is opposite an estate of prefabs at the eastern gateway to the village. As the Domino in the 1970s, says Hannah, it used to be "a druggy hell-hole" with a sign advising customers that "Drug use in this bar will not be tolerated – go outside and take them". The change of name to the Village Inn was part of a make-over to clean up the pub's act, but the old Domino's reputation seems well travelled: the Scottish thriller writer Iain M. Banks has a dodgy character in one of his novels known as Domino Waunarlwydd.

We turn right off the new Swansea Road into the old, passing the Welsh-medium Zion Baptist Chapel (1860-1872), its austere, Pennant sandstone frontage severely assaulted by the breeze-blocking of a window and by a hideous porch extrusion. "Good choir here," says Hannah, many of whose dead are buried in the cemetery at the rear, which lies at the bottom of her garden. The road swings left in front of the Masons Arms, and we pass several houses with names that testify to former roles, such as the Old Bakery and the Bird in Hand. Number 122 is also known as Yr Hen Rhif Tri (the old number three): Welsh still has a presence here, notably at the Welsh-medium primary school Ysgol Gynradd Cymraeg Login Fach down by the rugby pitch and the railway line. There's also a little Welsh in the pubs.

Although, with an English father and a *mam di-Gymraeg*,[19] Hannah's was not a Welsh-speaking upbringing, she came round to the language in later life. "At Waunarlwydd Junior we had bits of Welsh, but it was half-hearted. Peripatetic teachers. An afterthought. I had absolutely no interest in the language and dropped it as soon as I could. Then I went to university in England and came across these really bigoted people who were prejudiced against the Welsh. So I went in the opposite direction and became as Welsh as I could. I went to evening classes at Login Fach, and I really enjoyed it. I love speaking Welsh now." It saddens her that, as elsewhere in the more anglophone parts of Wales, the kids at Login Fach make little use of the language outside the school gates.

At the Farmers Arms, we bump into Hannah's father, Ian, and join him for a pint in the sun. Ian recalls being pulled up by the police in the Highlands of Scotland and asked for his address. "When I spelled out Waunarlwydd, the officer told me that if I was taking the piss I was in big trouble."

The only tension in balmy Waunarlwydd this Indian-summer afternoon has been on the rugby pitch. The ref's whistle, the lone impassioned shouts and the roars of the crowd have been the soundtrack of our walk. We make our way to the rugby club during the last minutes of the game, which is being played on

Waunarlwydd's distinctive leylandia-bordered pitch with its ram's head goalposts. Pitch and club house are connected by the narrow, 6'3" high tunnel which takes Roseland Road under the railway and which is far too cramped for a beer dray. Essential supplies have to be delivered to the club via a circuitous route through Fforestfach.

Although the club was founded in 1900, it pursued a famously epic struggle to achieve WRU status. Beginning in 1934, it did not succeed until 1964, thanks in no small measure to consistent support for their case from their old friends and rivals Bonymaen.

We reach the club just before the post-match rush. Their beaming faces, as the fans surge through the doors, declare victory for 'the green and blacks', with a score of 21-14 to Waunarlwydd. Hannah's not the only woman present, but, as in most clubs, the gathering is overwhelmingly male (the club's insignia is a ram's head), reflecting, she says, a generally macho culture that doesn't give women their due. "I was Ian's daughter first of all," she says, "and then I became Biff's girlfriend." I wonder if the many people we've said hello to must think she is scraping the bottom of the barrel with the bearded oldie she's been seen wandering around with today. "Aye," she says, "they'll have me pregnant by tomorrow morning."

The biggest issue in Waunarlwydd for decades is Timet's plan for three giant wind turbines to help cut the company's power bills. Over 2,000 residents have signed a petition protesting – on safety, noise and visual grounds – against the 68-metre turbines, which will be taller than the DVLA building at Morriston. If social bonds have been somewhat loosened in recent times, the campaign to resist these turbines seems to be reviving a sense of communal purpose that hasn't been seen for years.

notes

1. There's a village called Singleton on the south side of the Sussex Downs.
2. These names are among many others to be found on early maps reproduced in Bernard Morris's definitive account of Singleton *The Houses of Singleton: A Swansea Landscape and its History* (1995).
3. This would presumably have been some years after JHV's time.
4. Known anciently as St David's Ditch, and later as Cockett Stream or the Bryn Stream or Brynmill Brook or Brynmill Stream.
5. Later Parc Beck nurses' home, now flats.
6. It was not until the Newport National Eisteddfod in 2004, when two huge beer wagons appeared on the *maes* like *dei ex machina*, that the Eisteddfod's prim teetotalism was finally abandoned.
7. Where the 2011 Urdd National Eisteddfod was also held.
8. It was Graham who opened the Glynn Vivian Art Gallery, in 1911, in his dead brother's stead.
9. Jones himself acted as anaesthetist.
10. The date of birth is given, wrongly, as 1893.
11. The *Samptampa*'s crew are buried at Nottage Cemetery. The disaster is commemorated in Tim Lewis's striking stained glass window (1977) in All Saints parish church, Oystermouth.
12. In 2009, Swansea's dwindling Jewish congregation, which dates back to 1730, had to sell its synagogue in Ffynone Road to finance the upkeep of its two cemeteries.
13. These are Morriston, Kingsbridge, Rhydgoch, Coedgwilym, Cwmgelli and Danygraig. The council deals with around 2,100 cremations and 1,000 burials each year.
14. It wasn't until July 2012 that work commenced.
15. Aberystwyth, Bangor, Colwyn Bay, Llandudno and Penarth are the other five. A seventh pier, Beaumaris, is made of timber.
16. That a relatively small-scale structure could have had such an impact on the movement of sand has caused some to sound a note of caution about plans – which have generally been welcomed – to site in Swansea Bay a very much larger construction, the world's first tidal lagoon for generating electricity.
17. And possibly a small number of women.
18. The poet Maura Dooley (1957), who has family in Swansea, has reworked this material to haunting effect in her own 'The Women of Mumbles Head' (*Sound Barrier: Poems, 1982-2002*, Bloodaxe, 2002).
19. A non-Welsh-speaking mother.

WORKS CONSULTED

Baines, Menna; Davies, John; Jenkins, Nigel; and Lynch, Peredur, *The Welsh Academy Encyclopaedia of Wales*, University of Wales Press, 2006

Balchin, W.G.V. (ed.), *Swansea and its Region*, Swansea, 1971

Broady, Maurice, *A Vision Fulfilled – The Story of Celtic Studios and Swansea's architectural glass tradition*, West Glamorgan Archive Service, 2010

Campbell, Rhoda, *Water Under the Bridge*, D. Brown and Sons Ltd., 1997

Coles, David, *The Difficult Birth of the Driver & Vehicle Licensing Centre in Swansea*, The Author, 2010

Cuthill, Robert, *'That Tin Shack' – The Story of the Vivian Hall, Blackpill*, 1990 (publisher not known)

Bywgraffiadur Cymreig 1951-1970, Y, London, 1997

Davies, Brian E., *Mumbles and Gower Pubs*, Tempus, 2006

Davies, John, *A History of Wales*, Penguin, 1994
Wales: the 100 places to see before you die, Lolfa, 2010

Davies, James A. (ed.), *A Swansea Anthology*, Seren, 1996
Dylan Thomas's Swansea, Gower and Laugharne, University of Wales Press, 2000

Davies, Russell, *Hope and Heartbreak – A Social History of Wales and the Welsh, 1776-1871*, University of Wales Press, Cardiff, 2007

Dictionary of Welsh Biography Down to 1951, The, London 1959

Dumbleton, Bob, *The Second Blitz*, Bob Dumbleton, Cardiff,1977

Dunthorne, Kirstine Brander (ed.), *Drawn from Wales: a School of Art in Swansea 1853-2003)*, Welsh Academic Press, Cardiff, 2003

Gabb, Gerald, *The Story of the Village of Mumbles*, D. Brown and Sons Limited, Cowbridge, 1986
The Life and Times of the Swansea and Mumbles Railway, D. Brown and Sons Limited, Cowbridge, 1987
Swansea and its History, Volume 1, Swansea, 2007
Gower (1948-), the journal of the Gower Society

Graham, Ellie, *Swansea: Urban Characterisation*, unpublished MA dissertation (NGR: SS65042 93453), 2011

Griffiths, R.A. (ed.), *The City of Swansea. Challenges and Change*, Sutton, 1990

Hughes, Stephen, *Copperopolis, Landscapes of the Early Industrial*

Period in Swansea, Royal Commission on the Ancient and Historical Monuments of Wales, 2000

Jones, Alan, *The Story of the Grand*, Christopher Davies, 1983.

Jones, W.H., *The History of Swansea and of the Lordship of Gower, Volume I*, Carmarthen, 1920
　　The History of Swansea and of the Lordship of Gower, Volume II, Royal Institution of South Wales, 1992
　　History of the Port of Swansea, Carmarthen, 1922

Kilpatrick, J. Ramsay, with Kilpatrick, Felicity, *Down the Memory Lanes of My Hafod*, Worktoad Publications, 2009

Lang, Jeff and Scoville, André, *Then & Now Morriston*, Tempus, 2000

Marshall, Ray and Gabriel, Derek, *The Great Pub Crawl, A Story of Swansea Pubs*, Raydek Books, 1994

Matthews, Mervyn, *Mervyn's Lot*, Seren Books, 2002

Miskell, Louise, *'Intelligent Town', An Urban History of Swansea, 1780-1855*, University of Wales Press, 2006

Mitchell, Adrian and Steadman, Ralph, *Who Killed Dylan Thomas?*, Tŷ Llên Publications, 1998

Morgan, W. Ll., *The Castle of Swansea*, George Simpson & Co., Devizes, 1914

Morris, Bernard, 'Swansea Houses: Working-class Houses, 1800-50', *Gower*, xxvi (1975), 53-61
　　'The Earliest Views of Swansea, 1678', *Gower*, xxxiii (1982), 6-12
　　The Houses of Singleton: A Swansea Landscape and its History, West Glamorgan County Archive Service, 1995

Morris, Richard, *Penllergare, A Victorian Paradise*, The Friends of Penllergare, 1999

National Waterfront Museum, National Museum of Wales, 2005

Newman, John, *The Buildings of Wales: Glamorgan*, Penguin, 1995

Owen, J Alun, *Swansea's Earliest Open Spaces*, Swansea City Council, 1995

Plummer, Barry (ed.), *Evan Walters: Moments of Vision*, Seren, 2011

Porch, Richard, *Swansea: History You Can See*, Tempus, 2005
　　Swansea City Centre Heritage Trail, City and County of Swansea, 2007
　　Swansea's Heritage, The History Press, 2008

Read, Peter, *God's Botherer*, Swansea Poetry Workshop, 2001
　　Read Only, Pinewood Press, Swansea, 2008

Rees, Ken, *My Life and Swansea*, privately published, Swansea,

2003

Rees, Ronald, *Heroic Science,* Wales Books, 2005

Roberts, Alun, *Discovering Welsh Graves,* University of Wales Press, 2002

Roberts, Ann, *Estuary People,* self published, 2001

Robins, Nigel Alan, *Homes for Heroes: Early Twentieth-Century Housing in the County Borough of Swansea,* City of Swansea, 1992

Rogers, W.C., *A Pictorial History of Swansea,* Gomer Press, 1981

Historic Swansea (ed. Bernard Morris), West Glamorgan Archive Service, 2005.

Scoville, André, *Morriston's Pictorial Past,* D Brown & Sons Ltd, 1988

Morriston's Pictorial Past – Vol 2, D. Brown & Sons Ltd, 1994; *Images of Wales: Swansea,* Landore, Clydach and Morriston, Tempus, 2000

Images of Wales: Morriston, Tempus 2002.

South Wales Evening Post, The

Stead, Peter, *Swansea City Guide,* Christopher Davies, 1992

Stony Stories, Swansea City Council, 1985

Strawbridge, Don, *Swansea Bay … the coastal route,* Gower Society, 2007

Ross, J.E. (ed.), *Letters from Swansea,* Christopher Davies, 1983

Swansea History Journal (Minerva) (1993-), The Royal Institution of South Wales

Thomas, N.L., *The Story of Swansea's Districts and Villages* (2 vols., Neath, 1964; Swansea, 1969)

Of Swansea West: The Mumbles: Past and Present, Swansea, 1978

Towns, Jeff (compiler), *'Salzburg-on-the-Tawe': Vernon Watkins' Swansea,* Tŷ Llen publications, 2006

Vaughan Thomas, Wynford, *Portrait of Gower,* Robert Hale, 1983

Walters, E., 'The Development of the Walters Road Area of Swansea', *Gower,* xxx (1979), 45-51

Western Mail, The

Whittle, Elisabeth, *A Guide to Ancient and Historic Wales – Glamorgan and Gwent,* CADW, HMSO 1992

Williams, Glanmor, *Swansea, an Illustrated History,* Christopher Davies, 1990

Williams, Haydn, *Angels in Hobnail Boots,* Hafod Books, 2003

THE PHOTOGRAPHS

ACKNOWLEDGEMENTS

Among the many people whose memories, suggestions, company on walks and all manner of practical assistance have been invaluable in the writing of this book, I am particularly grateful to (in alphabetical order) Chris Bird-Jones, Brian and Maybellene Breeze, David Britton, Kaye Byrne, Robin Campbell, Paul Davies, Stevie Davies, Lyn Cousins, Jo Furber and staff at the Dylan Thomas Centre, Ellie Graham, Richard Havard, Lionel Hopkins, Paul Hopkins, Dave Hoskin, Gemma Howell, Angharad and Branwen Jenkins (my daughters), Martyn Jenkins (my brother), Ruth Jenkins, Felicity Kilpatrick, Hannah Lawson, Gloria McLeod (my mother), Antonio Montinaro, Margot Morgan, Susan Morgan, Bernard Morris, Malcolm Parr, Paulette Pelosi, Terry Phillips, Barry Plummer, Richard Porch, Jon Powell, Lynne Rees, Neil Reeve, Ioan Richard, Peter Richards, Sarah Richards, Andy Sherman, Steve Stokes, Ray Tilley, Rhys Owain Williams, Jen Wilson, Noel Witts (my cousin) and ever-helpful staff at Mumbles library and at Swansea University library. I am grateful to both the series editor Peter Finch and Seren for commissioning this book.

A version of the section on the Old Central Library first appeared in *Planet: the Welsh Internationalist*, no. 200, autumn 2010. 'Brothels' first appeared in the on-line journal *Swansea Review* (http://www.swanseareview.com/), edited by Fflur Dafydd for Swansea University's creative writing programme. Most of the haiku (the short, generally three-line poems) are taken from my two haiku collections, *Blue* and *O For a Gun* (Planet Books, 2002 and 2007 respectively), and from the anthology *Another Country: Haiku Poetry from Wales* (eds. Nigel Jenkins, Ken Jones and Lynne Rees; Gomer Press, 2011). Most of the longer poems come from my collections *Acts of Union: Selected Poems 1974-1989* (1990), *Ambush* (1998) and *Hotel Gwales* (2006), all published by Gomer Press. Both Planet and Gomer are gratefully acknowledged.

THE AUTHOR

Nigel Jenkins was born in 1949 and brought up on a farm in Gower. He worked as a newspaper reporter in the English Midlands and studied literature and film at Essex University, returning to Gower in 1976 as a freelance writer, teacher and broadcaster. Living in Mumbles and teaching creative writing at Swansea University, he is the author of collections of poetry and essays and co-editor of *The Welsh Academy Encyclopaedia of Wales* (University of Wales Press, 2008). His travel book about Welsh missionaries in north-east India, *Gwalia in Khasia* (Gomer Press, 1995), was Wales Book of the Year in 1996. Seren published his *Real Swansea* in 2008 and Gomer the following year published his *Gower*, a book of essays, poems and photographs produced in collaboration with the artist David Pearl. He is currently working on *Real Gower*.

INDEX